MARTIN McGUINNESS

MARTIN McGUINNESS

From Guns to Government

Liam Clarke and Kathryn Johnston

MAINSTREAM
PUBLISHING

EDINBURGH AND LONDON

First published in Great Britain in 2001 by
MAINSTREAM PUBLISHING COMPANY
(EDINBURGH) LTD
7 Albany Street
Edinburgh EH1 3UG

ISBN 1 84018 473 6

A catalogue record for this book is available
from the British Library

Typeset in Van Dijck
Printed and bound in Great Britain by
Butler & Tanner, Frome and London

Contents

Introduction: October 2001

I have to point out that those purporting to be writing autobiographical (sic)
accounts of my life are doing so without my cooperation or approval'

Martin McGuinness, 21 August 2001

What has McGuinness got to hide?

Letter in *Irish News*, from
'No to Censorship', Dublin, 27 August 2001

For years Martin McGuinness has complained that his views have been
censored, yet when we asked to interview him he ignored the first two
requests and replied to the third with a solicitor's letter.

Barra McGrory, McGuinness' lawyer, advised us solemnly that our letter
to 'the Minister for Education, Mr Martin McGuinness, MP, MLA seeking a
meeting with him to discuss your forthcoming political biography of him,
has been passed to me for reply. Mr McGuinness wishes me to make it clear
to you that he will not be cooperating in any way with this project.'

It was a reply worthy of Howard Hughes and it didn't stop there. In
August 2001, McGuinness interrupted his holiday to issue a press statement
'to ask republicans to withhold cooperation' with us. Timing is everything;
and his was poor. By now all our interviews had been completed and the
final manuscript was sitting on the publisher's desk.

As George Orwell wrote in *1984*, 'Who controls the past . . . controls the
future: who controls the present controls the past.' Right through the

research process, McGuinness' power and influence were evident. Sources, even some who were sympathetic to him, asked for their names and personal details to be changed for fear of annoying him. The usual explanation was 'I have to live in this town.'

When a request was made to the RUC press office for cooperation it went straight to Sir Ronnie Flanagan, the Chief Constable, who instructed his staff to write to us saying, 'his decision is that we should not assist in the project'. An RUC spokesperson later made it clear that Flanagan's refusal was not to be taken personally; it was due to the 'sensitivity' of the peace process and of the subject matter. A personal meeting with Flanagan produced a promise to get a senior officer to consider a list of questions but none of them was answered.

Every police officer and every republican who assisted in our research had to be willing, to some degree, to break ranks in the interests of setting the record straight. It is gratifying that there were so many of them. We appreciate their honesty and courage and are proud to count many of them as friends. The insights belong to them, the mistakes are our own.

Special mention must be made of the excellent resources at the Linenhall Library, Belfast, and the outstanding CAIN Archive (Conflict Archive on the Internet), at the University of Ulster's Derry campus, under the direction of Project Manager, Dr Martin Melaugh. We would also like to thank Peter Heathwood for giving us generous access to his unique private video archive of television news broadcasts and documentary programmes.

Colleagues we would like to thank personally for contributing material or recollections are Trevor Birney of UTV Insight, photographer Kelvin Boyes, Stephen Grey of the *Sunday Times*, Hugh Jordan of the *Sunday World*, Walter McAuley, Chief Librarian of the *Belfast Telegraph*, Eamon Melaugh, Dr Martin Melaugh of the University of Ulster's CAIN Archive (http://cain.ulst.ac.uk/), Dean Nelson, Scottish Editor of the *Sunday Times*, Rebecca North of the *Sunday Times* picture desk, Barrie Penrose, Jonathan Miller and Nic Robertson of CNN, journalist Ted Oliver, photographer Crispin Rodwell, Pat McArt, editor of the *Derry Journal* and our solicitor, Paul Tweed.

Liam Clarke would like to thank Fiona McHugh, the Irish Editor of the *Sunday Times*, and his other colleagues at the *Sunday Times*.

We would like to acknowledge the serenity and fortitude of all the staff at Mainstream Publishing in Edinburgh, especially Sharon Atherton, Bill

Campbell, Tina Hudson, Peter MacKenzie, Jess Thompson, Becky Pickard, Fiona Brownlee and in particular, to our editors, Ailsa Bathgate and Alison Provan.

This book could not have been written without the tolerance and understanding of our families; their many offers of help and support were deeply appreciated. Finally, we would like to thank our sons Adam and Daniel, and our daughter, Alice. They showed great patience during the writing of this book in summer 2001, and we are grateful. This book is for them.

If you have any comments about the material in this book please contact the authors at fromgunstogovernment@yahoo.co.uk

Interviewees

Quotations attributed to 'author interview' refer to previously unpublished interviews which McGuinness gave to Kathryn Johnston in 1992. Several people asked that their identities be kept confidential. For this reason and for legal reasons, a number of people have been given pseudonyms. The names we have given them are: Burke, Des Clinton, Charlie Coogan, Chick Donnelly, Peter Doherty, John Joe McCann, Stubby Wall, Paddy Lawlor and Martin Ingram.

The following are deceased: Kevin Agnew, Gerry 'The Bird' Doherty, Jimmy Drumm, Kathleen and Willie Gallagher, Cathal Goulding, Eamon Lafferty, veteran republican Sean Keenan, Malachy McGurran, Sean MacStiofain, Micky Montgomery, Daithi O Conaill, Phil O'Donnell, J B O'Hagan, Seamus Twomey, Kevin Ward, Eddie McSheffrey, George McBrearty, Charles Maguire, John Gerard Holmes and Paddy Deery.

Dennis Bradley: Former priest, founder member of the Link, Oscar winning film-maker
Willie Breslin: Former teacher and Derry Labour Party activist
Willie Carlin: FRU agent in Derry Sinn Féin
Pat Devine: Former SDLP Mayor of Derry
James Doherty: Nationalist Party politician and businessman, employed Martin McGuinness at the start of the Troubles

Martina Donnelly: Wife of Michael

Michael Donnelly: Former 'hooded man', attacked by IRA in 1998

Brother Egan: Teacher at Brow of the Hill Christian Brothers School

Monsignor Denis Faul: Campaigner on human rights abuses

Raymond Gilmour: RUC agent within the IRA, later gave supergrass evidence. Interviewed prior to his confidentiality agreement with MI5

George Harrison: Irish American activist

John Hume MP, MEP: SDLP leader

Pat Hume: Wife of John Hume

'Martin Ingram': Former FRU agent handler and intelligence collater

Phil Kent: Irish activist living in North America

Pat McArt: Editor of the *Derry Journal*

Martin McGartland: Former RUC agent within the IRA

Paul McGill: Education journalist

Peter Mandelson: MP for Hartlepool

Lord Ken Maginnis: Ulster Unionist Party Security Spokesman

Sir Patrick Mayhew: Former Secretary of State for Northern Ireland

Eamon Melaugh: Civil rights and political activist

Liam O Comain: Former organiser for Sinn Féin in Derry at the start of the Troubles

Michael Oatley: MI6 agent, known as 'Mountain Climber'

David Shayler: Former MI5 agent facing charges of breaching the Official Secrets Act

Peter Taylor: Journalist and broadcaster

Jill Uris: Photographer

Paddy Ward: Former IRA member

Sammy Wilson: MLA, DUP Education Spokesman

Norman Walmsley: Civil rights activist

CHAPTER ONE

A Boy from the Bogside

I don't regard my story as being important. My background is very much the same as everybody else who grew up in the Bogside and my story can be replicated in every town and village in the six counties. The experiences that I have been through, other people have been through.

Martin McGuinness, author interview, January 1992

July 2001

As the Member of Parliament for Mid-Ulster left Stormont Buildings for the last time before the summer recess, he took his seat in the dark-green Ford Mondeo he had chosen over the armour-plated Mercedes provided for his protection when he became Minister for Education in the Northern Ireland Assembly. When the car, driven by one of his regular bodyguards, moved slowly away from Stormont towards the motorway which would take him on the first part of his journey home, Martin McGuinness must have wondered when, if ever, he would return. Talks between the main parties in Northern Ireland were close to breakdown, and McGuinness, as Chief Negotiator for Sinn Féin, would play a make or break role over the summer months. As the Mondeo left the motorway for the ascent to the Glenshane Pass, the steep mountain road through the Sperrins, he might have looked out at the barren, rocky outcrops of the rural constituency he had just been re-elected to serve in the House of Commons. Just over two hours after leaving Stormont, McGuinness was being swiftly driven across the River Foyle, the serpentine river which divides the east and west banks of Derry. Within a few minutes the car had reached the familiar Bogside streets where McGuinness played as a child. Sometimes he would ask the driver to wait while he visited his mother, Peggy, who still lived in the house where he grew up. McGuinness and his wife, Bernie, lived just a few streets away and as his car drew smoothly to a halt outside his Westland Terrace home, he looked quickly up and down the street before hurrying in, closing the door sharply behind him.

The terraced houses of Elmwood Street, where Martin McGuinness played as a child, were, like the rest of the Bogside, built for the families from neighbouring Donegal who came to Derry looking for work in the building boom of the nineteenth century. Derry lies on a bend in the River Foyle, in the far north-west of Ireland; a network of back lanes and roads connect it to the neighbouring Co. Donegal in the Irish Republic, partitioned from the North in 1921. Derry's history is that of a bitterly divided people, where the very name of the city itself is contested. The Protestant minority know it as Londonderry, the Maiden City which repelled the advances of James II in the siege of 1689. The Catholic majority prefer to use the city's original name – Derry.

When Martin McGuinness was born in 1950, Derry was already displaying signs of the trouble that was to come. In 1936, following a warning from the first Minister for Home Affairs, Dawson Bates, to Northern Ireland's Prime Minister, Lord Craigavon, local electoral boundaries were redrawn to ensure that the Unionist minority controlled the City Corporation. The number of electoral wards were reduced to three: two, which were largely Protestant, returned twelve Unionist councillors between them, and the third, the mainly Catholic, South Ward, returned eight Nationalist councillors. Gerrymandering ensured that the Corporation remained in Unionist hands until it was abolished at the end of 1968 after civil rights campaigners marched in protest about discrimination in Derry.

On 31 May 1950, William McGuinness left his home at 5 Elmwood Street in South Ward to register the birth of his second son, born eight days earlier in Waterside General Hospital. William and his wife Peggy, who was several years younger than her husband, had just celebrated the first birthday of their oldest boy, Thomas, born in Elmwood Street on 15 May 1949. The healthy baby boy was registered James Martin Pacelli McGuinness. He would be known as Martin, after his grandfather and his uncle – a priest who later became Bishop of Nottingham. The couple were committed Catholics and McGuinness was named Pacelli after the family name of the then Pope, Pius XII, known as 'Hitler's Pope' because of the accusation that he had been a wartime collaborator with the fascists. Dennis Bradley, who became an Oscar-winning film maker and was a priest in Derry in the '60s, remembers the family well. 'They were certainly a religious family, as was everybody else in that community – after all, you were talking about 100 per cent attendance. They were a typical Derry family, and Martin's father in particular was a lovely man.' Like most Bogside families, the McGuinness family supported the Nationalist Party, whose leader, Eddie McAteer, was their local MP. But the church always came first. As Martin McGuinness would later remember, 'We were reared in the nationalist, Catholic tradition, with the greater emphasis being on Catholic.'

When he looked back on it later, Martin McGuinness would remember his childhood as happy and uneventful. He was the second oldest in a family of seven – six boys and one girl, who were brought up in the same house that Peggy McGuinness, who was widowed in 1973, still lives in today. Martin is a frequent visitor to the house, just a short distance from his Sinn Féin office on Cable Street, and often meets journalists there. John Hume, Social Democratic and Labour Party MP for the Foyle constituency, Member of the European Parliament (MEP) for Northern Ireland and winner of the Nobel Peace Prize, was a neighbour when McGuinness was growing up, 'I knew Elmwood Street, where McGuinness was born, well – in those days I lived in Beechwood Avenue, just a couple of streets from him. He was in the bottom house, round the corner from Bradley's pub, the Celtic Bar it is now. In those days I was very active in running the credit union, because it didn't have any full-time staff at the time. I was the treasurer, which meant that I was actually the manager and I ran it on a Friday night and on a Saturday, so I knew all the families in the area. The McGuinness family were a decent family, they weren't republican at all – I think he would have been the first one.'

While unemployment was the norm in Derry following the wartime boom, William McGuinness, who worked in an iron foundry like his father before him, managed to stay in work throughout Martin's childhood. John Hume remembers his own father, a lifelong trade unionist, warning him of the importance of bread and butter issues, 'You can't eat a flag', he would say. McGuinness has said, 'We were lucky that my father did have work - he worked all his life in Brown's Foundry, as a foreman. My background is much the same as everybody from the Bogside, Creggan, or Brandywell areas, just a working-class background.'

Apart from his older brother Tom, who always kept a close eye on him, the greatest influence in those early days on Martin McGuinness was his mother, Margaret, known as Peggy. Peggy was 'the backbone of the house', a neighbour remembers. 'She was always very supportive and very proud of all the family. Martin is very like her, in looks as well as everything else.'

Peggy's family was from the Illies area of Donegal, just outside the busy seaside resort of Buncrana, where she met Martin's father at a dance. McGuinness spent long parts of his school holidays in her childhood home, a small farm where his grandmother lived with his mother's brother. Martin's Uncle John was known as John 'Walls' Doherty; a well-known Derry member of the same clan was known as Paddy 'Bogside' Doherty.

McGuinness thrived as he roamed the hills of Donegal and during the school term he often yearned to return. Peggy remembers that 'He loved the country – cutting turf and corn, setting the potatoes.' He was a quiet child, and her favourite photograph of him is on the dry-stone Donegal wall outside the farmhouse, where her seven children sit side by side, their knees browned by the summer sun. McGuinness has often spoken of his love for the county: 'I have a very close affinity with Donegal – probably it goes back to the fact that my mother was born and reared there. I spent most of my summer holidays there when I was young, before the Troubles started and I love it very much.'

The McGuinness family grew steadily. On 12 July 1951, the day when the North's Protestant Orange Order celebrates the victory of the Dutch King William over the Catholic King James in 1690, Peggy McGuinness presented Tom and Martin with a new young brother, Paul Oliver, born at home in Elmwood Street. And just three days after Martin McGuinness' third birthday, on 26 May 1953, his only sister, Mary Geraldine, was born, again in the family home. Two years later another brother, William Columba McGuinness, was born, on 8 June 1956. Willie, who was instantly recognisable by the port wine coloured birthmark on his face, would become the only member of the immediate family to follow Martin into the republican movement. But for now, Martin's life had assumed a stolid and agreeable pattern, which remained largely untouched by the outside world. As he remembers it, 'My childhood was very quiet and uneventful and nothing very exciting happened. We were only interested in things like going to school, playing football, having a good time. Probably the most exciting thing to happen would be if an RUC man chased after you for playing football in the street.'

Outside events rarely intruded on his young life, 'There was no politics discussed whatsoever, to my recollection, in the house, although I was aware that, on my mother's side, there had been an involvement of grand uncles and things like that in the struggle for freedom in the 1920s. But we were a very, I would say, non-political family.' Willie Breslin, a teacher and member of the Derry Labour Party, knew the McGuinnesses: 'The whole family were lovely people. There was no history of any violence or aggression, any republicanism, nothing like that – no politics at all. They were good Catholic people who would probably have voted nationalist and when John Hume came along they probably would have voted for him. The mother was a very typical Derry mother, a very nice wee woman.' In fact, although the family voted for Nationalist MP Eddie McAteer, William McGuinness senior's best friend was a Protestant man he worked with in the foundry, Willie McNeill, and the family were brought up in a non-sectarian atmosphere.

As the boys grew older, McGuinness hero-worshipped his older brother Tom and frequently looked to him for protection in the rough and tumble of street games in the Bogside. One boy who played with McGuinness at the time remembers 'If anybody so much as looked crooked at Martin, he ran in to get Tom out to fight them for him.' The Bogside was a lively place, where children ran around freely in the days before the Troubles. Although it was an urban community, many kept chickens and pigs in their backyards – families who contributed scraps of food to the 'brock man' (who collected them for pigswill) were rewarded with a gift when the animal was slaughtered. Many remember being woken when they heard the roosters crowing at dawn.

By 1955 McGuinness was a pupil at the 'wee nuns', in Rosemount Street near the old gas yard, which would later become an important centre for IRA activity. Officially, it was called St Eugene's convent school, a Victorian building in the shadow of the cathedral. The school, which had outside toilets and no proper plumbing, was supervised by Sister Xavier from Leitrim. Forty-five years later, Martin Bowen, now a Derry school principal himself and McGuinness' best friend at school, told *The Guardian* newspaper that the young Martin 'was not a boy to get into the sort of devilment other boys got into. He was extremely polite to the nuns'. In an interview with the *Irish Times* in May 2001, McGuinness looked back on his first day at school, saying that he 'might have blubbered for a moment or two – nothing more than that – then I caught myself on'. He enjoyed his years there, and remained until 1957, when he left to go to the Christian Brothers Primary School.

Paul McGill, who lived in Marlborough Street at the time and later became an education journalist, was a contemporary at the Christian Brothers. He remembers it as a hard school, which laid great store on corporal punishment. McGill explained, 'There were 54 kids in our class and we got thumped all the time, especially in Brother Harney's class. He was a traditionalist and the whole point of the school was to get people past the eleven-plus. Corporal punishment was the day-to-day routine, but it was also Brother Harney's secret weapon in getting pupils through it.' For four years, McGill and McGuinness practised eleven-plus tests continually. If, according to McGill, you failed to answer a question correctly, you joined a line of pupils. When the line was long enough, the teacher would start to beat everyone on the hands with his leather strap. To safeguard further against failure, pupils were taken across to St Eugene's cathedral the day before their first test to say their confessions. Despite the flogging, McGuinness failed the eleven-plus. He later explained that he had no trouble with the work itself and blamed his failure on sitting the examination in an unfamiliar setting. In September 1961 he followed his older brother Tom to the Christian Brothers Brow of the Hill Technical College, where he spent his spare time playing soccer. The Brow of the Hill was the senior counterpart of the primary school and shared a site with the elite St Columb's College, where John Hume taught history.

At the technical college, violent attacks on pupils were very much the order of the day. As some pupils remember, while the Christian Brothers were very tough, some of the lay teachers were actually worse. Most used a leather strap to reinforce their teaching methods. The school was poorly resourced, and most of the classrooms were huts. Many thought the school day was dull and unvaried. Pupils studied French, Irish, RE, English, Physics, Chemistry, Maths and Applied Maths, Woodwork and Metalwork, Art and History. McGuinness was an undistinguished pupil, but one teacher, Brother Egan, who has since retired to live in Belfast, has fond memories of him, 'He was always quiet and cooperative with me, and, I believe, with other teachers. I wouldn't have said that he shone at school and I was somewhat surprised to see where he has gone, I would not have picked him out as going where he has gone.' He remembers that McGuinness enjoyed geography and English, although not Egan's own subject of mathematics. Brother Egan is a kindly, scholarly man and there is no suggestion that he used violence unfairly against his pupils, although McGuinness mentions the 'oppressive atmosphere' in several classes, including mathematics, where he said that his feeling going into their classes 'was one of dread – and I know I wasn't the only one'. 'In the training college,' Brother Egan recalls, 'we were taught that we could hit the boys if they did something wrong deliberately or refused to work, but not if they made a mistake. I couldn't say if all the brothers and the teachers kept to those guidelines.' Former pupils allege that some members of staff flagrantly breached them, and every opportunity to instil 'respect' was taken. On one sunny day during McGuinness' time at the school, a classroom door had been left open to let in some fresh air, and a little dog ran in, wagging its tail. The Brother teaching the class walked calmly over to it, his face impassive. As he reached the dog, he suddenly kicked it three or four feet up into the air. As the dog fell, it hit the door, which swang back against the wall. The dog was concussed for several minutes, before running off whining. As the dog ran off, the Brother turned to the class, who were staring at him, frightened, 'Little dogs are like little boys, when they get hit, they squeal, and then they don't get hit any more.'

Another of McGuinness' teachers 'was a maniac and ended up in a straitjacket' remembered one former pupil. Another explained, 'Everybody's parents tried to do their best for their children, turn them out very well, tried to give them the best education they could. It wasn't easy at the Christian Brothers, you needed football boots, kit – I suppose it was the same at any school then, but you were coming from an area where there was very high deprivation.' In frustration at the parents' inability to meet the kit requirements, the former pupil continued, the teacher cracked and took his anger out on the boys. The final straw came when he had them all lined up for checking. The first check was for football boots; some of the boys had none. As the list of missing kit grew, and he worked along the line of boys, 'he got more and more frustrated as time went on. He just started to pound them. He beat one boy to the ground, and then had to be pulled

off him – by boys as well as staff. Later that night, the wagon came for him.'
Some pupils went further still, blaming incidents like these for creating a
culture of violence in the school among the students. One boy who
witnessed an incident which involved McGuinness remembers it clearly. He
says:

> I wish this wasn't my strongest memory of Martin
> McGuinness, but it certainly is a very vivid memory. This was
> the first time I noticed his dress – Teddy Boys were going then
> and I would say that he must have been nearly 15 at the time.
> Martin wasn't a very loud Teddy Boy but he was very style-
> conscious, wearing drainpipes: not overly tight but they would
> have been that style, with a suit jacket and black pointy shoes.
> He was a striking person, with long, curly, bushy, fair hair.
>   I can remember it as well, it's funny how things stick in
> your mind, because I remember him standing outside one of
> the classrooms in the playground, I think it was room D and E.
> Two boys in darker suits stood on either side of him. Suddenly
> these two boys went over to another boy, standing on his own
> in the playground. They both hit at him until he was on the
> ground, then Martin came over and hit him when he was
> down. It wasn't an overly vicious attack or anything, I think
> maybe this boy had done something to McGuinness, but I
> didn't ask any questions, I stayed away. That's an incident
> that's always been with me and would have been, even if he
> hadn't become well known. A school playground bully. But in
> a different environment he would have been a team leader, as
> he later proved. It was the atmosphere we were surrounded
> with.'

Outside school, football was one of McGuinness' main pastimes. The family
home in the Bogside was close to both Celtic Park where Gaelic Athletic
Association (GAA) football was played, and to Brandywell Park, where
Derry City Football Club played. Soccer was traditionally the bigger sport
in Derry, following its promotion by the Catholic Church in the nineteenth
century due to fears that the playing of Gaelic games would influence the
young men of the parish towards nationalism. The entire family were

regular attenders at both grounds and all the brothers showed promise at sports. McGuinness would later tell how the brothers had won something like 12 medals for Gaelic games in Celtic Park. Tom was particularly skilled. He played Gaelic football for the local club, Sarsfields, and was a member of the victorious Derry Under-21 side, who won the Ulster title in 1967 and the All-Ireland Championship in 1968. His brother Paul was a talented soccer player who was right-back for Derry City Football Club for a period. Paul once played in a League of Ireland Select XI against Diego Maradona, the legendary Argentinian member of the World Cup-winning team. Martin preferred soccer to Gaelic football and one of his dearest memories was when his father took him up to Belfast by train in 1964 to watch Derry beat Glentoran 2–0 in the Irish Cup Final at Windsor Park.

Soon after reaching his fifteenth birthday in 1965, Martin McGuinness left the Brow of the Hill to seek work. Despite the fact that his father had a reasonably good job as foreman in the Foundry, money was tight with nine mouths to feed. Declan Anthony McGuinness had been born on 5 July 1957, soon to be joined by another brother, John Eugenio, who was born on 23 October 1958. Tom had already left school, and had started work in the building trade. At the time jobs were scarce and the growing Catholic population were encountering discrimination. Derry had a birth rate which was more like the profile of a Third World country rather than that of the United Kingdom and the 1961 census revealed that Martin McGuinness was one of the 40 per cent of the population of South Ward who was under 15. He applied for a job as a mechanic in a local garage. The firm would ask potential employees which school they had attended, a back-handed way of gauging his religion. As soon as McGuinness answered that he had attended the Christian Brothers, he was shown the door. 'I was shell shocked,' he said later. It was his first experience of the discrimination which so many young people had encountered in Derry. 'There was nothing for us in Derry, for young people. There wasn't any work, the levels of unemployment were very high – I think a lot of people were conscious of the massive discrimination which was being used against them by the Unionists.' He later found work as a shop assistant at the Home and Colonial Store on Ferryquay Street, where he stayed for six years. In 1971 his father got him an interview at Doherty's Butchers, where he became an apprentice.

Meanwhile, in August 1966, a weekend meeting of the Wolfe Tone Society was held in the comfortable Maghera home of the prominent republican solicitor, Kevin Agnew. After dinner, guests listened as the new strategy of the republican movement was set out in a paper read by Eoghan Harris from Cork, in whom Chief of Staff Cathal Goulding (who became a Marxist while in jail in England), had placed his trust. The paper outlined a long-term strategy to unite the Protestant and Catholic working-class people of Northern Ireland by mounting a civil rights campaign, which in the short term would put pressure on unionism for political reform and in the long term would alert the Protestant working class to their real interests. The way would then be clear for a united working class to fight for socialism, leading to a united socialist republic. This plan, the 'stages theory', was initiated in January 1967 when the Northern Ireland Civil Rights Association (NICRA) was formally established in Belfast, with some short-lived unionist representation within its membership. Initially there was only one representative from Sinn Féin – Kevin Agnew – on the executive, and by and large NICRA was a strange hybrid of members of the Communist Party of Ireland and liberal middle-class Catholics. They called for a number of reforms; one of which was for 'one man, one vote', that is, a universal franchise for local government elections. At the time only ratepayers were entitled to votes, and there were other anomalies concerning additional votes for companies. NICRA also pressed for the end to gerrymandering of electoral boundaries; the end to discrimination in the allocation of public sector housing and appointments; the repeal of the Special Powers Act; and the disbandment of the 'B-Specials' (Ulster Special Constabulary) which was a largely Protestant paramilitary-style reserve police force. By November 1967, NICRA's membership and influence were growing, and other radical groups were springing up, particularly in Derry.

A small group of young Derry men had already become active on social issues in the early 1960s and soon started a Derry branch of the youth wing of the IRA, the Fianna Eireann. Paddy Ward, from the Creggan housing estate in Derry, was a member of the Fianna: 'To the best of my knowledge, the Derry Fianna was started in about 1963, and the aim was to kind of start an armed revolution, people felt that the older republicans in Derry had had their day and were happy enough just running the Easter commemorations.' John Joe McCann became a member in 1965: 'I joined the Fianna when I was about 13, and I worked with them until we went over to the Provos – at the end there were men in it as well as boys, but we just kept them on anyway. We had virtually no guns, but we did have a uniform – a green tunic, a Sam

Browne belt, and a beret. We spent our time learning Irish and going on demonstrations at the Guildhall on a Saturday.' The demonstrations were to extend the city boundary to provide for more public housing for the working-class people of Derry, who were mostly Catholic. The Unionist-dominated Derry City Corporation refused to build more houses, claiming a shortage of land.

To all real intents and purposes, however, there was precious little remaining of the IRA in Derry at the time, a fact acknowledged later by Martin McGuinness, 'When the Troubles actually started, apart from a few very creditable families in the city who had a republican position, there wasn't any republican movement in Derry at the beginning of the civil rights. There were a number of people and families who regarded themselves as being republican, but there was no real republican movement in terms of hundreds and thousands of people supporting Sinn Féin policies.' Liam O Comain, who joined the IRA in 1955 when he was just 15, lying about his age, was sent to Derry to reorganise the republican movement. 'There was a romance there at that time, but the reality that I actually experienced over the years was far removed from my idealism then.' O Comain worked with Sean Keenan, in whose house he often slept, and Gerry 'The Bird' Doherty, who got his nickname in the '30s for his tight-lipped response to queries – 'a little bird told me'. Doherty became a legend after his escape from Crumlin Road Prison in 1941 when he scrawled 'the bird has flown' on his cell wall.

O Comain was appointed joint organiser, with Malachy McGurran, for Sinn Féin in the North: 'I was full-time and I did the West: Derry, Tyrone, Donegal, Fermanagh. Malachy did the East part of the six counties. As part of that particular structure, I was automatically co-opted onto the Ard Comhairle of Sinn Féin at the time. I was also on the Army Executive, Army Council. Within the movement, there were all the left ideas, certain documents came up from Dublin to be discussed . . . I remember one meeting Sean Keenan came along too. Now, everyone knew Sean Keenan wasn't for this particular thing at all, and he drifted away after that and wasn't seen again till the beginning of the Provisionals. The McGuinness family were not involved in any of this at all. Martin was not recruited into the IRA until much, much later.'

As unrest built in the North, Martin McGuinness steered clear of the protests. He had found a new job, as an apprentice in James Doherty's butcher's shop. Doherty was a senior Nationalist Party politician in Derry at the time and remembers McGuinness well, 'Martin McGuinness was a quiet lad, a good worker. A very solid, sound fellow. His background was traditional Derry, a first-class sound background. I had no idea then what his views were, his father would have given me a ring. We had started a sideline, packaging bacon, and he worked for a couple of years in Waterloo Place, packing bacon. We were a large butcher's shop, which developed a small factory and we supplied all the grocers in Derry. The front of the shop was retail, and the back production. He had other duties too; when we had a bottleneck of any kind, production staff came in and helped in the shop. It was an old-fashioned method, but it met the needs of Derry at the time.'

As Martin McGuinness settled into his new job, preparations were being made for the event which would provide the spark that lit the flames in Derry.

CHAPTER TWO

Sticks, Stones and Good Old Petrol Bombs

It seemed to me as plain as daylight that there was an army in our town, in our country, and that they weren't there to give out flowers. Armies should be fought by armies.

Martin McGuinness, quoted by
Nell McCafferty, *Irish Times*, 19 April 1972

'Four incidents,' Martin McGuinness once said, 'made me a republican.' Although he was not personally there, the Duke Street march of 5 October 1968 was one of them. That Saturday, most Derry people gave the march a miss. The civil rights movement had not yet captured nationalist imagination, although there were signs that local apathy was breaking down.

The march had been banned by Minister for Home Affairs, William Craig, and Gerry (later Lord) Fitt, Republican Labour MP at Stormont, had brought three British Labour MPs with him as observers. The organisers expected trouble, and had tipped off RTE (the Irish equivalent of the BBC). Before long trouble had flared up when the RUC attacked sections of the crowd as they ordered them to disperse. That night the television coverage of marchers being beaten by the RUC was shown worldwide. Millions saw Gerry Fitt try to reason with the RUC, blood dripping down his face from his wounds. British Prime Minister Harold Wilson was among the viewers who saw one senior officer pursue a demonstrator while waving a blackthorn stick around his head, before cornering and attacking him.

The lesson for McGuinness was that 'peaceful protest wasn't going to change things. You could only take so much violence from the state, from the RUC and from the "B men" . . . The inability of the civil rights movement to actually achieve anything forced me to have a complete look at the entire situation. I very quickly came to the position that justice could only be achieved in the context of a 32-county united Ireland.' For the first time, the 18-year-old McGuinness started to take an interest in civil rights. He watched closely as 1969 opened with attacks on the People's Democracy (PD) marchers who walked from Belfast to Derry, in imitation of Dr Martin Luther King's march from Selma to Montgomery. Seven miles from Derry, they were ambushed at Burntollet Bridge by loyalist gangs, armed with cudgels, iron bars, bottles and stones. The RUC failed to protect the marchers from the gangs; many were convinced that they were in league. That night, a group of policemen invaded the Bogside, and the next day the following slogan appeared painted on a gable wall appeared 'You are now entering Free Derry'. The gable wall is still standing today and is preserved as a historic monument.

By Easter that year, it was obvious that attitudes were hardening. On Easter Sunday, the veteran republican Sean Keenan shared a platform with the young radical, Johnny White. Keenan, whose diminutive stature and dapper appearance were at odds with his reputation as a veteran IRA man, appealed to the crowd to join the republican movement, telling them 'The enemy is still England.' Shortly afterwards, Keenan went to America where he worked the circuit of Irish emigrant groups to found the Irish Northern Aid Committee. Over the years it raked in millions of dollars, which they claimed to send 'home' for prisoners' dependants. No doubt some money did reach legitimate groups, if only for accounting purposes. However, Noraid, as it is better known, provided the cover for one of the most efficient arms dealing operations ever. The first shipment of several hundred Armalites left Philadelphia for Ireland in August 1970 and other weapons were later smuggled over on the QE2 and secretly unloaded at Southampton and other ports.

A few days after the Easter commemoration, the RUC were chasing a group of rioters who managed to escape through the door of a Bogside house. In frustration the RUC attacked the occupant, Samuel Devenney, who was standing chatting to a neighbour at his front door. The severe beating he received from the police resulted in a fractured skull and a subsequent heart attack. Devenney died of his injuries shortly after the annual 12 July Orange parades. The mood in Derry darkened, as it seemed to many that the RUC could literally get away with murder. His death had a lasting impact on Martin McGuinness who later said: 'My first, if you like, touch with death was when I heard that Sammy Devenney had been beaten in his house in William Street by the RUC.' Rumours swept the city as the annual Apprentice Boys parade on 12 August drew closer. The marching season is often an opportunity for triumphalism and that this year fears were growing that the marchers would invade the Bogside. Sean Keenan had gone to Dublin to ask Cathal Goulding, the IRA Chief of Staff, for support. Goulding turned him down flat, saying he had neither the men nor the guns to defend the Bogside, although he could arrange for the Northern Ireland Prime Minister and Minister for Home Affairs to be assassinated. Keenan, who was impatiently waiting for the promised consignment of Armalites to arrive from America, chose to make his own arrangements. The Derry Brigade of the IRA had already decided, as Sean Keenan told a packed meeting in the Stardust Ballroom, not to use what few weapons they had. Instead they would 'defend the Bogside with sticks, stones and good old petrol bombs'.

On the day of the march, the city was buzzing. After the Apprentice Boys had marched, the RUC, closely followed by loyalist mobs, manhandled their way through the barricades. When the Bogside residents fought them off, CS gas cylinders were fired at them to push them back. This was to be the pattern of events for the next two days as the Battle of the Bogside began.

The third day of rioting dawned on 14 August. The Bogsiders had so far managed to keep the police and B-Specials out.

Police resources were stretched to breaking point as riots broke out in Belfast and other towns in response to pleas from the Bogside for people to take the heat off Derry. As Martin McGuinness put it, 'The fury of a united people had finally exploded.' As McGuinness joined the rioters to hurl petrol bombs at the RUC, police responded by firing 1,105 tear-gas shells at the rioters in a thirty-six-hour period. McGuinness later told journalist Kevin Toolis, 'I threw stones, petrol bombs, whatever else I could lay my hands on . . . After work I would go home, get my dinner, and go back down and throw stones and whatever else was to hand until twelve o'clock at night.' Hundreds of people were injured during the three days and few slept, fearful that the RUC would enter the area and burn the Bogside to the ground. Elsewhere in Derry, there were reports that loyalist gangs had already started to burn out Catholic families. The Taoiseach, Jack Lynch, sent Irish troops to the border, assuring nationalists that he 'would not stand by and see innocent people injured, and perhaps worse.'

On Thursday, 14 August, late in the afternoon, British Prime Minister Harold Wilson sent British soldiers onto the streets of Belfast and Derry. At 5.00 p.m., the First Battalion of the Prince of Wales' Own Regiment marched onto the street. Initially, the soldiers were welcomed and local girls competed to serve them tea, but the honeymoon period was brief. McGuinness now believed that the troops had been sent not to protect the people of the Bogside, but to help the Unionists contain the situation, which was no longer under their control. 'In those circumstances,' McGuinness believed, 'confrontation with the British Army was inevitable.' Before long, there were complaints about the army's behaviour. One lunchtime McGuinness was returning to Doherty's after buying a snack at a local shop when he was stopped by an army patrol, who forced him to take off his socks and shoes before searching him. The soldiers then told McGuinness, still barefoot, to face the wall with his arms spread-eagled and fingertips touching the wall. Willie Breslin remembers what happened next. 'Martin was a very shy wee boy, and the soldiers humiliated him in front of all the girls from the shirt factories. They were on their break and stood around staring. Until then, he was a very quiet young fellow but after that Martin went down with the rest, throwing stones. He never would have done that before.' Paddy Ward heard about it from his older brother, Kevin, who worked in Doherty's at the time, 'Kevin told me McGuinness was absolutely raging. He seemed to take more of a part after that.'

By October the British Army were no longer seen as the saviours of the nationalist people. McGuinness was now a regular participant in the daily street battles and later told the *Irish Times*: 'All this time there was fighting in the streets and things were getting worse in Belfast. You could see the soldiers just settling into Derry, not being too worried about the stone throwing.' The army called the rioters the 'Derry Young Hooligans' and renamed the area near William Street where they threw stones 'Aggro Corner'. Saturday afternoon riots were known as the 'matinee'.

The trouble ran on into the autumn, when Martin McGuinness was part of a group of Catholic demonstrators who were protesting outside Strand Road RUC station after the police had intervened to halt skirmishes between them and a rival Protestant crowd. Sean Keenan, afraid that the British army would attack the crowd, appealed to them to move on. They ignored him, pushing abandoned buses together to form makeshift barricades, as the soldiers drew their batons to charge. During the fighting McGuinness was arrested for the first time for shouting abuse at the soldiers. On 27 October at Londonderry Petty Sessions he was found guilty of disorderly behaviour and fined fifty pounds, as well as being bound over in his own recognisance in the sum of fifty pounds for two years. It was the first time that anyone had been convicted on the basis of long-distance identification by British troops – a group of soldiers lying on the roof of the nearby Embassy ballroom had spotted McGuinness through binoculars trained on the crowd.

Some former pupils of St Columb's school, who were now members of the Fianna, broke into the school to raid the science labs for anything they could use against the army. Although McGuinness was not in the Fianna, he had tagged along with the boys. One of them would later become the IRA's top explosives expert in Derry and he was planning to experiment with a form of home-made explosive in his bedroom. Luckily, however, a local priest, Father Mulvey, caught them before they could attempt to convert the stolen sulphuric acid into an acid bomb.

Paddy Ward had joined the Fianna with his friends. 'A bunch of us were in a football team – we were all buddies and all brought up in Creggan so it seemed the right thing to do at the time, especially when we saw how the British Army and the police were behaving in Derry, in particular, the killing of Sammy Devenney. We were at that vulnerable age.'

Shortly after the Derry Fianna was started in 1963, a group of left-wing republicans were beginning to revive the IRA. Peter Doherty is a former member of the IRA who became active at that time. As he recalls, they were well organised and during 1969 were running border training camps, where volunteers were taught how to fire and strip down weapons, the use of explosives and so on. The camps were jointly run. Their leaders were a former soldier in the Irish army, and the legendary Phil O'Donnell, a burly man, already in his 30s who had once been a paratrooper in the British Army. At the time, Doherty says, some of the new recruits were suspicious of O'Donnell's army membership; others joked that he claimed to have fought in Korea, but had only played in the army band.

When Martin McGuinness finally joined the IRA in 1970, they were mainly drilling and training at weekend camps across the border in Donegal. Peter Doherty attended several training camps with McGuinness, whom he had known since school. 'You would stand around at pre-arranged pick-up points, in twos usually, before you would be picked up. The drill would be three or four car runs up a country lane, then into a barn, and up a trap door to the top of the barn. It was mostly weapons training, and after the basic stuff, guns would be fired in the hills. IRA men involved in the '50s campaign told us all the best venues – valleys, where the sound could be kept low, that sort of thing. On one occasion, the FCA (Irish equivalent of the Territorial Army) were on manoeuvres on the mountain opposite us, and we waved to each other.' The camps, which generally ran from Friday evening to Sunday night, were popular events, not least for the boy scouts atmosphere. McGuinness, who had enjoyed the country life during holidays at his grandmother's house in the Illies, loved them. In the evenings there were political discussions in front of a turf fire, held after volunteers had eaten the meals they cooked using gas cylinders they 'liberated' from Derry building sites.

Meanwhile, rumours that the IRA was secretly preparing for a campaign had reached London and some journalists were making discreet enquiries of republican contacts in Dublin. Following an approach from the BBC programme *Nationwide*, broadcast on 25 May 1970, the IRA agreed to let them film a camp, set up for that purpose. The young McGuinness, heavily armed with a machine gun, wearing a camouflage jacket and only lightly disguised in a stocking mask, frisked the crew and checked their identification as they arrived. The camp, in an old semi-derelict cottage at the end of a country lane, seemed to impress the crew, according to an IRA man who took part in manoeuvres and drilling for the cameras. After a staged sequence where another volunteer was roughly searched, Phil O'Donnell, the former Para, crouched on the rough floor to demonstrate stripping down a weapon. There was no attempt to disguise his voice, and his heavy chin and bulbous nose are clearly visible through his stocking mask. In another sequence, Martin McGuinness bursts through a door, masked and armed with a machine gun.

By the end of 1969, tensions within the IRA had come to a head resulting in an acrimonious split, after sections in Belfast, who wanted to return to armed struggle, contacted representatives of the Irish state. They were offered financial support, on condition that the IRA stayed north of the border. Sean Keenan was one of the earliest members of the new IRA. By January 1970, Sinn Féin had also split. The new IRA issued a statement calling themselves the 'Provisional' IRA, a title they had intended to be temporary. But the press latched on to it, and soon the two groups were called 'Officials' and 'Provisionals'. The Officials were later also referred to as 'Stickies', because badges they sold at Easter had adhesive backs, whereas the Provisionals used pins. The split left Derry largely untouched at first, in spite of Provisional IRA Chief of Staff Sean MacStiofain's frequent visits to Sean Keenan. Keenan had already been expelled from the IRA by Goulding for meeting Irish military intelligence who were trying to destabilise the IRA, but by February 1970 he had founded the Padraig Pearse cumann of Sinn Féin. He was also secretly recruiting for the Provisional IRA, with little initial success. Liam O Comain says that Keenan had been in close contact with Daithi O Conaill, the first Quartermaster of the Provisional IRA. 'O Conaill at the time was teaching at Glencolumbcille in Donegal and saw Sean Keenan regularly. Together, they tried to take some of the Officials with them, including McGuinness, but they refused. McGuinness stayed with the Officials for quite a number of months after that.'

The Fianna, although nominally neutral, were secretly working closely with Daithi O Conaill in Donegal. Although he was high on the wanted list of both the British Army and the RUC, O Conaill slipped across the border to Derry, where he attended a public meeting to recruit for the Provisional IRA in the Harps Hall in Brandywell. O Conaill told John Joe McCann that he planned to set up flying columns on the border, which would strike at the British Army before retreating to the safe haven of the Republic. As far as McCann was concerned, O Conaill's plan was stamped with the failures of the past. 'The Fianna wouldn't go near the meeting in the Harps Hall, we thought it was ridiculous. You're going to form the Provos at a public meeting? Flying columns on the border? We were in the '70s not the '50s, and this was a lot of hot air, just the usual waffle.'

After the army shot dead a republican petrol-bomber in Belfast at the end of July 1970, the Official IRA adopted a policy of defence and retaliation. Liam O Comain was given clearance to carry out an operation shortly afterwards. 'I discussed the matter with the late Cathal Goulding at a meeting in Brockaghreilly Hall near Maghera. I told him that Derry were of the strong opinion that there should be retaliation for this particular murder in Belfast. To be honest, there was a certain amount of competition to do the right job before the Provisionals got a chance . . . I came back from the meeting and conveyed that decision to the Derry City Command of the movement where a decision had been taken to carry out an op along the Derry/Donegal border.' The plan was to lay a landmine for an army patrol of two Land-Rovers and Goulding had guaranteed O Comain 50 lb of commercial explosives. The unit delegated to lay the landmine included Martin McGuinness.

O Comain said, 'within three weeks of me conveying that decision, I got word to go to a meeting in Dublin, where Cathal told me that the order was countermanded and the attack was suspended. When I brought the word back to Derry there was an argument and Phil O'Donnell and Martin McGuinness went away very angry. I would be friendly with Martin, but I am convinced that he is a very ruthless man. Martin wasn't political, Martin was a gunman, who had a primitive, physical force philosophy about the soldiers, send them home in boxes and free Ireland. In retrospect, I think if that particular activity had been carried out, I think Martin might well have stayed with the Officials.'

Peter Doherty remembers that he and some of the other volunteers decided to go ahead with the operation anyway; reasoning that the explosives were on their way, and even if they didn't arrive, the men might be able to take a couple of shots at the patrol. The night before the operation, some volunteers spent the night in a barn at Holywell, on the border, just behind the newly built Creggan housing estate. They had learned the art of laying landmines at training camps and had worked out that laying a mine with 50 lb of explosives buried a few inches beneath the level of the road would cause a 12-foot crater. The next day, however, they were forced to abandon the operation when the explosives failed to arrive.

By October, Peter Doherty had decided he had had enough of the Officials and set up an independent organisation, taking a few other men with him. Although McGuinness wasn't among them, he tagged along with another volunteer who lived near him and who had told him of Doherty's plans. When Doherty realised the difficulties of working on their own, he decided that they needed help to get their hands on modern weapons and approached Sean Keenan, who set up a meeting in Convoy, Donegal. 'The Provos started off in my front room,' Doherty remembers, 'that's how small we were.' At a second meeting Doherty brought Martin McGuinness along, where he joined four other men on the Brigade Staff as Finance Officer. It was an informal occasion, as Doherty remembers. 'MacStiofain said that swearing in to the Sticks was good enough. We'd all come that way, so none of us took the oath. McGuinness' duties were simple. 'As Finance Officer, any money that came in, or any money paid out, he would have been in charge of. At the start there was very little money, most of the money was going in PDF. There were no robberies at that time, just collections and gifts. If the IRA wanted money to do something, people threw a few pound in, and that was the petrol money.'

In 1972, McGuinness told *Irish Times* journalist Nell McCafferty, who had been a neighbour of the McGuinness family in her native Derry, of his reasons for leaving the Officials. 'The Officials would not give us any action. All this time there was fighting in the streets and things getting worse in Belfast. You could see the soldiers just settling in to Derry, not being too worried by stone throwing. Occasionally the Officials gave out Molotov cocktails which wouldn't even go off and I knew that after 50 years we were more of an occupied country than we ever were.'

So far, Doherty's defection had remained secret, although the Official leadership suspected all was not well and had sent a delegation composed of Tomas McGiolla, Malachy McGurran and Seamus Costello to try to convince them to stay. A few weeks after the aborted attack on the UDR patrol, Derry Command Staff of the OIRA were meeting in Micky Montgomery's house in Creggan. It was a casual affair, where the senior Officials discussed policy and gossiped over a cup of tea. It was a dark October night and when Montgomery answered a knock at the door the other men were alarmed to hear someone pushing their way into the house, announcing that he had come to take over the command in Derry. The OC and O Comain watched in horror as the man waved a gun erratically in Montgomery's direction. Montgomery, who was sharp, noticed that the safety catch was still on and grabbed it off him while the OC and O Comain wrestled him to the ground. They then tackled his companion and relieved him of a Russian hand grenade.

O Comain suspected Sean Keenan of being behind the attack and decided to look for him, accompanied by Montgomery and a third man, who had a car – at the time still comparatively scarce in Derry. As they left Montgomery's house to get in the car, they stopped dead in their tracks as a voice called out 'Halt, O Comain, or you're dead.' As O Comain looked around, he saw two boys silhouetted in the street lights. He recognised them straight away. McGuinness was the one carrying a gun. 'That was the first time I knew that Martin McGuinness had left. I started off to be diplomatic and I said, lads I'm going off to see Sean Keenan, what we need at this particular time is unity rather than bloodshed. While I was talking, Micky Montgomery had disappeared into his house, where he and the OC came out the back and jumped McGuinness and the other fella on the street. That was the third weapon we got.' One man who was there that night remembers other volunteers complaining about McGuinness. 'He was a bundle of nerves when the Officials chased us out. He was ready to run for home when he saw the Stickies chasing us out of the house. They finished up with an extra one or two weapons that day. But then we took a whole lot of theirs later, so that was all right.' When Montgomery and O Comain inspected the hand grenade, they discovered that the inexperienced Provos had failed to notice that the pin was missing, so they drove to the Craigavon Bridge and threw it into the Foyle.

Keenan had gone to ground, fearing trouble from the Officials, and O Comain finally tracked him down in Duffy's Bookmakers on Chamberlain Street a couple of days later. Keenan demanded the return of the weapons, which O Comain refused, before asking Keenan to agree to talks between the two groups. 'He just said, no, the Provos are taking over the town. That was it. That was when that particular unit left – they were young lions in a way, but it was purely physical force. They had no time for the politics.'

McGuinness was by now actively headhunting Officials he believed had promise and asking them to join the Provos. He approached Paddy Ward, who was now in the Official Fianna, asking him what weapons they had: 'McGuinness was in the Bogside at the time and we were in the Creggan. We told him we had 22s, which was true, and we were running round trying to start gun battles with the army. He told me that we would be better trained with better weapons in the Provos and asked me to coax as many guys over as I could. They all came save one. We always dealt with McGuinness directly after that. If there was a "move" on, an operation, he would tell the Fianna to go in and scout it, stake out the place, give warnings and stuff like that.'

Far from being well equipped, the Derry Brigade were, in fact, desperate for weapons. Peter Doherty contacted a Derry man who had been a member of Saor Uladh, a leftist republican breakaway group, in the '50s. The Saor Uladh man was suspicious of the Provisional leadership, particularly Ruairi

O Bradaigh, whom he suspected was right-wing. But he liked Doherty's enthusiasm and commitment and agreed to help. Doherty was delighted how things turned out: 'He told me "I can get youse a gun called an Armalite." It's funny looking back on it, but we had only vaguely heard about it, and going back in the car we wondered how good a plastic gun could be.' The Saor Uladh man told them that they would only have to raise the money to buy the guns in America, he would be responsible for the rest. Doherty had already bought guns from dealers in Donegal and brought them into Derry. 'It was unbelievable some of the weapons they had that the government didn't know about, Webley revolvers and Magnums. They were so cheap that you could buy them out of what was left from the spare wages after running the house. It was about twenty pounds for a short and sixteen or seventeen pounds for an Armalite.'

The operation hit a snag when Doherty was arrested and remanded. McGuinness, the Finance Officer, had the money for the Armalites and sent a message to Doherty in jail asking him how to proceed. The weapons were already on their way from America and when McGuinness returned back to Derry with a boot load of Armalites, his reputation as a hardline operator was sealed. Before long, O Conaill and MacStiofain had heard how the bold young Derry volunteer had independently armed the Derry IRA. His role as Finance Officer, however, came under some scrutiny from local volunteers, who found him wanting in several respects. 'We had nothing, nothing at all. We were running around freezing, and eventually my own mother went down to the city centre and bought six Parkas, like combat jackets, and handed them out to the volunteers. She would have bought more, but that was all the shop had. Every week, she went down and bought a few more until everybody had one. McGuinness was one of the first to get one.'

It would be some time before the Derry Brigade of the Provisional IRA were ready to use the Armalites. For the time being, they were at the height of a commercial bombing campaign. John Joe McCann, who had joined the Provisionals at the same meeting as McGuinness, had already been trained in bomb making and took on the task of briefing the others. 'At that time, things were very crude. People would put a timer in with a two or three minute fuse, at that time it was fuses, people would just light a fuse in their hands, put a bomb in and then run. It became more sophisticated later on. At that stage they were just very simple, very crude devices, you just went up the town with a bomb, lit the fuse and that was it.' Volunteers went out on bombing missions in twos. At that stage the IRA still had a separate women's wing, Cumann na mBan, who had gone with the Provos at the split, and their members teamed up to work with the Provos. Couples would walk casually through the city centre, embracing like a genuine courting couple to fool security forces surveillance, before casually leaving their bombs at commercial premises. The campaign was a success and many city centre premises were razed to the ground.

John Joe McCann knew McGuinness well at that time. 'I was quite friendly with him then. He was a very quiet guy, he wouldn't have been around drinking, smoking, or running around with women. He would have had high morals. I'd say he probably hasn't changed much from that stance. You'll never catch McGuinness with another woman, that will never happen. He would have been quiet in that sense.' Around this time, Sean Keenan's son Colm, who had deserted the Officials for the Provisionals, introduced him to Bernie Canning. She was from a republican family and came from Ann Street, in the neighbouring Brandywell area of Derry. McGuinness, who had only had one previous girlfriend, was soon going out with her on a regular basis. On their first date, although neither drank at the time, he took her to the local Bogside Inn.

As the marching season approached in July, tensions again mounted to fever pitch, with daily riots against the army. Late on the night of 7 July, when a 17-year-old youth darted from a crowd throwing stones at soldiers in an attempt to retrieve a soldier's helmet which had been knocked off in the rioting, an unarmed man, Seamus Cusack, ran out to help him. As they tried to run back to the safety of the crowd, a soldier aimed his rifle at Cusack at point-blank range, hitting him in the thigh. Local people feared that Cusack would be arrested for rioting if they took him to the local Altnagelvin Hospital. Not realising that the blood which soaked his trousers was spurting from his femoral artery, they drove him 20 miles to Letterkenny Hospital in Donegal, where he died at 1.40 a.m. on 8 July. In a later hearing which angered those who had witnessed the attack on Cusack, Lord Justice Gibson, who was later murdered by the IRA, apportioned blame for Cusack's death equally between the dead man himself and the soldier who had killed him.

Later that day, volunteers travelled across the border to a weapons dump, where they swiftly made up a cache of nail bombs. Nail bombs were simplicity itself to manufacture – a stick of gelignite was stuck inside a beer can packed with six-inch nails. The top was then sealed with tape, leaving a small hole for a detonator, which had a couple of matches attached to it. Volunteers who delayed throwing the bombs after the matches had been lit risked losing a limb or worse. Eamon Lafferty, the 19-year-old Commander of the Creggan unit, had been out all day making them up and bringing them back over the border. John Joe McCann and Doherty had been with him for most of the day and that afternoon they walked back together to William Street on the edge of the Bogside, where they met McGuinness, hanging about on what became Free Derry Corner. Doherty said 'We knew there was going to be trouble that day. When we got back to William Street, the army were trying to get into the Bogside. It was obvious they wanted trouble. One volunteer told McGuinness that we were going to throw nail bombs at the army. He just turned his back and sloped off.' When Doherty got up to the Lecky Road, he found a crowd of about 70 people stoning the army. Later that afternoon, at around 4 p.m. two soldiers from the Royal Anglian Regiment fired into the crowd; 19-year-old Dessie Beattie fell to the ground, fatally injured.

Although McGuinness was not present at either death, these were the final two incidents which influenced him:

> The turning point was those two shootings. There was tremendous anger and resentment amongst the community and that's what forced many young people into a position of deciding that you couldn't achieve the right to march in your own streets and the right to do what you want in your own streets through peaceful protests. That's what turned the people against the British Army. They were just two young fellows from respected nationalist families here in the city.
>
> The one which I have the greatest memory of is the killing of Beattie. He was shot on Lecky Road and he was brought from Lecky Road to Elmwood Road, at the bottom of the street where I was reared, Elmwood Street, and I remember his body being taken out of a car. He was quite clearly very, very badly injured at that time, had been shot around the lower body and there was blood everywhere.
>
> I remember being very scared and frightened by this at that time. It was the first time I had seen anybody killed by a bullet. In my opinion they were the most significant

shootings, acts of violence if you like, used by the state against the people of this city and were far more formative in people's experiences and forming their opposition to the state than anything which happened afterwards.

CHAPTER THREE

The Volunteer

*A lot of people look back with fond memories, to the very courageous stand that
the people took and the very courageous stand that the IRA took against what
was unbelievably superior military forces, in terms of arms.*

Martin McGuinness, author interview, January 1992

In 1971, Derry was still, on the surface at least, the city that Martin
McGuinness knew as a child. Ladies were welcome in the Royal Bar on
London Street; Sidebottom Bros announced that they were fishmongers and
poulterers to HM Forces; and the shirt factory girls still traipsed in and out
of Tillie and Henderson's, which Karl Marx had visited and later wrote
about in *Das Kapital*.

In other ways, however, the city had changed beyond belief. The Derry
Brigade had swollen in numbers, and McGuinness was proud to be a part of
it. He later explained the influx of recruits to the journalist Eamon Mallie
when he told him, 'good operations make the best recruiting sergeants.'
Other journalists had discovered that a visit to Barney McFadden's house in
Stanley's Walk, near the gasworks, was a good starting point for information
on the IRA. McFadden was a storeman at the gasworks and his nine-
bedroomed house came rent-free with the job.

Peter Taylor, the journalist and broadcaster, met McGuinness for the first
time early in 1972:

I met McGuinness after someone pointed him out to me as he

marched in a candlelit protest about Bloody Sunday. 'There is the person you want to watch,' I was told. 'That is the person you want to be talking to. He is the rising star of the Provos in Derry.' He wasn't OC when I met him, that was another man, a rather weak character who I interviewed for *This Week*. He didn't last long. I had several meetings with McGuinness near the gasworks; I always remember him saying to me that he would much rather be digging his garden than living life on the run and going round doing what he was doing. I actually believed him. That is the other side of McGuinness.

McGuinness was by now a familiar sight to the British Army and the RUC. Rarely leaving the Bogside, he would lounge around in a pair of flared trousers, sometimes wearing heavy-framed glasses to correct his short sight. Occasionally McGuinness would even dye his hair as well. He had already been arrested in one of the frequent RUC swoops, which took men off the streets, locking them up in custody for up to seven days to disrupt IRA operations. One Derry policeman questioned McGuinness at this time in the RUC Barracks on Strand Road, once the site of the city's lunatic asylum. 'We had about eight interview rooms in Strand Road, where suspects were put after their arrests in the early hours of the morning. Most of them kept their mouths shut and didn't even complain – I had the impression by then that it was going to be a long, long war and that they were prepared for that.'

The officer knew Derry well and his interview with McGuinness followed the pattern he found worked well:

> There was no point in asking him specific questions, like his whereabouts on a particular night, because he just sat there tight-lipped. I explained to him that I knew housing was bad, and things weren't right, but there was no point in killing police or civilians. OK, I agreed, the Unionists were unfair and yes, I expressed sympathy with the civil rights demands. Over seven days I went over everything. He realised after a while that there wasn't going to be any heavy stuff and I could see that he had switched off and was just sitting there, staring at the wall. So on the third day, as I was going over all this, I

suddenly thumped the table. He nearly jumped out of his skin. Psychologically, you have to make them listen to you.

The RUC had built up an intelligence file on McGuinness by this time, where they noted that he was 5 ft 10in., of medium build, fair/ginger hair, blue eyed, with a fresh complexion.' They believed that he had stayed with the Officials until 'early in 1971', but did manage to get it right when they recorded that he had left them after he 'became disillusioned due to their lack of military activity' and had intelligence, presumably gathered in some of the interviews in Strand Road RUC station, that he had been 'personally involved in a very large number of bombings and shooting attacks in Londonderry'.

By now the RUC believed that McGuinness was aware of plans to reintroduce internment. His file stated that 'McGuinness, with two others, represented PIRA in discussions with OIRA regarding possible mutually supportive action in the event of internment becoming a reality.' In fact, the IRA had been warned of the advent of internment by at least one sympathiser who worked in government offices at Stormont. A former British soldier who later defected to the IRA, Pete 'the Para' McMullan, also claimed that he had secretly passed information about internment to them. Forty-eight hours before internment, the senior Belfast IRA man, Joe Cahill, accompanied Sean MacStiofain on a secret tour of the North, as they briefed a select list of senior commanders that detention without trial was on its way. Leading Provos had been warned not to go away on any holidays that summer. That order was ignored by many, however, including one of the Dublin-based founders of the Provos, Ruairi O Bradaigh, who went to France, and Martin McGuinness, who went to Donegal. The Derry Brigade simply did not believe that the British would be so stupid as to hand them a propaganda tool on a plate.

However, rumours about internment were well founded and the British government reintroduced it on 9 August 1971. Operation Demetrius, as it had been code-named, was up and running. In a series of raids across Northern Ireland, 342 people were arrested and taken to makeshift camps. The gloves were well and truly off and within forty-eight hours, seventeen people had been killed, ten of whom were Catholic civilians shot dead by the British Army.

The Unionist-dominated Stormont government was delighted at news of the swoops, while the SDLP and the Irish government reacted with fury. Within days the SDLP announced that it was launching a civil disobedience campaign and withdrew their representatives from public bodies. A week later, over 8,000 workers went on strike in Derry to protest at internment. The senior Belfast IRA man, Joe Cahill, told journalists in Belfast that only 30 IRA men had been interned. However, he went on the run to Dublin, where he set up house in Ballymun. There were more arrests in the weeks to come and by the time internment ended in December 1975, almost 2,000 people had been detained; 7,000 were forced out of their homes because of sectarian intimidation, most of them in Belfast.

Although internment had only limited success in capturing known IRA men in most of Northern Ireland, it decimated the Provos in Derry, where Phil O'Donnell and Sean Keenan were among the first to be lifted. The Derry Brigade were still desperately short of resources, and few volunteers had cars or could drive, including McGuinness. Even the Brigade OC, older and steadier than the others, had originally been recruited because he could drive and had a car. John Joe McCann says that they took dramatic steps to overcome their shortcomings; hijacking cars from the local branch of a car hire firm. 'We took the cars and taught our people how to drive them in the liberated streets of Free Derry.'

There were still enough of them to wreak havoc on the streets, however. And they were determined to rival Belfast's record of killing soldiers. There has traditionally always been fierce rivalry between the Belfast and Derry IRA Brigades, and the Derry men were embarrassed that they had so far failed to shoot a soldier. During one unsuccessful attempt, McGuinness was part of a four-strong team which included Eamon Lafferty. After the others had fired at the soldier, one of them tossed the brand new .303 rifle, equipped with telescopic sights, to McGuinness. 'Don't be giving me that', he said in alarm before throwing it back, 'I'm blind as a bat.' According to one volunteer, that was par for the course. 'That was the usual pattern with Martin. He might have been involved in planning things, but he was never what you might call hands on.'

On the morning when internment was introduced, the Derry Brigade shot up Rosemount Barracks and mounted an almost constant attack on the army base in the old BSR factory, known locally as Essex. The next day the IRA murdered Paul Challoner, a 22-year-old bombardier. Bombardier Challoner was hit in the shoulder after the car carrying the four-strong IRA hit team had flashed its lights and sounded its horn to warn a civilian to get out of the way. Challoner was on observation duty at the army post at Bligh's Lane, in Creggan. Lafferty, now Adjutant of the Derry Brigade, fired the fatal shot. Eight days later, he too lay dead, shot down by an army bullet in a gun battle which lasted hours.

After the reintroduction of internment, the Derry Brigade had been directed by Daithi O Conaill to go to Letterkenny, across the Irish border in Co. Donegal. Believing that they would be trained, armed and organised, the volunteers were instead ordered to take collecting tins round the cathedral and the local Finn Harps football ground. The men quickly tired of this and returned to Derry. On the morning of 18 August at about 6.30 a.m., a large contingent of troops started to remove the barricades in an ultimately unsuccessful bid to reopen Free Derry. Soon the IRA and their supporters in the Auxiliaries were on the streets, supported by local people, who were rebuilding the barricades as fast as the soldiers could dismantle them. John Joe McCann was at Eamon Lafferty's side in Kildrum Gardens, Creggan, as the IRA tried desperately to halt the approaching soldiers:

> We had a big car, like a Granada, and the boot was just crammed with ammunition. At that stage we had just got a new .303 with telescopic sights, which Eamon wouldn't let out of his sight. The army had just come over the wall from the cemetery. To this day, I don't know what Eamon saw, but he suddenly said 'cover me', and walked down the hill towards them. We were safe, because the army had to fire up the hill at us, but they shot him as he walked down towards them. He was lying there, mortally wounded, but we wouldn't leave him. The thing went on that long that the women all came out and started praying behind us while we kept shooting at the soldiers down below us. Then the man beside me panicked, thinking that Eamon was alive. Did you ever see a rabbit still pulsing after it's dead? That's the way Eamon was. He got him into a car and drove to the Diamond, where the army pulled Eamon's body off him and arrested him.

Martin McGuinness had been in a safe house in Foyle Road with another volunteer and missed the whole thing. It was a disaster for the Derry

Brigade. Lafferty, although only 19, was one of their most experienced operators, and had joined the IRA three years previously. His importance was recognised when he received the ultimate accolade of a rebel song being written about him:

> Their guns engaged and battle raged
> Ah, but two guns let them down
> And left but one undaunted son
> To take on the British Crown
> On bended knee for liberty
> His rifle blazed away
> 'Til through his head a bullet sped
> The price he had to pay.

Lafferty's death had dealt the Provos a crippling blow. The OC, who was relatively inexperienced, had relied heavily on him. Promotion in the IRA is often a matter of 'dead men's shoes' and within days of Lafferty's funeral he had promoted McGuinness to Adjutant and second-in-command. The OC would later regret this deeply.

Internment had compounded the IRA's problems and news of the appalling brutality in the camps was causing morale to plummet. Fourteen internees were singled out for sensory deprivation techniques, where they were systematically hooded; deprived of food, drink and sleep; and subjected to 'white noise' (a constant high-pitched hissing designed to disorientate them). They were also beaten and shoved out of helicopters, believing that they were flying at a great height, when they were really only a few inches from the ground.

Michael Donnelly, a 22-year-old married man with one son from William Street in the Bogside, was accused of being a Provisional and remembers passing out several times after being beaten. Donnelly was transferred to the internment camps, where he would be one of the last released when internment ended in 1975. He later received compensation for his treatment. The Irish government reported Britain to the European Court of Human Rights, who found in 1978 that the 'five techniques' involved inhuman and degrading treatment. It was a partial vindication of the suffering of the hooded men. But in 1971, news of their treatment caused problems for the IRA when support from the families faltered. The IRA needed to prove they were not beaten, but it would be some time before the raw young recruits on the streets could shape themselves into the ruthless killing machine they later became.

One early operation ended in failure after an IRA driver took McGuinness and John Joe McCann out the Buncrana Road and drove the short distance across the border into Donegal from where they planned to walk back into Northern Ireland carrying explosives to blow up a British customs post on the border. As they turned a corner just in front of the border with Northern Ireland, McCann stopped dead in his tracks when he saw what he thought at the time was 'half the British Army':

> It was so ridiculous. They had Saracens, Saladin cars, big Saladins with huge guns. Then there was me standing there, looking across at them, with a bomb in one hand and a revolver in the other. I thought we had no option but turn around and take the chance that they wouldn't shoot us in the back. But the next thing I knew, McGuinness ran into a field and jumped on to a horse, leaving me on my own with a bomb and a gun. Off he galloped, into the sunset, bareback on a white horse. McGuinness was back in the Bogside before me.

Gossip that McGuinness had lost his bottle spread like wildfire through the crowded streets of the Bogside. Other operations were more successful, however, and by the end of the year the Derry Brigade had avenged Lafferty's death with the deaths of seven more soldiers.

By this time the IRA in Derry had been ordered into full-time active service and McGuinness stopped working in Doherty's butchers. He has always said that he gave up his job voluntarily, but Paddy Ward claims that he was sacked. 'I mind the time he got fired out of Doherty's butchers very well, he was insubordinate to the foreman. He refused to do what he was told, there was some scuffle in the butchers and he got sacked. My brother Kevin told my dad and I about it – my dad and the foreman's dad were very close. My dad worked with him at the Derry docks.' James Doherty, who still owns the business, says that while McGuiness certainly left his work for a while after the introduction of internment, he was not aware of McGuinness leaving after an argument. 'I saw him around Derry on more than one occasion at that time, and he certainly stayed in the city. I do remember that he was arrested at one stage. I understood that for a while he wasn't there, he disappeared, but then some people came and asked could he come back and I said, of course, certainly. The foreman probably wasn't happy with his level of attendance.' Doherty remembers trying to calm McGuinness on one occasion when he was talking to customers in the shop. 'Naturally I am not a hard-line employer; what you do in your own time is your own business, but I did remonstrate with him before he disappeared from the shop. You don't want to bring your labour relations into your political activities.'

By this time McGuiness had given up his occasional drinking and smoking to lead the traditional abstemious life of the active service volunteer. Although he was constantly on the watch for the British Army, he still found time to wear the goalie's jersey in a local amateur football team. There was little social life for the volunteers, although there were occasional fund-raising socials for internees' dependants in the 720 bar on Chamberlain Street, or the Bogside Inn near McGuinness' Elmwood Street home, where he still lived with his parents. At the socials, collections were taken as the rousing chorus of one of the first republican songs to be written about internment boomed out over the PA system:

> Armoured cars and tanks and guns
> Came to take away our sons.
> Every man must stand behind
> The men behind the wire.

McGuinness found life on the run to his liking. 'When you're young, at that age, it's quite exciting. It was very dangerous, it was a situation where the British Army and the RUC were constantly trying to arrest me. The first time my home was raided was in October 1971. I was long gone, although I was still in the city. The British Army arrived down our street in a furniture van, about 20 or 30 of them, in the back of a furniture van, pulled up outside the front door and burst into the house, on a Sunday morning, very early, I suppose expecting us to be sitting taking our breakfast.' Describing the opposition of the people to the presence of the troops, he recalled: 'The bin lids were in operation. If the British Army appeared in the middle of the night or attempted to move into a house to snatch someone out of it, the women were out with the bin lids. It was a brilliant early warning system, everybody knew exactly what was happening.'

While he later told the *Irish Times* in 1972, 'I don't feel like a big shot, travelling around the area in a stolen Ford Avenger,' privately he revelled in it. In an unguarded moment, he later said nostalgically:

> There was a really exciting aspect to being on the run, living from house to house and travelling about. We used to travel about Creggan in the middle of the night in cars, from eleven o'clock at night until seven or eight o'clock in the morning and it was only when it broke daylight that we went to bed, for fear that there would be a constant raiding of houses. We were out there with the community and I would say that many young people felt that it was exciting and that it was dangerous and that it was, you know, a change from the monotony of what went before. That whole Free Derry situation – everybody talks about it who was alive at that time, about how exciting those times were. A lot of people look back with fond memories to the very courageous stand that the people took and the very courageous stand that the IRA took against what was unbelievably superior military forces, in terms of armaments. Gradually and slowly but surely many of those people, including myself, politically advanced. We realised what was actually going on – that the British Army and the RUC had to be opposed, that there had to be some sort of an opposition to the British state.

McGuinness was certainly determined to be part of that opposition. But the vendetta against the British Army was not just fought against the troops. In those early days, many ordinary people were well disposed towards the army. Derry people had a long and distinguished record of service in the British Army. Hundreds had joined up to fight in both World Wars, and German U-boats had surrendered at Derry's Lisahally quayside, before being towed out into the Atlantic and scuttled. John Hume had even criticised the Irish Republic's neutrality during the war, saying that 'it would always bear the mark of Cain for refusing to go to war on the side of Britain against Nazi Germany'. And local girls saw no reason why they should not date the soldiers, who offered them a better future than the dole queue in Derry. The IRA, however, saw the dangers of what they deemed to be fraternising with the enemy. Worried that pillow talk would lead to arrests, they determined to make an example of the girls.

Marta Doherty, a 19-year-old woman from Drumcliffe Avenue, close to Martin McGuinness' Elmwood Street home, had been going out with a soldier. On 9 November 1971, three women dragged the screaming girl from her door and tied her to a lamp-post. A jeering crowd, some shouting 'soldier lover', watched the women shave her head before pouring molten tar and feathers over her. The previous night a 20-year-old woman had also been marched through the Bogside after she was abducted from her home at 3.15 a.m. Wearing only a nightdress, she shivered in the November frost as her attackers blindfolded her before shaving her head. The girl, ironically, had already served a four-month jail sentence for throwing stones at soldiers. 'I was terrified, both for my own sake and for my mother who is a widow. They told me it was my final warning. Next time I will be shot.'

Deirdre Duffy from Westway, just beside the army base at Essex, had actually asked permission to go out with a soldier, promising that she would never bring him into the Bogside. Paddy Ward, then in the Provo Fianna, kidnapped her on 11 November 1971 in a hijacked taxi as she walked home after saying goodnight to her soldier fiancé at an army checkpoint after a concert. Ward handed the girl to some women from Cumann na mBan at the back of the Bogside Inn, where they roughly cut her hair with blunt scissors before pouring red lead over her. He says the IRA wanted to stop the girls hanging around with the soldiers. 'They were out to get these soldier dolls because a bunch of them were spotted in the services club in Bond Street. There were tons of them and they all ended up marrying soldiers. The day she was done there was uproar in the papers, a wig company even donated wigs to her. The red lead did some damage to her eyes as well. Funnily enough, her brother Hugh later ended up as a very close associate of McGuinness.' Willie Breslin, a teacher and Labour Party activist, heard of the attack and went to the scene where he tried to free her. The IRA denied responsibility for the action, but the women refused to release her to Breslin until McGuinness arrived and apparently gave them permission, at which point Breslin took her to hospital. He already knew Martin McGuinness. 'I was in the Oak Leaf Athletic Club with his brother Tom, who was a County Derry Gaelic star at that time.' Breslin found McGuinness open to negotiation. 'He mightn't have done anything about what you were complaining about but he always listened and was courteous at all times. He is still a very amicable character, though obviously there are teeth there.'

It wasn't just 'soldier dolls' who were the targets of 'The Young Avengers' as they sometimes called themselves. McGuinness gave orders for others to be punished. Tony Miller, who had earned his spurs throwing stones and petrol bombs in the Battle of the Bogside, was still with the Officials. As Paddy Ward noticed, 'Miller was very unlucky – every time he did something he got caught. McGuinness gave orders that he was to be shot in the leg.' Miller later joined the Provisional IRA. McGuinness also ordered several Provos to be tarred and feathered after they left a small bag of explosives behind the seat of a car which had been lent to them by the brother of a volunteer. Ward remembers that the man had lent the car so that the bombing team could transport nitrobenzene in it. After the car had been returned, as the man and his wife travelled to Buncrana across the border in Donegal one Sunday night to play bingo, the army stopped him at a checkpoint. When they searched the car, they found the explosives and arrested the man. 'There was hell to pay after that,' says Ward.

The IRA were learning new tactics quickly. By this time they sometimes took advantage of the presence of the young rioters who regularly attacked police and troops. As Major Robin Alers-Hankey of the Royal Green Jackets led his men to the defence of firemen, under attack from stone throwers while they tried to put out a blaze in a timber yard, a sniper's bullet tore through his stomach when a gunman suddenly appeared as the crowd melted away. It was just a short walk from Martin McGuinness's home in Elmwood Street. Major Alers-Hankey, who was married with two children, was sent home after a six-week stay in the modern Altnagelvin Hospital on the outskirts of the city. He died of his injuries four months later.

On 27 October, 29-year-old David Tilbury and 18-year-old Angus Stevens, who both served with the 45th Medium Regiment of the Royal Artillery, were killed in an IRA bomb attack on Rosemount Barracks in the Creggan. Two men in their 20s had thrown bombs over a wall onto the sandbagged emplacement at the back of the RUC station, while a third man stood guard. The men, who were unarmed, ran off after the blast.

In the middle of November, McGuinness had a lucky escape when soldiers raided a house as the IRA made up a bomb. McGuinness panicked when he heard soldiers breaking down the front door and tore out the back door of the house in South End Park, followed by other IRA men. One man, 22-year-old Kieran Conway, from Dun Laoghaire in the Irish Republic, was caught by a soldier when he delayed them to let McGuinness get away. A pistol and 218 sticks of gelignite were found in the house.

Sean MacStiofain, Chief of Staff, sent out orders to all Brigade Staff after internment that, from then on, policy had changed. RUC and UDR personnel, like British soldiers, were now to be considered 'legitimate combatant targets at all times, whether on duty or not, armed or not, in uniform or not'. IRA men across the North rallied to his call, and by the end of 1971, had murdered five UDR members and eleven RUC men. The IRA's capacity to strike almost at will was causing problems for the Conservative government of Edward Heath. Home Secretary, Reginald Maudling, had distinguished himself the previous year by his reaction to his first visit to Northern Ireland: 'For God's sake bring me a large Scotch. What a bloody awful country!', he is reputed to have said after boarding his homeward flight to London. In response to the upsurge in IRA activity, Maudling now drew the fire of the Unionist population by conceding that the IRA would 'not be defeated, not completely eliminated, but have their violence reduced to an acceptable level'.

The New Year dawned quietly in Derry, with no foreboding of the bloody turmoil to come. But behind the scenes, a flurry of secret briefing papers had been exchanged between senior army officers, embarrassed that teams of IRA bombers could slip in and out of the Bogside unhindered to make forays into the commercial centre of Derry, which they were rapidly reducing to rubble. Major-General Robert Ford, Commander of Land Forces (CLF) for Northern Ireland, visited Derry in the first week of January. At the end of November, Ford had instructed Pat MacLellan, Commander of the Eighth Infantry Brigade, the army's most senior officer in Derry, that his priority was 'to recreate the state of law in the Creggan and Bogside as and when he could'.

What he saw convinced him that the policy of containing the IRA in the no-go areas had failed. In addition, there was a new problem which was undermining the army's ability to defeat the IRA. In a confidential report to the General Officer Commanding (GOC), Lieutenant-General Harry Tuzo, Ford wrote that the IRA were exploiting young unemployed teenagers as decoys for their gunmen and bombers. Calling them the 'Derry Young Hooligans', Ford told Tuzo that, in his opinion, CS gas and rubber bullets had failed to keep the rioters under control. Firmer measures, he believed, were called for. To restore law and order to the streets of Derry,

Ford believed, it had now become necessary 'to shoot selected ringleaders among the Derry Young Hooligans, after clear warnings had been issued'. The Conservative government went along with Ford's new policy without a single misgiving.

In the meantime, an impromptu march to protest at the opening of a new internment camp gave a hint of what was to come. On Saturday, 22 January, several thousand civil rights marchers gathered on the desolate eight-mile stretch of silver sand at Magilligan, 20 miles from Derry on the North Atlantic coast. As the protestors, who included the SDLP MP John Hume, approached the outskirts of the camp, they were halted in their tracks by soldiers from the resident local regiment, the Green Jackets. For the first time, they were joined by soldiers from the First Battalion of the Parachute Regiment. One Para, as they were known, were based in Belfast, 70 miles away, where there had been numerous allegations that they used unnecessary force in riot situations. As the marchers surged forward, arm in arm, they were met with a barrage of rubber bullets and CS gas. John Hume accused the soldiers of 'beating, brutalising and terrorising the demonstrators'. He was deeply concerned about the level of violence used against the crowd, who had been peaceful. McGuinness, who never attended the civil rights marches, had stayed in Derry, where he watched pictures of the march on the television news.

The following Monday, Frank Lagan, the Chief Superintendent of the RUC in Derry, briefed Pat MacLellan, then Commander of the Eighth Infantry Brigade, that NICRA planned a non-violent demonstration against internment in Derry on Sunday, 30 January. Lagan, who was a Catholic with good links to the local community, had been assured by the organisers that the march would be peaceful, and that neither wing of the IRA would carry guns. He trusted his contacts and advised MacLellan that the march should take place without military intervention. MacLellan agreed to recommend this approach to the CLF. Ford, however, had not been impressed with Lagan when they had met earlier in the month. His officers had told him of the rumours that Lagan was secretly sympathetic to the civil rights movement and that his wide network of local contacts went as far as republicans. In his secret memo to Tuzo, Ford had outlined his dissatisfaction with both the senior RUC officer in the area and the Brigade Commander. 'I was disturbed by the attitude of both the Brigade Commander and also, of course, by Chief Superintendent Lagan,' he wrote.

Convinced that 'military action is necessary', Ford had already briefed Prime Minister Edward Heath at a meeting of the Northern Ireland Committee of the Cabinet. Rejecting Lagan's advice, he gave command of the arrest operation on the day to the man who had directed One Para's snatch squads in the Belfast riots, Lieutenant Colonel Derek Wilford.

As Ford finalised his plans for the civil rights march, the Provo OC was facing a revolt in the ranks. He was aware that his Adjutant, Martin McGuinness, was secretly undermining him, sniping that he was indecisive and lacked the stomach to take on the Brits. Volunteers were saying openly that he could not cope with his position and ignored his orders, turning instead to his deputy. For some time now, McGuinness had taken over day-to-day operations as he gradually sidelined the OC. His prominence had been noted by military intelligence, who warned the Joint Security Committee at Stormont on Thursday, 27 January to expect 'a new rash of attacks on RUC personnel'.

As the committee met, a gold-coloured Hillman Avenger carrying five RUC men drove up the steep hill that leads from Creggan Road to Rosemount RUC station. They were heading away from the city centre shortly before 8.30 a.m., when a lone IRA gunman stepped out from an alleyway to open fire on the car. The RUC drove on, thinking the attack was over, but just 40 yards further up Helen Street on their left, two more gunmen fired on them with a Thompson submachine gun and an M1 carbine. By this time the RUC patrol were only minutes away from Rosemount police station, and the driver sped towards the safety of the barracks. A soldier from the Coldstream Guards managed to fire four shots after the IRA unit, but they were already out of sight. 26-year-old Sergeant Peter Gilgunn, a Catholic from the small Co. Fermanagh village of Belcoo, who was married with an eight-month-old son, lay dying. Peter Gilgunn had joined the RUC in 1966, well before the start of the Troubles. He had been promoted to Sergeant in November 1970, around the same time as Martin McGuinness had joined the Provisional IRA. He and another RUC officer, 20-year-old Protestant, David Montgomery, were the first of many policemen to be killed in the streets of Derry.

As Frank Lagan already knew, both the Official and Provisional IRA had held meetings where they discussed their plans for the day. The Provo OC had given his word to march organisers that none of his men would carry arms and issued orders that all weapons should be kept under armed guard until further notice. However, he was exhausted after a series of meetings to organise the removal of weapons from the Bogside. In a fateful decision, he sent orders to his young Adjutant that he would give the march a miss to catch up on his sleep so that he would be alert when the march was followed by the predictable riots that night. McGuinness, he told the Brigade Staff, is in command.

CHAPTER FOUR

Bloody Sunday

A decision was taken that under no circumstances would any member of the republican movement be involved in any military contact with the British Army or the RUC on that day and that's what actually happened. Most of us republicans went on the march. I was on the march, as were most of my friends, and the rest is history, we all know what happened.

Martin McGuinness, author interview, January 1992

The clear skies of Sunday, 30 January 1972 heralded a fine but chilly start to the day. It was ideal weather for the march and organisers were pleased.

In his home in the Bogside, John Hume was worried that there would be trouble at the demonstration. After Magilligan, he was convinced that the army wanted an all-out confrontation with the civil rights marchers and had decided neither to attend nor support the march. The previous day's newspapers had announced Hume as one of the platform party, even though he had already spoken publicly against the march. 'I had seen the injuries they had caused to peaceful demonstrators on a deserted beach,' he later said. 'It didn't take much imagination to work out what could happen if those demonstrators had been facing the army on the streets of Derry. I thought the march was irresponsible.'

As people returned home after midday mass, they were shocked to see convoys of troops coming over the Craigavon Bridge. Army barriers were being erected and snipers had been seen taking up rooftop positions, some on buildings where IRA graffiti warned that 'all soldiers will be shot on sight.' Father Edward Daly (later Bishop Daly) was in St Eugene's Cathedral. As Communion ended, another priest approached him at the altar to tell him that heavily-armed paratroopers had surrounded the cathedral and the adjoining streets. Daly appealed to the congregation to remain calm and to make sure that the afternoon's march was peaceful.

Meanwhile, General Ford, Commander of Land Forces, had arrived at Ebrington Barracks to join Lieutenant Colonel Wilford as an 'observer'. General Carver, Chief of the Defence Staff, had personally briefed Edward Heath and his Cabinet on the planned 'scoop up' of the 'yobbos'. As Brigadier MacLellan put it in Brigade Order 2/72, which he had drafted a few days earlier, the aim was 'to prevent any illegal march taking place from the Creggan and to contain it, with any accompanying rioting, within the Bogside and Creggan areas of the city.' Military intelligence believed that there were around 80 members of the Provisional IRA in Derry, mostly 'skulking in the nest of militants in the Bogside'. Soldiers were warned of probable 'IRA terrorist activity to take advantage of the event, to conduct shooting attacks against the security forces . . . almost certainly snipers, petrol bombers and nail-bombers will support the rioters.' They were specifically told to expect sustained and accurate sniper fire from Rossville Flats. The army's plan was to pre-empt the IRA. The army would halt the marchers as they attempted to enter the city centre, the Paras would disperse legitimate marchers, the nail-bombers would be isolated and the 'scooping up' operation could begin. If IRA snipers should be foolish enough to make an appearance, army marksmen were waiting for them.

Only one Derry man knew for certain what the army had planned. Chief Superintendent Frank Lagan had listened in horror as Brigadier MacLellan outlined his plans at the coordinating conference at Ebrington Barracks. Lagan had been in secret contact with one of the march organisers, Ivan Cooper. Cooper, a Protestant, had originally been a member of the Unionist Party before becoming a founder of the SDLP and a local MP. Lagan trusted Cooper, who later confirmed that he had obtained assurances from the IRA that they would be unarmed on the march and would not attack the army.

Following the OC's orders that all weapons were to be taken out of the Bogside and Creggan, at 2.00 a.m. on the Sunday morning several cars had taken weapons up to the Creggan until after the march. The OC had told one former IRA man of his fears. 'Like everybody else, the OC had relatives and friends going on the march, so ordered that all the gear was to be put out of the area and held in those cars. All McGuinness had to do was to carry out orders and make sure everybody else did too.'

Paddy Ward, at 17, was in command of the Derry Fianna. He met McGuinness late the night before Bloody Sunday in one of the four or five lock-up garages at the back of the Bogside Inn that were surreptitiously used by the IRA. McGuinness told him to bring the Fianna to the garage the next day before the march and handed him a list of targets. The targets were all premises around the Guildhall and included the tax office; Liptons (the shop where McGuinness had once worked) a bank; a travel agency, which McGuinness said belonged to a Burntollet UDR man who had attacked the People's Democracy marchers in 1969; Chada's shoe store and the Guildhall itself. That Sunday lunchtime, McGuinness and two IRA men handed Paddy Ward and the other seven Fianna members in the garage two nail-bombs each. 'McGuinness told us to join the march when it moved off from the Bishop's Field. When we got to the Guildhall, McGuinness told us to pick our target and throw the nail bombs at it. He told us that this was to cause havoc once we got into the city centre.'

It was just what Ford had predicted.

Around the same time, Martin McGuinness went to check the weapons that had been placed for safe-keeping in the boots of the two cars, as the OC had instructed him the night before. But, according to Peter Doherty, McGuinness had secretly planned to attack the army after the nail bomb attack led by Paddy Ward. To do this, McGuinness needed to convince other volunteers to disobey the OC's orders. 'McGuinness was Adjutant, and he had three or four fellas who always followed his lead . . . They weren't bluffers. There was always the fear that the Brits might have come in the back way into the Brandywell and the man in the car was there partly to defend the Brandywell, and partly to keep the guns under control. He wouldn't give out the guns in any circumstances. But some of the other boys there were militants; like McGuinness, they thought the OC was just a stick in the mud. But McGuinness got the gear in the Bogside car; what went out of that car was two shorts and a Thompson.'

As the time drew near for the march to begin, thousands of people were making their way to the rallying point. The march began at the summit of Derry's highest hill, in the Bishop's Field beside the Creggan estate. Shortly before 2 p.m., Chief Superintendent Lagan drove in to Ebrington Barracks to join Brigadier MacLellan in observing the march from the army operations room. As he drove through the security checks, General Ford was leaving, escorted by a heavily-armed detachment of Military Police, for an inspection of army positions. Two Sioux military helicopters were hovering over the Creggan, one filming the marchers, the other monitoring their progress. The drone of their engines drowned out the noisy arrival of Thomas McGlinchey's flat-bedded coal lorry, which would lead the marchers into the city centre and provide a platform for the speakers. In Hume's absence, they would be Bernadette Devlin, and Lord Fenner Brockway, the elderly Labour peer.

As the march set off, McGlinchey drove, accompanied by veteran IRA man Gerry 'The Bird' Doherty, who had helped to provide stewards for the march, some of whom were armed. McGlinchey, who was an IRA volunteer and later lost both legs when the Ulster Volunteer Force tried to murder him, had been told the route to take the previous Monday evening by Barney McFadden, whose house in Stanley's Walk was often visited by Martin McGuinness. Also on the lorry was Kevin McCorry, a member of the NICRA executive. The afternoon was bright and sunny and the clear skies offered excellent opportunities for the army to monitor the march. There was no sign of trouble as they left the Bishop's Field. A band played, and one of the marchers, Dr Raymond McClean, remarked that they set off 'in an almost carnival mood' and found the atmosphere so relaxed that he decided to leave his medical equipment behind. As they marched behind the civil rights movement banner, the crowd sang 'We Shall Overcome'. Father Edward Daly joined the march at the end of a funeral service he had conducted in the nearby City Cemetery. He was on his way to visit some of his elderly parishioners in the Rossville Flats, as he usually did during riots in case they were frightened or affected by the CS gas. And as the march passed by Brandywell Recreation Ground, where Derry Harps were playing against Letterkenny Rovers, both teams abandoned the game and joined the demonstrators.

In the meantime, tension was building among the waiting British soldiers as word spread that Major Robin Alers-Hankey had lost his fight for life in a London hospital. Many remembered how he had been shot four months earlier by an IRA sniper who had suddenly appeared as a crowd of young rioters faded into the background.

Paddy Ward and the other seven Fianna members were at the head of the parade, as McGuinness had instructed them. But the army had erected a barricade blocking William Street, which led to the Guildhall. McGuinness sent another IRA man to call off the operation. Gerry 'Mad Dog' Doherty intercepted Ward just after he had dispatched his team so that they were ready to take action. 'Mad Dog said it was too risky to go on. The army had put a spanner in the works because they erected a barricade and we were to bring the gear back. We rounded up everybody except for one, Gerry Donaghy. He was just out of jail after doing six months for rioting. We ran back to behind the Bogside Inn and left the gear there where we got it. There was nobody there, we just ditched the gear in the lock-up. The crack then was that we went back and threw stones at the Brits at Sackville Street.' Years later Gerry Doherty did go on to bomb the Guildhall, reducing it to rubble.

At their Monday night meeting, Barney McFadden had instructed McGlinchey to turn down Rossville Street. As the coal lorry swerved sharply to the right, many of the confused marchers followed the group of youths who had continued on down William Street towards the army barrier. As hundreds of people streamed towards the waiting soldiers, Kevin McCorry jumped down from the lorry and ran back to try to redirect them, but he was too late.

It was now 3.30 p.m. and by this stage the youths, who started off jeering at the soldiers, were now hurling stones and missiles at them. Unknown to the marchers, they were now surrounded by army snipers. General Ford, observing the rioters behind the army barrier, saw an RUC Inspector warn them through a loud-hailer to disperse. His warning enraged the youths, who continued to defy the stewards' attempts to bring them under control. After the crowds briefly scattered when a water cannon sprayed them with purple dye, two of the young rioters lit CS gas canisters and threw them at the army, who loaded their baton guns with rubber bullets. Father Daly recognised their distinctive thump as he spoke with passers by. Most of the crowd at the army barrier had by this stage started to move away from William Street and towards Free Derry Corner, where Bernadette Devlin and Lord Brockway were waiting to address them. Around 3.45 p.m., Daly warned Patrick 'Barman' Duffy, one of the civil rights stewards, that he had seen some young people behaving suspiciously at the back of some nearby shops. One of them was Martin McGuinness.

McGuinness and his fellow IRA men looked like all the other young rioters as they mingled with the crowd on Chamberlain Street. As the firing intensified, they began to kick in the door of Duffy's Bookmakers. One of the youths who helped McGuinness was Des Clinton, an IRA sympathiser although never a member. 'The army barrier was across the road, just where the old picture house used to be, and the crowd was not that many yards away. I went round the back of the bookies, the High Street entrance, and I put the back door in, me and another fella. Then McGuinness and the rest of us went into the bookies.' Clinton had been on the civil rights march since the start, where he had met up with another friend who was in the IRA, who told him that weapons were on their way down to the city centre. As he looked around the bookies, Clinton believes he knew what McGuinness planned to do. 'It was an ideal place for a bomb. The window upstairs looked on to William Street and we were actually looking down on the soldiers, they were only a few yards from us. You could do a lot of damage to the troops, but the crowd would have been safe because there was a gap between them and the soldiers. You could have blown every one of them up and still have got away. Then McGuinness got word that the army was coming in – I think from a walkie-talkie – and there was no time to put a bomb there. We all ran out the back.' Just before McGuinness and the others escaped from the back of the bookies, a shot was heard. One person who was there alleges that, just before McGuinness left, and as he heard that the soldiers were coming, McGuinness had fired a shot from the Thompson at the door.

James Donal Deeney later told the Bloody Sunday Inquiry that he had been in the bookies himself. 'We had broken down the door at the back and then both went through to have a look at the soldiers' positions (not that we were going to do anything as we were not tooled-up). I could see a number of troops behind barriers in riot gear and, behind them, further troops with military vehicles lined up. Most of these troops were not in riot gear and I would describe some of them as "top brass". All I could see from my vantage point were a number of military targets. They swaggered about like Marines.'

There are other accounts of McGuinness' activities that day. References to him have been found in security service debriefing notes of a Provisional IRA informer, code-named 'Infliction'. According to the documents, which were telegrams sent from the Hague in April 1984, 'Martin McGuinness . . . has admitted to Infliction that he had personally fired the shot (from a Thompson machine gun on "single shot") from the Rossville flats in Bogside that precipitated the "Bloody Sunday" episode.' However, David Shayler, a former MI5 agent who dealt with Infliction, described him as a 'bullshitter'. 'His file was marked "source whose reliability is being re-assessed". In MI5 speak that means "we can't trust this bugger as far as we can throw him." Infliction was later discontinued. We stopped using him.' Shayler intends to give evidence to the Bloody Sunday Inquiry.

Other evidence unearthed by the Bloody Sunday Inquiry includes 'a highly controversial memo' where Ivan Cooper is quoted by a *Sunday Times* journalist. Cooper has repudiated its content, saying 'I find this account poisonous and disturbing and I reject it in its entirety'. The disputed account claims that McGuinness and two other men were trapped in a house in William Street where they planned to fire through a doorway at soldiers. 'The troops moved in, and the trio were trapped. Ivan Cooper says that Martin McGuinness panicked, and thought he was going to be caught. McEvoy said to dismantle the Thompsons and put them up their jerseys. They did and ran off with the crowd.' In a later passage, Cooper is quoted saying he saw 'six gelignite bombs, and a couple of revolvers and at least one Thompson' in the back of a car.

The journalist Nell McCafferty later wrote that a young Derry priest, Father Tom O'Gara, who has since died, told fellow priests that he saw 'two armed members of the IRA, in the vicinity of the slaughter, about ten minutes before the soldiers swept into the Bogside.' This incident was left out of the collective statement issued by the priests of the diocese; as McCafferty noted, 'Father O'Gara's information, had it been divulged, would have been a propaganda godsend to the British Government in the immediate aftermath of Bloody Sunday.'

Meanwhile, 15-year-old Damian 'Bubbles' Donaghy was hunting for a rubber bullet. The bullets were popular trophies, and visiting journalists offered good money for them. Paddy Ward saw what happened next. 'The first one I saw firing a shot was the Major at the barricade in Sackville street and he pulled out a short arm, which was on a rope or lanyard. His first shot got Damian Donaghy, Bubbles. Then he shot John Johnston at the corner of Colm Bradley's pub – nobody could believe their eyes. I remember myself and another man were sheltering behind this sheet of tin when the Brits were firing rubber bullets at us – we were coming out from behind it and throwing stones at them. Your man just came out and let go. Bang bang, two went up. After that, there was just a mad rush up Rossville Street in panic.'

Johnston, a 59-year-old shop manager, on his way to visit an elderly friend, died as a result of his injuries in June 1972.

The Bogside unit of the Officials had one of their staff cars, a blue Avenger, parked nearby in Glenfada Park. After hearing the shots which wounded Donaghy and Johnston, one of their volunteers took a .303 rifle from the boot. Striding up to a first-floor balcony which the Officials had earlier earmarked as a good sniping position, the man fired at the soldier he thought had shot the two men. He missed, hitting a nearby drainpipe instead. Before he could continue, three Provisionals tried to disarm him in a furious argument, which only ended when the Official agreed that he would not fire again. A man in the flats who witnessed the incident later said that it was the first time he had seen the Provos 'with their arms both the same length' for some time.

Meanwhile, McGuinness, Clinton, and the others were running up Rossville Street, where Clinton took shelter behind a low wall. It was now 4.10 p.m. and Father Daly joined the crowd running from 'C' Company of the Paras as they charged through Barrier 14 on William Street. Fleeing marchers had been shocked when they heard General Ford encouraging his men, 'Go on, One Para, go and get them.' As Daly approached the flats, he heard a soldier using a loudhailer warning his men: 'Please do not fire back for the moment unless you identify a positive target.' 'At that stage all hell broke loose. It was just like a war film, there were bullets flying in all directions and the ricochets and the whistling of the bullets – it was horrendous. The first thing I remember in the clearest detail was a young boy, a parishioner of mine, running beside me, laughing. I think he was excited, nervous. I ran into the courtyard of the flats to try and get out through an exit, to get cover, or just to get away out of the area. He was running towards me, and as he ran towards me, a shot rang out, and he gasped. And then he fell. Just beside me.' Jackie Duddy fell in the car park of the Rossville Flats, watched by Daly and the others who had now crouched down behind the low wall at the back of the garages at the rear of Block Two of the flats. Des Clinton's heart was pounding. 'I was running beside young Duddy when he got shot. I just kept on running and when I looked up from behind the wee wall, the bullets were still flying around. It happened within minutes. Where Martin McGuinness went, I don't know.'

By this time the car park was deserted of all but the Paras, and Daly decided that he had to go to Jackie Duddy. Waving a white handkerchief he had taken from his pocket, he started to crawl out from behind the wall. As he gave the dying boy the last rites, he was joined by Charlie Glenn from the Knights of Malta, a voluntary medical corps, as well as two other men, Liam Bradley and Willy Barber. Not realising that Duddy had died, they came under a hail of bullets as they lifted him gingerly and carried him to shelter. As they moved off, Father Daly glimpsed a man taking aim at the soldiers. 'I remember at that stage one of the things that frightened us was a civilian came along with a short arm. That was the only time I saw any civilian with a gun that day. He fired a couple of shots from the gable at the end of Chamberlain Street. Well, of course, we screamed at him and told him to clear off. We didn't say that, we used other language. And he did.'

The man, who was captured on film and became known as 'Father Daly's gunman', belonged to the Official IRA. Liam O Comain, who left the Official Republican movement soon afterwards, confirms that several Officials fired at the army that day. 'There is an interesting twist to Bloody Sunday. For a while there was an element in the Officials who disagreed with Goulding's thinking on the ceasefire and they definitely made a decision to open up on Bloody Sunday. I was on the fringes then, but I tell you this, there was an element there, and their thinking at the time was that if we can have some form of death on Bloody Sunday, it might pull the Officials back into line again and put some heart into the leadership.'

By 4.35 p.m., the order had gone out to the soldiers to hold their fire. By now, many had fled the scene of the shootings in terror. Eamon Deane told the Bloody Sunday Inquiry that he had left Free Derry Corner with his girlfriend when they heard the first shots. As they ran up Westland Street, they met Martin McGuinness at the gable end of Blucher Street, not far from his home in Elmwood Street. McGuinness, who was with five or six other men, asked them what was going on. Deane told him 'that the Brits had come into the Bogside and were shooting people.' He later recalled that McGuinness' reaction was one of shock and disbelief. As they ran on, McGuinness and the others were looking down in the direction of Free Derry Corner.

Sheila Ingram, who was 21 at the time, also told the Bloody Sunday Inquiry that she saw Martin McGuinness at around this time. 'The next thing I remember as we made our way down the Lecky Road is seeing Martin McGuinness and a couple of other men I did not know coming towards us from a little walkway which ran between the shopping precinct in Meenan

Park and the Lecky Road. I do not think they were running, but they were certainly walking quite quickly and they were moving towards where we had come from. It was apparent from their faces that they were wondering what on earth was happening and I think one of them must have shouted "what is happening?" I distinctly remember shouting "so much for your protection then, they are killing people down there." I knew by that time that the Army was killing people, you did not need to see it to know what was happening. I have always assumed since that moment that Martin McGuinness and his friends must not have been on the march that day.'

In fact, Martin McGuinness later claimed that he had been on the march. 'I remember walking down Southway from Creggan with thousands of people. I remember feeling very, very proud that I was a part of a people who were prepared to stand up and defend the rights of others. It was a great day. It was a great feeling coming down until we reached William Street.' The IRA was hurt by the accusation that they had failed to protect the marchers and actually complained to *The Observer* newspaper the following Sunday that, 'After the shooting, some of our members went off to Creggan to get weapons. Feelings were running very high. Known Provisional marksmen were attacked by women in the streets after the shooting, hysterically asking where the IRA was and why we were not defending them.'

At Free Derry Corner, the march organisers were trying to work out what had happened. Willie Breslin was at Free Derry Corner when the soldiers opened fire on the crowd. A little later, Breslin saw McGuinness and asked him if the IRA had fired at the army. McGuinness told him, he says, 'There are no Provisional guns in the Bogside.' 'He took me from Free Derry corner to the back of the Bogside Inn and showed me his car, opened the car door, and invited me to see that there was nothing there.' After the shootings, McGuinness stayed in the Free Derry Corner area, waiting for more men and weapons to arrive from the Creggan.

Des Clinton was devastated. He had gone on the march with workmates, neighbours, friends he played football with. Now 13 of them were lying dead in the streets. He met Big Pat Harkin, an IRA man known as 'The Gentle Giant', who told him that Paddy Doherty, 'The Skelper' had been shot dead. 'I had only seen him a few nights before. His last words to me were, "watch yourself, because you were nearly shot the other night.' We had been caught in a riot and I was crawling along the road – I thought I was going to be shot in the sole of the foot. Instead it was Paddy.' Doherty had been shot as he tried to crawl to safety. As he lay dying, he cried out for help. Several people tried to reach him, but were forced to retreat when they came under fire. Barney McGuigan, a 41-year-old man from the Creggan who had earlier warned marchers to be careful as he feared that there might be trouble, took a white handkerchief out of his pocket. As he slowly walked towards Doherty's body, he waved his handkerchief above his head to show the soldiers that he was unarmed. After only a few steps, McGuigan crumpled and fell to the ground, shot once in the back of the head. Sean Canney watched in horror as Barney McGuigan was hit. He told journalists at the time: 'There was a large pool of blood around his head. I have a vivid memory of steam rising from the blood.' When the firing ended, marchers placed the civil rights banner that had been carried in the march over him like a shroud.

As Clinton and Harkin left Free Derry Corner for the Bogside Inn, they saw a man armed with a rifle about to open fire. 'I thought it was a .303. Big Pat Harkin started shouting at him, "What the fuck are you doing with that?"' Paddy Ward took a different view: 'He was the only one I saw with a rifle that day. I was raging. I just shouted, "Are you going to fire that fucking thing or not?"'

This man was an Official, but by this time both wings of the IRA were preparing to take authorised action against the army. Anger and bitterness gripped them; in their frustration they blamed each other for what had happened. As one Official IRA man walked home, without a weapon, he was attacked by a group of Provos walking down Westland Street towards the Bogside Inn. The Provos threw him to the ground as one of them shouted, 'You're the bastard that let the soldier go.' A few days earlier, a group of Officials had kidnapped a British soldier who was visiting his Creggan fiancée. When Martin McGuinness heard about it he decided to take over the kidnap since the soldier was being held in the Bogside, which he regarded as his territory. McGuinness and several other IRA men went to the house where the soldier was being held and tried to take him out at gunpoint, at which point they planned to kill the man. The Officials resisted this attempt and the man was later released unharmed.

Paddy Ward, one of the few Provo drivers at the time, took some Fianna members in a car loaded with weapons to attack the soldiers.

We got a car, a mark 2 Cortina estate, and parked in St

Columb's Wells with a load of gear in it, rifles. We made the mistake that if you go across St Columb's Wells, halfway across the houses are high and then they just stoop down to low houses. We had parked in front of the low houses and the soldiers on the walls could see it. We ran back to get the car, I got into the car and started it and they fired a shot at us through the roof. I can even tell you the registration of that car, it was RAT 141G, I'll never forget it. We reversed up St Columb's Wells again and headed out to the Lecky Road checkpoint. At that point there were people going down everywhere. After that we heard more shooting and we headed towards Brandywell. One IRA man, Chick Donnelly, had got himself stuck in a doorway halfway down Hamilton Street. It was a gateway to the Brandywell showgrounds where they play football. We started shooting at the checkpoint so the Brits kept their heads down – they had a sandbag post on top of the old Foyle Road milk depot. As we were firing, the man got away. We reported that to McGuinness because Chick was one of his men.

By this time, the cars from the Creggan had arrived at the Bogside Inn. One of them was a stolen Triumph 1300 which had been the getaway car when the IRA had murdered the two RUC men three days earlier. The six men who had been spotted on Westland Road earlier, leapt out of the cars and moved off towards Free Derry Corner. Heedless of the Sioux helicopter which was hovering overhead, they fired a volley of shots at troops on the walls, but failed to hit any. One round was returned.

That night the Brigade Command Staff met in the Bogside, where they pledged to make the British Army pay for what they had done. McGuinness told friends he was shattered. He later said, 'I don't believe until the day I die that I will ever get over the experience of what happened on that day and the cruelty and the barbarity of the paratroopers. I think the whole thing, even though it was regrettable and sad and tragic and many people have lost their lives, was inevitable and natural – in a situation where you put so many thousands of soldiers and RUC men, with so much power, into areas like these, there are only two responses: that people lie down and accept that there is no future for them, or that people fight. I am proud of the fact that

I was part of that community which was prepared to fight back. Basically, that's what happened and that's what happened in my life. I became one of those who was prepared to fight back.'

Only two of the dead were known personally to Martin McGuinness. He had grown up with Michael McDaid, who was 'a very quiet, unassuming young man'. He also knew Jim Wray, whose cousin, Raymond McCartney, joined the IRA after witnessing the army brutality on Bloody Sunday and was a very close friend of Martin McGuinness. McGuinness later said, 'I have an everlasting memory of Jim Wray standing on top of a British Army vehicle in the middle of Westland Street trying to rip the top off with his bare hands on the day that Damien Harkin was killed by a British Army Land-Rover.' None were members of the IRA, although Gerry Donaghy had been in the Fianna. (Donaghy had been the single member of the Fianna that Paddy Ward had been unable to find after McGuinness gave them the order to return the nail bombs.)

Later that night, McGuinness was in a car with some other IRA men. As they drove through the Bogside, people were boarding a bus to go to Buncrana to play bingo. McGuinness boarded the bus, where he told passengers that they should be ashamed of themselves, going off to bingo after 13 people had been shot dead. The passengers immediately left the bus. McGuinness later said that on reflection he believed he had been wrong to have tackled them.

When the IRA Brigade Staff met that night in the Bogside, they were determined to even the score. Although the OC was furious with McGuinness, he was powerless to move against him. Bloody Sunday had been the first day McGuinness had assumed sole command of the IRA. From then on, he would be unstoppable.

CHAPTER FIVE

The Blue-Eyed Boy

I have never said that I was in the IRA. I am not a member of the IRA. I was a republican activist in Free Derry. I make no apology for the fact that I stood in total opposition to the British Army and the RUC. The people of this city are well aware of my credentials and I don't feel that I have anything whatsoever to be ashamed of.

Martin McGuinness, author interview, 1992

On the day of the funerals, thousands marched on the British Embassy in Dublin, carrying 13 symbolic coffins and black flags. Rioting broke out as Gardai failed to control the crowd, and a petrol bomb set fire to the building, which burned down. In London, Edward Heath announced that there would be an official inquiry into the deaths, to be chaired by the Lord Chief Justice, Lord Widgery. Many eyewitnesses refused to give evidence to the Tribunal and the slogan 'Widgery Whitewash' appeared on gable walls around Derry. Lord Widgery was an obvious target for the IRA, and as a result the Tribunal sat in Coleraine, 30 miles from Derry. Lawyers were forced to rely on a large scale model of Derry made by the RAF. The closest most of them got to the streets of Derry was the officers' mess at Ballykelly Barracks on the outskirts of the city, where they were quartered.

As Derry mourned its dead, the IRA had more offers of help than they could handle. Two weeks after Bloody Sunday, the Provisionals retaliated when IRA men dragged Catholic UDR man Thomas Callaghan off the bus he was driving through the Creggan estate. Three hours later, his body was found nearby. He had been hooded, gagged and shot in the back of the head in a traditional IRA execution. There was widespread condemnation of his murder and that night about 30 young men gathered in protest at RUC headquarters. McGuinness, aware that IRA violence while the world was watching could turn public sympathy against them, ordered his men off the streets as he began to streamline the Derry Brigade.

His first priority was to arm the new recruits and within a week he was handed the opportunity he was waiting for. Although most of the Fianna members had sided with the Provos, 16-year-old Gerry Doherty had decided to stay with the Officials. When McGuinness made his move on the arms dump at the back of some shops in the Creggan estate, Doherty was killed trying to take a .38 short arm off one of the Provos. Paddy Ward was on the raid, on 25 February 1972. 'We got a Thompson sub-machine gun, a couple of short arms, and some .22s that they used for target practice. After we got away, the Stickies wanted their weapons back and actually raided a lot of the cars we had hijacked. They even burst open a Hillman Hunter in Inishowen Avenue, taking bomb material and timers from it. The whole thing escalated when the Sticks came into the Bogside and there was a shoot out. After we fired on them, the Officials opened up, firing 40 or 50 rounds. The only reason there wasn't another Bloody Sunday was that the army was watching the whole thing from Rosemount Barracks and opened up on all of us.' The two sides entered negotiations, and the feud ended before there were more deaths. The Provos agreed to hand back the weapons, but managed to hang on to them after the Official IRA declared a ceasefire later that year. The next month several crates of M1 carbines arrived from America and were buried in a local football pitch where the IRA had easy access to them.

By this time, Martin McGuinness' Derry Brigade of the IRA had 'managed to bomb the city centre until it looked as if it had been hit from the air', as Eamon McCann put it. A resourceful Derry volunteer had invented the Durex bomb; a test tube filled with sulphuric acid, which is sealed in wax before being tied in a condom. The condom is then placed in an envelope filled with sodium chlorate. When the test tube is squeezed, the acid eats through the condom in about an hour, igniting the chemicals.

Rumours spread that MacStiofain, a devout Catholic who often visited Sean Keenan in Derry, had refused to bring condoms to the Republic, where they were still illegal, so that other volunteers could be trained in the bomb-making technique because he feared they would be used for immoral purposes. He'd prefer to bring a Thompson, they joked.

Durex bombs were simple, but effective. Volunteers could simply walk from the Bogside to the city centre, with a bomb in a shoulder bag and a girl for cover. The explosives were mainly gelignite, stolen from quarries or plants like Irish Industrial Explosives in the Irish Republic. Gelly mix, or plaster gelatine, which looked like black cubes of jelly in a little satchel, was used in nail-bombs. Protests from the British government saw security increased around quarries in the South, and the IRA had to start making their own explosives from chemical fertilizers mixed with some other chemical, like diesel oil or nitro benzene, detonated by a charge of gelignite. The diesel oil gave off a lot of smoke, but it was cheap and readily available.

By this time McGuinness was one of the most wanted men in the Northern Ireland and rarely slept at home. The back doors of safe houses were often left unlocked at night, and it was not unusual for a family to find one or two stubbled faces sitting at the kitchen table when they came downstairs in the morning. One of Martin McGuinness' boltholes was the Elmwood Road home of Willie and Kathleen Gallagher. McGuinness had known Willie Gallagher, a doorman at the Embassy Ballroom, since he had attended his first dance there when he worked in Doherty's butchers in 1971. After internment, he was a frequent visitor to the house, where he was given food, a bed to sleep in, and was generally treated as a son. Their house was just around the corner from his family home in Elmwood Street, and sometimes he even risked going home for his favourite meal, 'spuds, cabbage and pork ribs, à la Peggy'.

By 13 March, the Widgery Tribunal had finished hearing evidence in Coleraine. Major Hugh Smith, secretary to the Army's legal team at the Widgery Tribunal, was spending his last night in Northern Ireland before returning to London. Hearing this, soldiers from the Royal Green Jackets, garrisoned at Ballykelly, had offered to make his last night one to remember. The Green Jackets were going to take Smith and Colin Wallace, an army public relations officer seconded to the legal team, on foot patrol in the Bogside. As Smith and Wallace pulled on combat kit, they looked like every other man in the 12-strong platoon.

Paddy Ward was on his way to help a relative fit a carpet that night when he saw a heavily-armed detachment of soldiers entering the Bogside. 'I went down to Stanley's Walk and gave them a wire that there was a whole heap of

Brits coming down. The heavy gear was handed out – I had a Sterling sub-machine gun and the other guys had carbines and stuff like that. There was a couple of other machine guns, sten guns, 9mm stuff.'

As the patrol entered Stanley's Walk, they realised that they had walked straight into a trap. Paddy Ward saw the platoon sergeant fall, blood pumping from a wound in his leg. 'The IRA had lifted a manhole and mounted a GPMG (general purpose machine gun) on the street and one man down the manhole. When he opened up down Stanley's Walk, all hell broke loose.'

Wallace and Smith pressed against a wall, desperately seeking cover as other soldiers helped the platoon sergeant limp out of range. They stopped dead in their tracks when a hijacked Morris 1800 screeched to a halt and two young men leapt out. 'It was Colm Keenan and Eugene McGillan. The Brits let them have it. Shot them dead. After that it turned into a heavy duty gun battle.' Ward says that the shooting lasted no more than four minutes. In that time, over 200 shots were fired. Wallace was uninjured in the fighting, but a bullet from an M1 carbine smashed Major Hugh Smith's right arm, severing an artery. It was amputated later that year. According to Paddy Ward, there were two IRA men, as well as Keenan and McGillan, killed that night. One was the man firing from the manhole, who came from Lifford in the Republic of Ireland, and another man, who was from Donegal. 'The IRA put their bodies in bags and buried them in Creggan cemetery that night on the sly without admitting the casualties. Every time I look at McGuinness I think of those two guys. After we ran out of ammo, we saw McGuinness hiding in the corner of the flats with a fully loaded weapon. He hadn't fired a shot.'

Sean Keenan, who was still interned, was released to attend his son's funeral. Chief of Staff Sean MacStiofain slipped across the Derry/Donegal border, to pay his respects, along with Ardoyne IRA man Martin Meehan. Although he was only 18, Colm Keenan had been a Lieutenant in the Derry Brigade, and was buried with full IRA ceremonial honours. His coffin, draped with a tricolour, was flanked by an IRA guard of honour in combat jackets and black berets. The cortege was preceded by a lone piper and young girls from Cumann na mBan carried wreaths. The Fianna marched behind the coffin. At the graveside, a firing party fired three rifle volleys over the grave in the Republican Plot of the City Cemetery in Creggan and a bugler sounded the Last Post. The family of Eugene McGillan, who was also 18, did not share their son's republican beliefs, and he was given a private funeral. The men, who were on active service, were unarmed and returning to a safe house in Stanley's Walk when they were killed.

Father Dennis Bradley attended the dying Keenan. 'I was a great believer for most of my adult life that there had to be engagement between the republicans and the British and that night confirmed it for me. I was sent for when the Brits were beginning to pull out, although there was still some firing. Colm Keenan was there, badly wounded. I anointed him and took him off to hospital. The next morning a British Army officer I knew slightly came to the door. He was in very bad shape and he told me that he thought he had fired the shot that killed young Keenan. He was very upset. It was the first person he had ever killed – if he killed him.' At the time, some people in Derry called Bradley 'the Provo priest'. 'It wasn't true, you know. We were at each other's throats in some ways,' he said at the time, going on, 'there's a great danger of creating other myths about the IRA, what they achieved and how principled they were. They created a myth that they were defenders of the people. That's a lot of bunkum.' In April, Father Bradley was sitting in a house in the Brandywell when he heard a massive explosion. 'When I went out to see what had happened I was called over to the scene. All I could make out was the top of a torso lying in the back yard and I remember not knowing if it was a human being or not. It turned out to be a soldier blown up by a booby-trap bomb. About three hours later the young fellow who had planted the bomb asked to see me. I knew him very well. It was the first person he had ever killed. There has always been a very strong thing in me which says that there has been far too much talk about the problem, whether it is in the Shankill, or in the Bog, whether it is in the British side, or in the Irish side. The problem is well known. What we haven't talked enough about through all of this is a solution.'

After an IRA no-warning bomb at the Abercorn restaurant in Belfast in March killed two girls and injured over 130 people, including two sisters shopping for a wedding dress, O Bradaigh and MacStiofain called a three-day ceasefire so that the IRA could meet Harold Wilson, leader of the opposition Labour Party. The two sides had little common ground and, as the ceasefire ran out at midnight, the Derry Brigade shot at troops in the Bogside. Prime Minister Edward Heath announced that the Stormont parliament was to be prorogued and Direct Rule from Westminster imposed from the end of March 1972.

In April, Martin McGuinness listened to Sean MacStiofain's oration in Derry City Cemetery on Easter Sunday. The Chief of Staff got a rousing reception from the 2,500-strong crowd when he rejected calls from the head of the Catholic Church in Ireland, Cardinal Conway and a group of priests in Belfast and Derry, that the IRA should call off their campaign. 'Concessions be damned, we want our freedom,' MacStiofain told them, while in Dublin Ruairi O Bradaigh warned that 'peace at any price' was not on offer.

The next day, the Derry Command announced that they would address the concerns of local people at a public meeting. The following Saturday, Martin McGuinness spoke in public for the first time as Daithi O Conaill and Maire Drumm listened. Visibly nervous, he gave the IRA line. 'Gerry Fitt and the SDLP are concerned at the moment with running down the IRA. These people are going around talking about peace. They're wasting their time. It doesn't matter a fuck what Gerry Fitt or John Hume say. We fight on. We're not stopping until we get a United Ireland.' As his audience cheered him on, some remained silent, concerned at the prospect of the lynch law which operated unchallenged in the streets of Free Derry.

Father Bradley had started a Bogside Community Association in the area. 'Daithi O Conaill approached me at that meeting and asked me would I set up a police force under the auspices of the Bogside Community Association. I told him to go and stuff himself.'

The IRA had taken over policing in Free Derry, setting up their own traffic courts where vigilantes could fine speeding motorists on the spot and petty thieves were stripped and beaten in the streets in front of journalists. They even issued press cards, telling English journalists they were to safeguard them against being mistaken for military intelligence by over zealous volunteers. The cards' real purpose was to let the IRA control the movements of any journalists investigating how they ran the Bogside. McGuinness mingled with the reporters as they drank in the bar of the City Hotel, swapping stories with those he favoured. One journalist even remembers dancing with his girlfriend, Bernie. But McGuinness showed a grimmer side to his nature in April, when he introduced journalists to an IRA gunman who had earlier shot a British soldier in the city. And after one reporter wrote that the IRA had ordered a priest out of the city at gunpoint, McGuinness told the journalist to leave the city. The story referred to an incident where Martin McGuinness' close friend, Barney

McFadden, had grabbed the microphone from a priest who was criticising the IRA in St Columba's Chapel.

Frank Thompson, a *Daily Express* writer who described McGuinness as 'fair-haired, handsome and with almost a schoolboy shyness about him', left town soon after McGuinness let it be known he was no longer welcome. McGuinness was 'acutely embarrassed' by Thompson's profile, 'The boy who rules Free Derry.' 'Me married? You must be joking,' he laughed. 'I'm too young for that,' McGuinness was quoted as saying as another headline in the story declared, 'Martin has more time for guns than girls.' Thompson went on to describe McGuinness as 'one of the most feared and wanted men in Ulster and a fanatical disciple of the Provos' Dublin-based leader Sean MacStiofain'. The City Hotel escaped the IRA's bombing campaign until June that year, when it was firebombed. It had escaped, not because it was used by the journalists that McGuinness worked his easy charm on; but because a republican supporter was a porter there. After he was dismissed, the hotel joined the list of targets. Another casualty around the same time was Doherty's butchers, which was destroyed in a bomb attack on a neighbouring bakery.

There was more violence after the Widgery Report was published on 18 April 1972. Lord Widgery found that the firing of some soldiers of the Parachute Regiment 'had bordered on the reckless' and that there was a strong suspicion that some of the marchers had earlier fired guns or handled bombs. Most Derry people shared the views of the City Coroner, Major Hubert O'Neill, who told the inquest in 1973 that the Paras had run amok and committed 'sheer unadulterated murder'. Seamus Costello, the Official IRA's Director of Operations, had issued orders after Bloody Sunday that all British soldiers were to be shot on sight. In May, the Official IRA kidnapped 19-year-old Derry man, William Best, a member of the Royal Irish Rangers who was visiting friends on leave when he was abducted. Costello's orders said nothing about the position of local soldiers and Ranger Best's body was found the next morning. He had been hooded and shot in the back of the head. The Provos did their best to make political capital out of Ranger Best's death, conveniently forgetting how they had attacked the Officials on Bloody Sunday when they released a British soldier unharmed instead of giving him to McGuinness for certain execution. Five thousand people attended his funeral, including the Bishop of Derry. Four hundred women from the Creggan and the Bogside marched on the Officials Meenan Park

Headquarters, where Best had been questioned after his abduction. Milking the situation to the full, the Provos issued orders banning the Officials from entering the Creggan or the Bogside. Shortly afterwards, rocked to the core, the Officials declared an indefinite ceasefire.

Liam O Comain left the Official Sinn Féin after Ranger Best's killing. According to O Comain, one of the Official Command Staff at the time told him that Best was an agent. O Comain argued with the man, saying that an agent wouldn't walk around Derry in a British Army uniform. 'The day after Best was shot, I was walking down to an education meeting and a local woman said to me, "the Provos shot a Derry man last night." So I walked into the meeting and there were two or three other men there and I said "You've done it now." Malachy McGurran was there at the time and I said, "Now that you've done it, don't claim it." The Provos are getting the blame for it. But they went and issued a statement claiming it. It was a damaging blow to the Officials in Derry and they never really recovered. After that, I said, "look, I'm moving aside for a time." Within a few days, women had been conditioned to come down to the premises and protest.'

McGuinness had learned a lot about tactics since Bloody Sunday. Mingling with journalists in the City Hotel had taught him the value of propaganda and now he was ready to use it. He was enjoying the media attention he attracted and was at ease with the title of Officer Commanding. In a television interview shortly after Bloody Sunday, as he strolled through the Bogside with the journalist Tom Mangold, he had answered a question about IRA policy addressed to him as 'Officer Commanding the Provisional IRA operation' without turning a hair.

By this time McGuinness had become a distinct asset to the IRA and had impressed Sean MacStiofain on his trips to see Sean Keenan. Father Dennis Bradley later said, 'A myth has grown up around McGuinness. He was a very nice young fellow like a thousand other young fellows – the difference with him was he had a good face.' John Hume noted, 'He just seemed to come out of the blue. There were rumours about his involvement, but the IRA were a secret organisation, I hadn't a clue who was in it.' Another observer said, 'McGuinness was young, articulate, the blue-eyed boy with no skeletons in the cupboard. He was the very image of an ideal volunteer.' McGuinness later told Anthony McIntyre, an ex-prisoner and former IRA commander for the Ormeau Road in Belfast, that he was not a member of the leadership in 1972. 'The prominent role that history has ascribed to me is inaccurate. It is based solely on my presence in the delegation that met Whitelaw . . . I was picked to go merely because MacStiofain made a decision and that was it. The leadership that I knew about and was part of was on the streets in Derry where the community were putting up resistance. I have no intimate knowledge about what political or strategic considerations informed the decision to call a ceasefire. I was very much on the ground. The political strategy was devised by others such as O Conaill and MacStiofain.'

McGuinness was being modest. In June, he had accompanied Sean Keenan to a meeting with MacStiofain where they outlined a plan to announce publicly that they would suspend IRA operations for seven days, on condition that Secretary of State for Northern Ireland William Whitelaw met them in Free Derry. MacStiofain jumped at the idea. In Brandywell Community Centre on June 12, O Conaill and MacStiofain joined McGuinness and Seamus 'Thumper' Twomey, the sinister-looking Belfast OC, often seen posing in a pair of dark glasses, as they outlined their plan, which was publicly rejected by Whitelaw. Significantly, the Provos had dropped their demand for an immediate end to internment or any major policy declaration from the British, asking only that the British Army ended arrests, searches, raids, and harassment of the civilian population. The next day, as an IRA bomb wrecked Derry's Guildhall, O Conaill and MacStiofain knocked on the door of John Hume's Westend Park home. 'After their press conference I had issued an immediate statement and the next day O Conaill and MacStiofain arrived at my door asking to see me. I had a chat with them – what they wanted was for me to arrange a meeting with Willie Whitelaw so they could have talks. That was all done very privately.'

Much to their surprise, Whitelaw, who said later that he had simply wanted to see the whites of their eyes, agreed to the meeting. On 20 June, following Hume's intervention, a meeting to lay down some ground rules took place at a secret location in Derry. There were only four men at the meeting. On the British side were Frank Steele, a senior MI6 man, and Philip Woodfield, a civil servant from the Northern Ireland Office; the Provisionals were represented by Daithi O Conaill, and Gerry Adams, the 23-year-old Adjutant of the Belfast Brigade, who had been released from internment to attend the meeting. The release of the gawky, bespectacled Adams had been one of the two pre-conditions set by the IRA; the other was political status for the prisoners.

Two days later, the IRA announced a 'bi-lateral truce', which was to come into operation at midnight on 26 June. The IRA were determined to show that the ceasefire was not a sign of weakness and murdered five soldiers and a policeman in the run up to the deadline. On 7 July, they travelled to the meeting point at Shantallow on the outskirts of Derry, where they joined Frank Steele in a minibus with brown paper taped over its window. The IRA delegation was MacStiofain and O Conaill, for the national leadership, joined by McGuinness to represent Derry and Adams to represent Belfast, along with Ivor 'Dinger' Bell. Ivor Malachy Bell, a former mechanic known as 'The Heathen', was a close associate of Adams – a devout Catholic like McGuinness. The final member of the delegation was Myles Shevlin, a lawyer from Dublin, who had observer status. To ensure their safe return, the Derry Brigade had kidnapped two British soldiers who had wandered into the Bogside the night before. Two members of the delegation were also armed, MacStiofain with a .38 Cobra Special revolver in a shoulder holster. Steele later said that MacStiofain provided a rare moment of levity when the minibus stopped behind some cows as they drove to the prearranged spot where a helicopter was to pick them up and fly them to Aldergrove airport, when he said, 'I do think the British Army could have given us a better escort.' The IRA delegation found the episode even more bizarre when an RAF officer saluted them as they boarded the plane.

They were flown to RAF Benson, 50 miles to the west of London, where two Special Branch cars drove them to the Cheyne Walk home of Paul Channon, one of Whitelaw's Junior Ministers, where Whitelaw and Channon were waiting to greet them. MacStiofain was impressed that Whitelaw 'had done some homework before the meeting', pronouncing his name correctly, while Adams noted that his handshake was 'quite sweaty'. The IRA delegation dismissed all attempts by the British to lighten the atmosphere, stiffly adhering to a list of demands read out by MacStiofain. The demands were a rigid recital of IRA policy that offered no prospect of negotiation and included a recognition of the right of the Irish people to determine their own destiny as a unit and a British declaration of intention to withdraw their forces, as well as an immediate end to internment and an amnesty for all political prisoners.

Whitelaw and Channon listened politely, and the meeting was cordial until Whitelaw denied that British soldiers had ever shot innocent civilians, at which point an angry Martin McGuinness drew his attention to Bloody Sunday. The meeting ended in stalemate and, accompanied by Steele and

Woodfield, the men flew back to Aldergrove. McGuinness later said, 'My initial impressions before we went into the meeting were that we were dealing with the most experienced diplomatic group of people in the world and we accorded the British the respect of understanding that they are very, very experienced, that in terms of diplomacy and so forth, we were very inexperienced and all that we had to go on, going into that meeting, was our own basic honesty, in terms of understanding the struggle we were involved in and what we were attempting to achieve through that struggle.'

After the meeting, he noted, 'I had learned in two hours what Irish politicians still haven't learned: that the British don't give easily.' Pending Cabinet discussions, the truce would continue until Whitelaw gave the IRA their response. MacStiofain was rather taken aback when they arrived in Derry to find that the two British soldiers held hostage against their safe return had already been released. Within forty-eight hours the ceasefire ended as the IRA and British Army became involved in gun battles in west Belfast following a dispute over the allocation of houses. The army shot dead five people that night, including a 16-year-old Fianna member, a 13-year-old schoolgirl, a priest, and two other men. The ceasefire was over, MacStiofain announced, and the campaign would resume with 'the utmost ferocity and ruthlessness'.

Later that month on 21 July the IRA set off 26 bombs in Belfast killing nine people and injuring scores more in an operation directed by Belfast OC Seamus Twomey and his Adjutant, Gerry Adams. Twomey was a militarist who had seen the ceasefire as a sign of weakness on MacStiofain's part. Bloody Friday, as it became known, was one of the worst days of the Troubles; and a major tactical setback for the IRA. The army had been urging Whitelaw for weeks to let them enter the no-go areas and take down the barricades. Two weeks to the day after Whitelaw's meeting with the IRA, Bloody Friday convinced him the army was right. Operation Motorman, the biggest British military operation since Suez, got under way at first light on 31 July as 12,000 soldiers with bulldozers and tanks smashed their way past the barricades. In a televised broadcast the night before, Whitelaw had warned that action would be taken to allow the security forces to move freely through all areas of Northern Ireland.

At a meeting of the Derry Brigade that night, McGuinness gave orders that most of the volunteers were to go on the run across the border to Donegal immediately. He would stay to lead the defence of the barricades.

At around ten o'clock he told the section leaders of the eight-man cells to dump all their gear. IRA volunteers took up position at the barricades at Westway; the top of Southway where Eamon Lafferty had been killed; the Lonemoor Road; Creggan heights; Piggery Ridge; and Broadway. The Saracen armoured cars were already on their way into the city and IRA resistance to Operation Motorman folded as the tanks rumbled into the city at dawn. The IRA had failed to predict the scale of Operation Motorman – at one stage, four landing craft from HMS *Fearless* sailed up the Foyle Estuary to set down Royal Marines and Royal Engineers with Centurion bulldozer tanks to clear the barricades.

Paddy Ward was desperately looking for somewhere to dump his section's weapons which he had hurriedly piled into the boot of a borrowed car. After narrowly avoiding capture several times, he abandoned the car to escape from a foot-patrol who had tried to stop him. As he ran through a house, he doubled back to watch as the army checked out the car. At this point, McGuinness walked casually up to him. 'I told McGuinness, "they are on to that car, if they don't blow up the boot, what will I do with those weapons?" "Whatever you like," he said. "I don't give a shit." He had tried to dye his hair auburn, hadn't he, and it had turned out purple. I just turned to him and said "You are some actor, man." Then he walked off.' The soldiers from the Black Watch Regiment blew up the boot. As they sheltered from the blast, the weapons were hurled all over the road with the force of the explosion and Paddy Ward watched the soldiers 'dancing and whooping up and down the street like Red Indians'.

When the coast was clear, Ward escaped over the border. The Provos had bought a bed-and-breakfast house in Buncrana to house the men on the run, but places were reserved for 'the top brass'. While the leadership whiled away their evenings drinking, other volunteers, like Ward, had to make their own arrangements, and he ended up sleeping in the back of a car for nearly a month before he decided to take his chances back in Derry.

On the same morning, 31 July 1972, IRA men in Derry planted three car bombs in the quiet village of Claudy, killing nine people. The bombers had failed to deliver a warning that bombs had been planted because a callbox they planned to use was out of order. The IRA issued an immediate denial of responsibility and Sean MacStiofain claimed that a later IRA court of inquiry carefully investigated the denials which were subsequently borne out. Few believed them. It was widely known that the bombs had been planted by an

IRA unit. However, the fact that one of the men responsible was an associate of Martin McGuinness was kept a closely guarded secret. McGuinness wandered around the barricades that afternoon, joking with local people as he took photographs of the tumbling barricades. Although his face was familiar to troops who had been issued with photographs of him, there were no attempts to arrest him. As he circulated, he told the teenagers he met in the Bogside and the Creggan that the army was to be stoned that night. As the army fired in the Creggan that night, two young men were shot dead and two injured. Under cover of the disturbance, Martin McGuinness slipped across the border, disguised as a woman. He headed for the Illies and his grandmother's farm, where he was joined by other volunteers on the run, including the man who had bombed Claudy that afternoon. As McGuinness later noted, 'After Operation Motorman, the whole thing moved on to a very different phase. The area was occupied and the barricades were taken down and the British Army moved in here with a massive military force, something akin to what the Americans were doing in Vietnam, only transferred to a western Europe scenario. And it was quite incredible how the resistance of the people continued on even after that, and has continued on to this day.'

McGuinness sat the rest of the year out in the Illies, although he would sometimes slip back into Derry to visit his mother. By now he was a well-known figure and visitors to Ireland often made the journey to the small farmhouse near Buncrana where he held court. In June, he had shown the actress Siobhan McKenna around Derry, which she had visited to present her one-woman show. Around the same time the writer Edna O'Brien met him in a house in the Bogside. Later that year, the American writer Leon Uris visited McGuinness in the Illies. Uris was travelling around Ireland with his wife, Jill, researching a book of photographs *Ireland: A Terrible Beauty*, which was published in 1975. Leon Uris photographed McGuinness for the book, gazing dreamily into the distance as light from an adjacent window played over his face. Uris based Conor Larkin, the IRA hero of his novel *Trinity*, on the conversations he had with McGuinness at that time.

On New Year's Eve 1972, McGuinness' country idyll came to an end, when he was arrested by Irish police near a car at Cappry, Co. Donegal, with another man, Joe McCallion. McGuinness, who had a Zapata moustache, which was dyed black like his hair, was caught red-handed with 250 lb of gelignite and 4,757 rounds of ammunition. The two men were remanded in custody and McGuinness spent the first night of 1973 in jail.

CHAPTER SIX

Prison/Truce

I am a member of the Derry Brigade of the IRA and I am very, very proud of it.

Martin McGuinness, Dublin Special
Criminal Court, 29 January 1973

When Martin McGuinness woke up on New Year's Day, he was facing the bare walls of a Donegal Garda station. The Irish police had been watching the red Cortina that McGuinness and another IRA man, Joe McCallion, had abandoned earlier. The car contained 50 lbs of explosives and a large assortment of ammunition. A senior Army officer in Derry said, 'It is great news. This chap has been on our wanted list for some time.' McGuinness and McCallion were remanded in custody on charges of having in their possession 250 lbs of gelignite and 4,750 rounds of ammunition, being members of the IRA and failing to account for their movements.

Two weeks later, McGuinness declined to request bail from 'any court that will allow itself to work for the same aims as Mr Whitelaw and Mr Heath'. He added, 'My place is in Derry City. As soon as this case is over, the better.' The Irish police commented dryly, 'McGuinness is safely bedded down.' While he was being questioned by police in Dublin, a Derry IRA man who had fled there after an encounter with the British Army visited McGuinness, pretending to be his brother. Shane Paul O'Doherty was one of the youngest members of the Derry IRA, and one of its most determined bombers. He had decided to visit McGuinness after being bluntly rebuffed by the man put in charge after McGuinness' arrest. The new man had taken a dislike to O'Doherty, whose self-confidence was sometimes mistaken for arrogance. McGuinness agreed to help provide him with another IRA contact in Derry. O'Doherty returned to the city where he worked as Explosives Officer for the Derry Brigade, training teams of volunteers to assemble and plant bombs.

In a court case in Derry on 10 January, the contents of an envelope were read out in court. They had been seized by police, who arrested an IRA courier as he tried to cross the border into Co. Donegal to deliver them to McGuinness who was still on the run in the Irish Republic, from where he directed events in Derry. Patrick Joseph McGilloway (18), who was described as an IRA Intelligence Officer, was found with the envelope by the RUC, which contained lists of policemen's homes, car registrations, descriptions of individual policemen and their families, along with their movements, and details of the policemen's religions. Another document, headed 'Explosives', was a list of 'operations which can be carried out within the next few weeks', which included the blowing up of the telephone exchange and a transformer. On the back of the list was a note of shops in Derry which were to have incendiary devices planted in them the following Saturday. Another sheet gave details of army and UDR movements. McGilloway said that he had been ordered to deliver the envelope to Martin McGuinness in Buncrana, but was unaware of the contents. One of the documents read, 'We should send our acting company CO out to kill at least two British soldiers a week.'

At the end of the month, McGuinness and Joe McCallion, from Lisfannon, Co. Donegal, were both convicted at Dublin Special Criminal Court of being members of the IRA, receiving a six-month sentence each. They were acquitted on four charges relating to explosives and ammunition. McGuinness, who did not recognise the court, made an unsworn statement, saying, 'In Derry City it is a known fact that every citizen killed has been killed by the British Army or the RUC. For over two years I was an officer in the Derry Brigade of the IRA. We have fought against the killing of our people. My comrades have been arrested and tortured and some were shot unarmed by British troops.'

Chief Superintendent James Doyle told the court he knew that the two men were members of the IRA, but not which Brigade they belonged to. Joe McCallion retorted, 'You know so much about us, but you don't know to what section of the IRA we belong to?' McGuinness proved the truth of the old saying that a man who represents himself has a fool for a client by telling Doyle, 'I am a member of the Derry Brigade of the IRA and I am very, very proud of it.' They were taken to the Curragh detention camp, just outside Dublin, where they joined a large contingent of IRA prisoners, including Sean MacStiofain and Ruairi O Bradaigh. McGuinness later remarked that he had found it easy to 'do his bird'. 'There's a camaraderie in prison which gets you over everything. There's people that I met in prison I didn't know before I went there and we've been lifelong friends ever since. There are people that I met there who I still regard as friends. I think that most people get by and are able to put up with prison as long as there is comradeship and as long as there is a camaraderie between the prisoners.'

On 16 May, after getting 'time off for good behaviour', or remission, as it's generally known, the two men were released. Peggy McGuinness and Joe McCallion's mother met them with a car at the prison gates. In an embarrassing turn of events, the car refused to start when the driver turned the key in the ignition. Two military policemen had to push them down the road before the car would pick up any speed. They were relieved when they arrived back at Martin's grandmother's farm in the Illies, for 'a good feed of ribs'. McGuinness, who had spent much of his time in prison reading from the sparse stocks in the library, was blasé about his experiences, telling friends who called round to see him that, 'prison was absolutely no problem to me at all, no problem whatsoever, because of the comradeship and the crack and the friendships and the relationships that you strike up with people.'

While McGuinness was still in the Curragh, his girlfriend, Bernie Canning, had been lifted in Derry. She had been arrested at a checkpoint near Craigavon Bridge on the Foyle Road when the army had stopped the white Ford Cortina she was a passenger in. The car was driven by Thomas McCallion (from Beechwood Street), a neighbour of the McGuinness family and a top IRA man. When soldiers searched the car, they found six 5 lb bombs containing home-made explosives, three No.6 electrical detonators, three alarm clocks, two of which were wired up to batteries, seventeen rolls of insulating tape, fifteen assorted brass nuts and bolts, and nine torch bulbs. The soldiers knew straightaway that they had stumbled on an IRA bomb team. The torch bulbs replaced the detonators in the bombs – it was a crude but effective safety device to avoid the alarming number of IRA personnel who had blown themselves up when arming bombs. If the bulb lit, there was a faulty contact somewhere. The detonator replaced the bulb at the very last minute, when the bomb was being planted. John Gerard McCool from Duncree Gardens on the Creggan estate and Marie Healey, a neighbour of Bernie Canning from Anne Street were also in the car. All four were taken to Victoria RUC barracks, where they were questioned by CID. Healey and Canning denied all knowledge of the explosives but when they appeared at a Special Court in Derry on 25 April, they were remanded in custody after being charged under Section 3B of the Explosive Substances Act, 1883. McCallion, McCool and Healey were subsequently convicted, while Canning was found not guilty.

The following month, McGuinness was given the honour of addressing the annual Wolfe Tone commemoration at Bodenstown Cemetery, Co. Kildare, in the Irish Republic. Seamus Twomey was joined by Sean MacStiofain, now released from the Curragh, as they listened to the emotional McGuinness: 'From the soldiers of the Irish Republican Army to the British government, I bring this message. "We are in a stronger position than ever before and we will not end this just war until you withdraw the murderous British Army and recognise the right of the Irish people to settle their own affairs . . . A rejection of this means a continuation of the struggle and the certain deaths of British soldiers."'

He had just been appointed to Director of Operations on GHQ staff, where he replaced the veteran Tyrone IRA man, Kevin Mallon, who was serving a 12-month prison sentence in Portlaoise prison. Shane Paul O'Doherty was still Explosives Officer and had been one of the first callers to see McGuinness in the Illies, where they soon renewed their friendship. McGuinness had heard that O'Doherty had been perfecting a prototype letter bomb, and was recuperating in Dublin after receiving injuries when one detonated in his face. Following his recovery, McGuinness asked him if he would be prepared to go to London, which O'Doherty knew well, to send letter bombs to a number of prominent targets. O'Doherty readily agreed. He received 30 life sentences at the Old Bailey in 1976 for single-handedly masterminding an IRA letter bomb campaign in London, where he selected his targets from the pages of *Who's Who*. His victims included the Conservative Home Secretary who held office at the time of Bloody Sunday; Reginald Maudling, who received injuries to his left thumb and fingers when he opened a parcel containing a book on horoscopes; and Edward Heath, Prime Minister at the time, whose secretary at 10 Downing Street threw the book containing the bomb into a waste-paper bin thinking it was a prank from a girls' school.

The top priority for the IRA during the early '70s was the bombing campaign in England, where the publicity generated by their activities confirmed their view that one small bomb in London was worth a hundred in Ireland. McGuinness threw himself into organising the offensive with enthusiasm, as Marion Price later remembered. Price, along with Gerry Kelly and her sister Dolours, was jailed at the Old Bailey in 1973 after planting four bombs in London, two of which exploded, killing one person and wounding 180. Referring in 2001 to Martin McGuinness' condemnation of continuing violence from dissident republican groups, she said, 'What I find nauseating is that those who went down that same path with me now condemn others for doing the same. People like Martin McGuinness now condemn them, but back when we were discussing the politics of armed struggle, he turned around and said, "I am not a politician, I am a soldier."'

Martin McGuinness' father, William, died in Altnagelvin Hospital at the end of June after a short illness. The coffin was wrapped in a tricolour as it was carried after Requiem Mass, from St Mary's Church, Cockhill, Co. Donegal, to the adjoining graveyard for burial. Martin and Peggy were joined by his brothers Tom, Paul, Willie, Declan and John, and by his sister, Geraldine, who had married IRA man Joe McColgan less than two weeks previously. Among the 40 or so wreaths placed on the grave were some from Provisional IRA headquarters in Dublin, as well as units in Derry, Donegal and Tyrone. Several hundred mourners attended the funeral, including Nationalist Party President, and former MP for Derry, Eddie McAteer.

At the end of August, McGuinness joined Barney McFadden at a graveside commemoration to mark the second anniversary of the death of Eamon Lafferty. He told a crowd of about 700 that the fight against the British forces of occupation would go on until they had realised Lafferty's dream of a United Ireland. McGuinness and Barney McFadden were loudly cheered when they condemned priests who had been critical of the IRA murder of Patrick Duffy, who they claimed was an informer. The IRA had claimed the murder of Mr Duffy, whose body was still missing, by inserting a notice in the *Derry Journal*.

McGuinness was arrested again on 11 February 1974, when the Gardai stopped a car driven by Liam Bradley, one of the men who had helped Father Edward Daly carry Jackie Duddy's body on Bloody Sunday. McGuinness had tried to escape after pulling a gun on the police, but was caught in a nearby field. At the end of February he was jailed for a year after being convicted of IRA membership and failing to account for his movements. McGuinness had matured since his earlier court appearance and told the police who arrested him that he had 'absolutely nothing to say'. Again, he passed the time in prison by reading. On this occasion he had been sent to Portlaoise jail, where his favourite book was the story of a mining family in a Welsh village, *How Green Was My Valley*, by Richard Llewellyn. 'It caused me to empathise with the miners and all workers ever since,' he later remembered. Other books enjoyed by McGuinness included Walter Macken's trilogy about the nineteenth century Irish famine – *Seek the Fair Land*, *The Scorching Wind*, and *The Silent People* – which he described as 'little gems'. McGuinness also joined the prison football team, where one prisoner remembers him 'in a pair of boots, hoofing a football around the yard'. The prisoners ran several teams and a football league, and they also had a sports committee.

He was released in November 1974. This time, Bernie Canning was there to meet him. She had been found not guilty of the explosives charges against her on 19 April that year.

The couple got married on 20 November 1974, just over a week after McGuinness' release. The marriage took place in the little church of St Mary's, Cockhill, where his father had been buried the year before. Bernie's sister, Eileen, and Martin's oldest brother, Tom, witnessed it. Father Dennis Bradley performed the ceremony and the couple travelled to Dublin for their honeymoon. The couple had intended to set up home in Buncrana, but later moved in with Martin's mother, Peggy, in Elmwood Street. It was a difficult time for Bernie, as Martin McGuinness later recalled. 'The first years of married life were very, very difficult because I was still on the run and being sought by the British Army and the RUC. Things were very difficult, in terms of trying to maintain a normal relationship. My wife and I were trying to find a home, where she could live in, where I could visit every now and again until such times as internment had ended and that brought about a situation where I was able to have some semblance of a normal life.'

The day after their wedding, 21 people died in two pub explosions in Birmingham. By now, Martin and Bernie were on honeymoon in Dublin, where Shane Paul O'Doherty met them that evening as news of the slaughter came through. McGuinness was furious about the bombing and told O'Doherty that if the IRA were found to be responsible, he would have no hesitation in resigning. IRA GHQ staff issued a statement in Dublin to deny any involvement in the Birmingham bombs. Few believed them, and they were later forced to admit they had lied. Around this time Councillor Pat Devine was one of four SDLP councillors who asked the IRA for a meeting. 'We wanted to convince them of the wisdom of stopping,' he says wryly. The meeting took place at night, in a house in the Bogside, where Martin McGuinness joined Shane Paul O'Doherty and two other IRA men. 'At times,' Devine remembers, 'the discussion got very heated. Shane was very arrogant at that time, and we had a serious ding-dong with him. We were older than them, and they were young and angry. It was Devine's first meeting with McGuinness, who impressed him as a 'tough cookie'.

While McGuinness had been in Portlaoise, the leadership had been involved in secret talks with the British. Merlyn Rees was the new Secretary of State following the general election of 28 February 1974, which had seen Harold Wilson put Labour back in power again. Unknown to Rees, MI6 had in fact been secretly meeting IRA leaders since 1973. Michael Oatley had recently taken over from Frank Steele, who had brought the IRA to meet Whitelaw at Cheyne Walk in 1972. By the end of 1973, Oatley had met the Derry man, Father Dennis Bradley, whose introductions would provide him with a unique insight into the thinking of the IRA, an advantage that would continue until his retirement in 1991. 'They hadn't a baldy about what was going on, but the one thing about the Foreign Office was that they were always prepared to learn. Having come out of Cambridge and Oxford and so on. Oatley in particular was an incredibly sophisticated man who was very comfortable in church circles with clergy, but hadn't a clue. When you scraped the surface, underneath all the sophistication you had colonial attitudes – they thought this was an uprising by an unruly group of people.' Father Bradley became Oatley's conduit into a world he didn't know existed, particularly in what he saw as part of his own country. Two Derry businessmen joined Bradley in the Link: a unique group, composed of Father Dennis Bradley and two Derry businessmen, which played a pivotal role in the relationship that slowly developed between the two sides. Father Bradley says that McGuinness was not involved in the talks, and he dealt with Daithi O Conaill, Ruairi O Bradaigh, Seamus Twomey and Billy McKee. 'What happened was Oatley began to come and chat and try to set things up and so forth and eventually they agreed to meet, and they met. I was the only priest and Oatley came round to see us.' It had been RUC Inspector Frank Lagan who had given the idea to Father Bradley. 'Lagan had said to me, "Look, this is crazy stuff and nobody is taking command, nobody can control it, nobody will do anything . . . It is just pure reaction and there is no one to put an end to it."' After the initial encounter, Oatley visited Derry regularly, where the meetings were generally held. They took place in private houses, with members of the Link sitting in the next room. Occasionally people taking a break from the meetings would ask them questions, as Bradley recalls: 'In my opinion it wasn't a good system, and we didn't have any authority or stature. We should have been chairing the meetings. Sometimes somebody would come out to the toilet and say, "we are fucking struggling, have you any ideas on it?" That would happen an odd time and there was a whole session afterwards where people obviously wanted to chat.'

At the end of December 1974, another extraordinary meeting took place between the IRA Army Council and a group of Protestant clergymen. The meeting was a coincidence, and was prompted by Canon William Arlow's invitation to O Bradaigh, O Conaill, McKee, Twomey, Kevin Mallon, and J.B.O'Hagan. While the Feakle talks, as they became known (held in Smyth's Village Hotel in Feakle, Co. Clare in the Irish Republic), were a genuine attempt at dialogue, another series of talks was initiated in Belfast as a smoke screen. Maire Drumm and a Belfast IRA man called Prionsias McAirt met once or twice a week as a decoy while the Link series of talks continued in secret. On 18 December, a deputation from the Feakle talks met Merlyn Rees at the House of Commons to hand him a document containing the IRA's terms for a permanent ceasefire. It presented the government with an ideal opportunity. Canon Arlow and his clerical associates had unwittingly broken the ice for the government, who could now present the product of the Link series of talks as if it had been the Feakle initiative that had come up with a solution.

On Christmas Day 1974, Father Dennis Bradley travelled to Co. Roscommon in the Irish Republic. He had not planned on making the journey, but Michael Oatley had asked him to deliver the government's response to the IRA's statement of their minimum terms in the Feakle communiqué. The IRA had already declared 'a suspension of operations' over the Christmas period to allow the British time to respond. The ceasefire was swiftly extended and on New Year's Eve, the Army Council invited Father Bradley to an Army Council meeting so he could authenticate the message from the British. The British, Father Bradley told the Council, wanted to meet Billy McKee in Derry. A week later, Billy McKee, accompanied by a witness, travelled to Derry for the historic meeting with Oatley. McKee who had been released from Crumlin Road prison on 4 September after serving almost three and a half years in prison, was in command of the Belfast Brigade, and had a seat on the Army Council. His support was essential to the success of negotiations, and the Contact, Father Dennis Bradley, who did not know that McKee was actually sitting with him at the Army Council meeting on 31 December 1974, had said that British officials wanted to meet with him. At a second meeting, James Allan, a colleague from the Foreign Office, accompanied Oatley, while O Bradaigh this time accompanied McKee. It was now clear to both that each side was willing to deal. And at a later meeting still, at the beginning of February, six points of agreement were broadly agreed – the most significant for the IRA being that a sustained cessation of violence would be met with a reduction in troop numbers and an eventual withdrawal to barracks, and that discussions between the government and Sinn Féin would continue with the aim of securing a lasting peace. Passes were to be issued to men on the run, who would be allowed safe passage home, and permits would be granted to IRA men to carry arms for self-defence. The discussions almost broke down over this point but the IRA was adamant that they risked assassination, and that they must be given the means to protect themselves. Eventually, the British gave way and two-dozen permits were agreed, for key volunteers.

When Merlyn Rees confirmed to the House of Commons on 5 February that if the IRA ended all offensive operations, the army would slowly be reduced to peacetime levels and ultimately withdrawn, Father Dennis Bradley heaved a sigh of relief. Four days later the IRA issued a statement announcing that a ceasefire would begin at 6.00 p.m. on 9 February. Meanwhile, most IRA members were bewildered by the turn events had taken. McGuinness went along with it. Since his release from prison in November 1974, he had created a new position. As Peter Doherty remembers, 'He called himself Executive OC, or something stupid like that.'

The British and the IRA had agreed that the truce would be monitored through a series of 'incident centres', which were to be maintained by Sinn Féin. In Derry, McGuinness installed himself in the incident centre on Cable Street, where he quickly learned how to bargain and negotiate on the hot line that gave him instant access to a desk at the Northern Ireland Office in

Stormont, staffed twenty-four hours a day by officials and with immediate access to the Secretary of State. Their experiences in the incident centres gave many active service volunteers their first taste of politics.

By now most of the internees had been released and some of them were finding it difficult to adjust to the new political climate. As Peter Doherty remembered McGuinness did little to soothe their sensibilities, 'When one man came out of internment, he would suggest ways of doing things to McGuinness. McGuinness said to him, "Who do you think you are? You sat on your arse in Long Kesh for the last four years. You needn't think you can tell us what to do."' Many dropped out, disillusioned, and some joined the new organisation – the Irish National Liberation Army – which had just split from the Official IRA. Seamus Costello had founded the INLA as the paramilitary counterpart of his Trotskyite party, the Irish Republican Socialist Party (IRSP or Irps). McGuinness hated them too, seeing them as a more ruthless and militant version of the Sticks, the Official IRA he had left in 1970. It was a bitter blow to McGuinness when his close friend Dominic McGlinchey, known as 'Mad Dog' later changed allegiance from the IRA to the INLA. McGuinness referred to the INLA as 'scumbags', and one of his first actions against them was to order the tarring and feathering of one of their Derry leaders. He later ordered the beating of another member, Patsy O'Hara, who became one of the ten hunger strikers who starved themselves to death for political status in 1981.

In Belfast the ceasefire period was marked by sectarian and internecine violence, as two bloody feuds broke out between republican factions. Derry appeared peaceful by comparison, with the Official IRA restraining themselves to describing McGuinness as 'a brainless figurehead controlled by Sean Keenan'. However, in one incident McGuinness nearly lost his life. John Joe McCann was still in the IRA, but was becoming increasingly frustrated. Eventually, he believes he reached a point where he had to challenge McGuinness' authority, no matter what the risk to himself. 'There used to be an open field where Celtic Park is now; my brother had joined the Irps, and him and his friends were going off to shoot some soldiers. McGuinness put out an order that they were to be stopped and there was a Mexican stand-off, they all pulled guns on each other.' The next day McCann and his brother pushed their way into the incident centre to tell women staffing the office to summon the Brigade Staff urgently. The two brothers and a third man ran upstairs, where they waited for the IRA to arrive as they took their seats around a huge boardroom table. A fourth man waited outside, to warn them if 'the big battalions suddenly turned up'. When McGuinness arrived, he sat down beside John Joe, who was nervous. 'I was hyper, the adrenaline was going. When you're in a feud, and it's family as well, you get like that. But they had to be stopped. How could these people claim to be republicans when they were going to shoot other republicans for shooting soldiers?' The Brigade Staff easily outnumbered them and McCann knew that if he wanted to stay alive he would have to take the initiative, 'McGuinness was on one side of me. I pulled my Webley out and put it to the mouth of the guy on the other side. He took a wobbler; he was like a chicken with no head. I told the other man with me, who was standing near the door, "kill him." We were freaked out. I said, "sit down," and he sat.' McCann went round each IRA man asking them individually if they intended to harm his brother. When they assured McCann that he and his brother were safe, he walked out, followed by the others. 'Before I went I said to them that if they try to get me and I could still crawl away, I'll do you, I'll do your houses, I'll do your granny, I issued all these threats. McGuinness said afterwards he thought he had 30 seconds to live; he probably had less, being honest.'

McGuinness, like the majority of the IRA, was jaded with politics and keen to get back to war. In July the Derry Brigade planted three bombs that caused serious damage to Crown Buildings in Derry in response to 'army harassment of nationalist youths'. McGuinness put his talent for making a virtue out of necessity into practice at a press conference the next day, claiming that a British statement that Derry had been the quietest and most peaceful part of the North was accurate, 'for the Volunteers of the Derry Brigade are disciplined and obedient'.

Father Dennis Bradley was depressed when it became clear that the ceasefire had broken down: 'I think the republican movement settled in the Good Friday Agreement for the same things that were achievable in 1974. The difference between 1974 and the Good Friday Agreement was 20 years of violence and so many people dead in between.' On 10 November, the Derry Brigade sent a message to the British about the future of the ceasefire, when they 'closed down' the incident centre in Cable Street by blasting it to rubble. In case they should have mistaken the message, McGuinness underlined it just before Christmas, when two members of the Forty-Two Heavy Regiment, Royal Artillery, were killed by a bomb that exploded at a car park near the Guildhall Square.

CHAPTER SEVEN

The Sinews of War

The Provisional IRA has the dedication and the sinews of war to raise violence intermittently to at least the level of early 1978, certainly for the foreseeable future.

Brigadier James Glover, *Northern Ireland Future Terrorist Trends*, 2 November 1978

Every year since 1972 had been proclaimed 'The Year of Victory' by the IRA; 1976 was no exception. But by spring the IRA knew that they had serious problems. When Merlyn Rees rose to address the House of Commons on 25 March, the IRA was close to defeat. Ruairi O Bradaigh might try to convince himself that Rees had 'seriously considered withdrawal'; but the truth was that the IRA had been outsmarted by the British. Merlyn Rees had never seen the ceasefire as anything more than 'an instrument of policy', and the Labour government had only entered talks with the Provisionals as part of a carefully planned strategy to split the movement. As Rees mused in his memoirs, 'Part of the art of government is to use events to one's own purpose,' and by releasing the internees and ending special category status, he had paved the way for 'criminalising' the IRA. 'Police primacy' made the RUC the leading element of the security forces. While the overall direction of security policy was the responsibility of the Secretary of State, the army were to counter the paramilitary terrorist threat by suppressing terrorist activities and giving the RUC the protection they needed to carry out their normal activities. The scale of the legislative and policy changes being undertaken by the Labour government clearly indicated the depth of their commitment to remaining in Northern Ireland.

McGuinness was under constant watch by both the Irish police and the RUC. It was several years since he had been directly involved in attacks, although he was still intimately involved in the planning, preparation and sanctioning process. Whenever possible he would observe the action from a safe distance. New recruits to the RUC were briefed to look out for McGuinness. As one man remembered, 'When I moved to Derry as a young uniformed officer, we were told he was the overall commander of PIRA in Londonderry – the buck stopped with him.' Young officers tried to make a name for themselves by trapping him. 'I was young, and one night I decided to follow his car and see where he was going, but he second-guessed me, and doubled back. So I ended up coming out in front of him, and we met at the junction. It was the first time I ever clapped an eye on him and he just stared me out.'

At the beginning of February, Martin McGuinness had been arrested again, this time in the Bogside, and was charged with IRA membership between 8 August 1973 and 7 February 1976. He was described in court as an 'unemployed labourer', and was casual and assured, even speaking in Irish about the death that morning of IRA prisoner Frank Stagg, who had gone on a number of hunger strikes as part of a campaign to serve his sentence in Northern Ireland. The bearded McGuinness appeared confident and relaxed, waving at a crowd of women supporters in the public gallery. Some cheered, and one shouted, 'Keep your head up,' to which he replied, 'My head will always stay up. See you later.' As he strolled out after being remanded in custody, he called over cheerfully to the Resident Magistrate, 'Bye-bye monkey'. One of the police on duty that day remembers that rioting broke out inside the court when McGuinness was remanded. 'McGuinness was led out, handcuffed to a policeman. Then he stood on the steps, raised his other hand in the air, clenched his fist, and shouted out "They will never beat us," before he was taken off in a pig with a big escort.'

By the time his case came up for full hearing on 2 March, McGuiness realised that the ending of special category status could mean imprisonment under a punitive prison regime as a common criminal. His subsequent court performance was sober and restrained, as he told the court, 'I am a republican, but being a republican and a member of the IRA are two completely different things. I believe my arrest was a political move to get me out of the way. They were just holding me in cold storage.' McGuinness blamed the press for his prominence. A newspaper report on 30 June 1975 quoted him 'as a former leader of the Provisional IRA', claiming that the Provos were in negotiations with the British government to secure a declaration of intent to withdraw. It stated that McGuinness had threatened that the IRA would 'once again go on the offensive until the declaration is made and the principles for which our dead comrades made the supreme sacrifice are realised'. In court, he denied that he was involved with the Provisional IRA, and claimed he simply wanted to return to the Bogside 'and live quietly with my wife and child and mind my own business'.

Smartly dressed in a tweed sports jacket, green polo neck sweater and slacks, McGuinness was surprised when charges were dropped after no evidence was offered against him. When he got home to Derry, where Bernie and his baby daughter, Grainne, were still living in her parents' house, McGuinness faced heavy criticism for recognising the court and dissociating himself from the IRA with the result that he denied his remarks in the *Derry Journal*. At the time, there was speculation that McGuinness had been arrested after a tip-off by a faction within the IRA, who had been blamed for the arrest of Daithi O Conaill in the Republic the previous year. By the end of 1976, McGuinness had been arrested twice more. On 23 August he was arrested in Derry after an RUC ammunition find before being released with no charge, and in October he was held under the Emergency Provisions Act, again being released with no charge.

McGuinness faced serious problems in Derry City. All over the North, the ceasefire had given the RUC and the army time to study the IRA's local structures and to collect vital intelligence from careless and disillusioned volunteers. Derry, some said, was 'riddled with informers'. Certainly operations were often aborted and volunteers were arrested regularly when army or police patrols appeared from nowhere. The hiatus during the ceasefire had contributed to a lack of discipline among volunteers, making them vulnerable to approaches from the RUC or the army. Men released from Magilligan and Long Kesh were resentful when they saw how some volunteers had lined their pockets while the families of internees received little support. Some had reported back for active service the minute they were released, only to be told that the positions they had held prior to detention had been filled by others. It was galling when boys they remembered as no more than stone throwers told them that they were too well known to the security forces and were now a liability. The IRA was in total disarray. Morale was so low at the beginning of 1976 that a Belfast IRA man, Billy McKee, featured in Peter Taylor's television series *Provos*, had actually discussed calling the campaign off altogether in a conversation with Seamus Twomey.

Seamus Costello's newly formed INLA recruited volunteers unhappy with the faltering military campaign. Their political wing, the Irish Republican Socialist Party (IRSP), made big gains in Derry, drawing on some former members of the Officials who had left in the '70s. Liam O Comain, for instance, joined the IRSP at this time and Paddy Ward later joined the INLA.

Using the excuse that he wanted to start a family following his recent marriage, Ward decided to leave the Provos for good:

> What brought it to a crux was when I was Intelligence Officer for Creggan. I had also been taught about explosives and had just joined the bomb squad. There were five of us making bombs and one day we had three bombs to go into the town to be planted opposite the Guildhall. At that stage the city centre was sealed off and you had to use delivery and beer lorries for cover to get into the town through the security gates and checkpoints.
>
> After the boys had planted the bombs and were on their way home, the Brits rammed their car on Beechwood Avenue. Somebody had tipped them off – they got 15 years each. Now somebody must have wired the Brits.

Father Dennis Bradley was still in contact with many of the volunteers. 'For the first time I realised how centrally controlled republicanism is. People were told, "Shut your mouth, we are doing what we are doing and it is not your business to ask questions." I suppose that is true of any army but the Northerners were very angry. The tensions arose between the Northern people and the Southern people and then they eventually overthrew the old leadership. It wasn't a night of the long knives, rather, a gradual change. As the young crowd from the North became more politically aware, they started to sideline the old crowd from the South.' Moves were taken to isolate potential dissidents; Billy McKee, for example, was ordered out of Belfast to look after 'internal security' in Dublin.

McGuinness, at 26, was one of the most senior IRA men in the country. By the spring of 1976, he was part of the caucus that would lead the next phase of the struggle. McGuinness had taken over as GHQ Director of Operations following the arrest of Kevin Mallon, a '50s man and a dedicated militarist with strong socialist views. Brian Paschal Keenan, a brilliant strategist and committed Marxist who had opened up weapons supply routes from Libya, was in charge of the mainland bombing campaign, where his hand-picked volunteers were known as the 'Brixton Brigade'. Another close associate was Pat Doherty of Carrigart, Co. Donegal, who had returned to Donegal in 1968 after living in Glasgow for some years with his brother, Hugh. Hugh was one of Keenan's bombers, and would later be convicted for his part in the Balcombe Street siege. Pat Doherty later became Vice President of Sinn Féin and Westminster MP for West Tyrone. Gerry Adams and his second in command, Ivor Bell, completed the team. At Army Council level, McGuinness could rely on the backing of his fellow Northerners, Seamus Twomey and Joe Cahill.

Adams was in prison – serving an 18-month sentence for trying to escape – where he organised a series of lectures on political theory, the study of international anti-imperialist struggles, Irish history, and lectures on weapons and explosives. These lectures were the basis for the *Green Book*, the IRA's manual, which was completed after his release from jail in 1977. *Republican News*, the Northern Sinn Féin paper, published articles he smuggled out under the pen name, 'Brownie'. His main contribution was his recognition that one of the IRA's fundamental problems had always been the lack of a coherent ideology, with volunteers united only by their commitment to physical force republicanism. Adams advocated 'the complete fusing of military and political strategy', envisaging a revitalised IRA, organised along cellular lines, fighting an incisive campaign directed against selective targets. Volunteers, particularly those who had become known to security forces through internment or imprisonment, would be channelled into Sinn Féin, where they could promote street politics and community structures as an alternative to British rule. At the same time, they could build up a political base that would provide support for the armed struggle.

While Adams lobbied from inside the jail, McGuinness and Bell were appointed to a new internal commission to assess the strength of the IRA and submit proposals for change to the Army Council. As they commenced their work, a one off 'spectacular' in the Irish Republic illustrated the potential of the new strategy. The attack, masterminded by Brian Keenan, was intended to provoke a breakdown in Anglo-Irish relations and gain worldwide publicity to demonstrate that recent arrests in London and Northern Ireland had failed to break the IRA. On 21 July, three volunteers detonated a 200 lb landmine under the car of Sir Christopher Ewart Biggs, British Ambassador to Ireland. It was only the twelfth day of his new posting. The Ambassador and a young civil servant travelling with him, Judith Cook, were killed instantly, while a British civil servant and the Irish driver were seriously injured. They had driven just 150 yards from the Ambassador's residence in Dublin on their way to a liaison meeting with Irish civil servants. It was a horrific and shocking attack that achieved the IRA's objective of worldwide publicity. Ironically, the main target escaped. The IRA had received intelligence reports that Merlyn Rees would accompany the Ambassador that morning, but his plans were changed at the last minute after Opposition leader Margaret Thatcher objected to the usual pairing arrangements when he flew to London. It was intended to show both the leadership in Dublin and the British government exactly what the IRA was capable of.

In September 1976, new graffiti announced, 'Stone Mason Shall Not Break Us', when Roy Mason took over from Merlyn Rees as Secretary of State. Mason was an outspoken and burly former miner from Barnsley who courted the company of soldiers and industrialists. He liked to pose for photographers reviewing troops, incongruously dressed in a safari suit, and drawing on a pipe. Mason was a stark contrast to the more restrained style of Merlyn Rees. He almost totally ignored local politicians, while at the same time lavishing public money on dubious job creation schemes designed to win working-class nationalist support away from the Provos while simultaneously promoting a tough security policy to achieve a military solution. His emphasis on police primacy divided the RUC, as Father Dennis Bradley remembered. 'Roy Mason's strategy was, on the one hand we'll buy them off, and on the other hand, we'll root the bastards out. [Chief Superintendent] Lagan totally disagreed with his policy of police primacy, which he believed would destroy the police. I thought initially he was overreacting, but that was his view: "When the police go into the front line to fight the Provos, we have become a paramilitary organisation ourselves." Politics went out the window.'

As Mason settled in to his new post, the Army Council gave the go-ahead for the establishment of Northern Command, with Martin McGuinness as its first OC. As McGuinness, who was now on the Army Council, prepared to supervise the reorganisation of the IRA, Maire Drumm was shot dead by loyalists in the Mater Hospital as she recovered from an eye operation. Just three months earlier, she vowed at a rally in Belfast, 'Belfast will come down stone by stone, and if it is necessary, other towns will come down, and some in England too.' Without Northern Command, her words would have been nothing more than empty rhetoric.

McGuinness and Bell had bluntly acknowledged in the Staff Report that the IRA was close to defeat. Two main causes were identified: it had failed to give volunteers the 'psychological strengths' to resist interrogation; and the 'inefficient infrastructure of commands, brigades, battalions and companies' was a burden to the movement. Their main recommendation was 'reorganisation and remotivation, the building of a new Irish Republican Army'. Ireland would be divided for organisational purposes into two units. Northern Command would control the six Northern Ireland counties of Antrim, Armagh, Down, Derry, Fermanagh and Tyrone, plus the five border counties in the Republic: Louth, Cavan, Monaghan, Leitrim and Donegal. The Command area was then subdivided into five Brigade areas: Belfast, Derry, Donegal, Tyrone/Monaghan and Armagh, each with their own Active Service Units, or cells. The cell structure was designed to halt the success of the RUC in arresting and extracting confessions from IRA volunteers. Only the head of each cell would, in theory, know the identity of its members; the members would only know each other by pseudonyms. Cells should strike as often as possible outside their own areas 'to confuse Brit intelligence and to expand our operational areas'. The commission acknowledged that this would have only limited success in rural areas, where the majority of IRA members were known to each other. In practice, the cell structure proved a failure, as the success of the supergrass system in the '80s proved, when hundreds of volunteers were held on lengthy remands on the uncorroborated word of former members: 'converted terrorists', as the RUC called them.

Northern Command directed the campaign, answerable only to the Army Council. Southern Command's main role was to act as Quartermaster, raising finance through robberies, buying weapons, and providing general back up. There was one Brigade in Dublin, which also had several ASUs, and there were ASUs in rural areas of the Southern Command area. There was also provision for coordinated province-wide operations, with the establishment of ten-strong commando units, loosely based on the flying columns of the '50s, which could operate on either side of the border. McGuinness had already promoted the idea of a flying column for Donegal/Derry in 1975, but had scrapped his plans after volunteers referred to it as the 'Buncrana Brigade', a reference to the men who had spent internment on the run across the border. It was a criticism that irritated the abrasive McGuinness, as one former IRA man recalls:

> McGuinness asked me what I wanted to do when I came out of jail. I didn't want a pile of stripes like some people; I said I'd just go where I was needed. But I never thought he'd say he'd like me to join Sinn Féin. At that stage Sinn Féin was almost like an afterthought. Then he told me I could go into the flying column – I said, hold on . . . the Buncrana Brigade, the long rifles? They never used to shoot anything, but they would direct things from Buncrana . . . People used to say they would need to have a gun with a 13-mile range. He wasn't pleased because he'd had a lot of stick about the Buncrana Brigade – we had a real bust up and I walked away.

Northern and Southern Command were accountable to the Chief of Staff and the Army Council. GHQ Staff remained as before, organised into the departments of Quartermaster, Finance, Engineering, Intelligence, Publicity, Security, Operations, Purchasing and Training. The mainland bombing campaign, which had ground to a halt after police captured the main players, remained under Keenan's control for the time being. Sinn Féin was to be reorganised, 'under Army organisers at all levels'. Army organisers would radicalise the party, whose members would then be directed to infiltrate other movements. Respect for the party, the commission noted, would lead to support for the cell.

Such root-and-branch reorganisation forced some volunteers into early retirement. McGuinness rationalised the number on active service, reducing them from an estimated 2,000 in 1972, to around 300 in 1976. He could call on as many as 3,000 active sympathisers for support. McGuinness' first priority was to convince the demoralised volunteers that they could still force the British to withdraw. To do that successfully, he had to lower their expectations. There would be no more talk of the 'Year of Victory'. The IRA were fighting a long war of attrition, which would only end with the attainment of a United Ireland.

The long war strategy intensified the struggle, with volunteers mobilised on a full-time basis. 'Ulsterisation' and 'police primacy' led to a widening of legitimate targets to include off-duty and part-time RUC and UDR officers, who were mainly drawn from the unionist community. The IRA answered the widespread criticism that such attacks were sectarian by countering that 'They are never off duty. They are armed members of the Crown Forces all the time, and if they came upon IRA volunteers they would attack them, whether they were on duty or not.' The IRA taught volunteers that the loyalists had a supremacist mentality, comparing them to the Pieds Noirs in Algeria, or the Afrikaners in South Africa. If loyalist paramilitary groups retaliated against the nationalist community, the IRA would come to its defence and loyalism would be clearly seen as an enemy. McGuinness also planned an economic bombing campaign to drive up the price of shoring up the North's economy.

International links would be strengthened. Limited collaboration with other anti-imperialist movements would create new arms networks, as well as providing a forum where human rights issues could be used to embarrass Britain on the international stage. A dedicated team would gather intelligence on 'symbolic' targets and a selective bombing campaign on the British mainland would demonstrate the IRA's ability to strike right at the very heart of the establishment.

Several departments were strengthened at GHQ level. The Education Department, responsible for lectures and discussions at weapons training camps, would from now on supplement the usual indoctrination lectures with training in anti-interrogation techniques. Weapons and explosives would be 'under the complete control of the Brigade's/Command's QM and EO respectively'. The Security Department would be responsible for the detection and punishment of informers, while the IRA would later exploit its achievements to the full with the merger of *An Phoblacht/Republican News* under the control of the Northern leadership.

By now Bernie McGuinness was expecting their second child and the family had left 9 Anne Street, where they had been briefly living with Bernie's parents, John and Christina Canning. They moved to 161 Lone

Moor Road, not far from Anne Street, in between Celtic Park and the City Cemetery. Just before Christmas, on 18 December, Fionnuala Mairead was born in Derry's Altnagelvin Hospital, and Bernie McGuinness brought her home to join her older sister Grainne, now just over one year old and starting to toddle around everywhere. On her birth certificate, Martin McGuinness gave his occupation as 'sales assistant – furniture'.

The IRA declared a Christmas ceasefire, to last from 25–27 December, as Roy Mason announced that 1977 would be 'the year the net tightens on terrorists'. In response, the IRA threatened that they would 'hot things up' in 1977, and by the end of January, volunteers from the newly formed Derry Active Service Unit had already ambushed a policeman as he took his car for a routine service in Derry. The leader of the Derry ASU, Raymond 'Raysie' McCartney, was a close friend of McGuinness, who had joined the IRA after his cousin, Jim Wray, had been shot dead on Bloody Sunday. McCartney had refused to go on the run during Operation Motorman, choosing instead to stay in safe houses in Derry, where British soldiers referred to him as 'Smiler'.

Desperate to pursue their policy of economic sabotage, the Provisionals embarked on a series of murders of prominent businessmen, who they argued were 'not Irishmen but colonialists', who represented 'grassroots British imperialism'. Within days of their attack on the RUC man, McCartney and the Derry ASU had murdered 59-year-old Jeffrey Agate, the English head of the Dupont Corporation's Derry division. There was widespread shock at his murder, and employees downed tools in protest. Undeterred, the IRA killed several more businessmen before calling a halt to their campaign, claiming they had achieved a victory: 'Already the business community is reeling under IRA attacks . . . the revolutionary strategy of the IRA has changed the nature of the capitalist bourgeoisie.' In fact, the IRA had not only been strongly condemned by trades unionists and politicians, they had also attracted bitter criticism from within the republican movement. Debates in the press saw them accused of abandoning the struggle, and betraying the principles of republicanism. In one last defiant statement, the IRA defended itself: 'Those involved in the management of the economy serve British interests . . . unlike British troops they are not expendable. Thus the outcry.' However, there were no more attacks on businessmen and the IRA's campaign dwindled to nothing. Not even Ian Paisley's announcement in May of a loyalist strike to protest against government security policy and to demand the return of majority government could stir up much of a response from the Provisionals. Despite massive intimidation the strike failed to attract significant support from the unionist community and the stoppage collapsed.

Before long the Provisionals were facing open criticism from within their own ranks, with some accusing the leadership of 'going Stickie', citing the drop in IRA operations and the tone and language of recent press statements as evidence. In June, the Army Council decided to act, choosing the annual Wolfe Tone commemoration at Bodenstown, Co. Kildare, to air the new direction for the first time. Bodenstown cemetery holds the remains of the founding father of Irish republicanism, Theobald Wolfe Tone and is the central event of the republican calendar. Each year, the republican faithful gather at the ruined church where Tone's remains lie. Bodenstown is traditionally an occasion for the reaffirmation of old certainties; in 1977, it became the launching pad for a revolutionary strategy.

Jimmy Drumm, whose wife Maire had been murdered by loyalists a year earlier, had served more time in jail than any living republican. His commitment to armed struggle was beyond doubt. He was the perfect choice to deliver the speech, which admitted that the strategy of the early '70s had been mistaken, before introducing the new concept, 'The isolation of socialist republicans around the armed struggle is dangerous and has produced a reformist notion that "Ulster" is the issue . . . We find that a successful war of liberation cannot be fought exclusively on the backs of the oppressed in the Six Counties, nor around the physical presence of the British Army. Hatred and resentment of the army cannot sustain the war.' As the republican movement absorbed Drumm's speech, the rest of the year remained comparatively peaceful. Deaths related to the Troubles had more than halved and Roy Mason felt confident enough to predict that 'The tide has turned against the terrorists and the message for 1978 is one of real hope.' His confidence might have been shaken if he had been aware of the contents of a pencil case found when the Irish Special Branch arrested Seamus Twomey at an apartment in Dun Laoghaire, south of Dublin, at the start of December. The raid was in response to an Israeli tip-off that an IRA arms smuggler, Seamus McCollum, was in the flat with Twomey. McCollum had organised an arms shipment from Al Fatah (the largest faction within the Palestine Liberation organisation), which was being seized by Belgian police at the same time. Hidden in the pencil case was a copy of the IRA commission's Staff Report. The Irish Special Branch passed a copy to the British, where an army intelligence report warned on 28 February that 'the Provisional leadership is deeply committed to a long campaign of attrition.'

Adams took over as Chief of Staff after Twomey's arrest, and, before the end of the year, had met Martin McGuinness, Peter 'the Para' McMullan and Brian Keenan, in a flat in Dublin, where they discussed VIP assassinations in England. According to McMullan, who planned to shoot Brigadier Frank Kitson in the heart with a Lee Enfield .303 rifle, the IRA had received new intelligence on Kitson, giving them details of his weekend movements, when he was unguarded. A man who worked for Kitson had met IRA leaders in Dublin where he had given them a general description of Kitson's movements and the woods and trails where he often walked alone on Sunday afternoons. McGuinness and his colleagues decided to proceed with plans to target the Brigadier, as well as upping the economic bombing campaign, both in Northern Ireland and in Britain.

The opening shot in Derry was the bombing of the Guildhall in January 1978, just seven months after it had been rebuilt following a firebomb attack in July 1972. In February a booby-trap car bomb killed a UDR man and his ten-year-old daughter in Co. Derry. Attacks on soft targets were to become a characteristic of the IRA campaign in rural areas. Many Protestants believed that the IRA wanted to drive them from their farms so that the land could be bought by Catholic families and, as a result and particularly in border areas, many joined the part-time RUC Reserve or UDR to gain access to weapons for their own protection.

Improved surveillance methods, an increased flow of intelligence from nationalists, and the growing professionalism of the RUC meant that more and more volunteers were being arrested. Once arrested, volunteers could be kept under seven-day detention orders in the dedicated interrogation centres of Castlereagh in Belfast and Gough Barracks in Armagh, where the IRA claimed that special teams of detectives systematically beat and tortured them until they signed incriminating statements. Once charged, volunteers then had to face lengthy remands; it could take years for a case to be brought to court. The Provos termed it the 'Conveyor-Belt' system and McGuinness continually stressed to volunteers the need to target the individual officers involved in it, particularly those in Special Branch. One middle-aged Special Branch officer who had been responsible for securing many convictions in Derry City had been watched for some time without success when the IRA discovered that he in fact lived in the mainly Protestant town of Limavady, about ten miles from Derry. Believing that Limavady was too dangerous for the IRA to penetrate, the man relaxed his guard at weekends and took regular walks in the same place on Sundays. When McGuinness was told about this, he approached a member of the INLA who knew the area. The INLA man recalled, 'Martin McGuinness wanted to set up a sort of a joint operation, for us to eliminate this Special Branch man. I knew the area and I knew the individual concerned. We were short of weapons, and McGuinness said he would see us right – the deal was that we would do the job, the IRA would get the glory, and we would get to keep the gun.' The plan came to nothing after the man spotted that he was being watched. He moved away from the area soon afterwards.

Gerry Adams was arrested and remanded in custody for several months after an experimental type of incendiary bomb killed 12 people, all Protestants. Four hundred people were attending functions that evening in the La Mon House Hotel in Castlereagh, on the outskirts of Belfast, including members of a collie club and a cycling club. The prototype incendiary was a blast bomb, made from a mix of recrystallised ammonium nitrate and aluminium filings, which were attached to a can of petrol. As the incendiary detonated, the blast showered the function room with a cascade of flaming petrol, and the entire hotel was an inferno in minutes.

Following Adams' arrest, the Army Council had appointed Martin McGuinness and Brian Keenan to work together as joint Chiefs of Staff. After La Mon, the IRA Publicity Department had briefed selected journalists that there had been a suspension of bomb attacks on targets where civilians might be at risk, specifically mentioning attacks on trains, buses and hotels. However, by the autumn, McGuinness was confident that the IRA was resilient enough to handle any condemnation and resumed the campaign at full-tilt. The IRA was as heedless of casualties as ever, and one woman was killed when four IRA bombs exploded on the Dublin–Belfast Enterprise train in October. Following protests from IRA prisoners about conditions in the jails, prison officers were now legitimate targets, and on 26 November, Albert Miles, Deputy Governor of the Maze Prison, was shot dead at his North Belfast home.

Before the end of 1978, there was more bad news for the Secretary of State when an army intelligence report (Northern Ireland Future Terrorist

Trends) dismissed Mason's description of the IRA as a 'criminal conspiracy' who were led by 'godfathers' and warned that the IRA had the means and dedication to continue the war of attrition for some time. The report, written by Brigadier Jimmy Glover of the Defence Intelligence Staff (DIS), described the IRA as 'intelligent, astute and experienced terrorists', with 'the dedication and the sinews of war to raise violence intermittently to at least the level of early 1978, certainly for the foreseeable future'. As Brigadier Glover had warned Roy Mason and Prime Minister James Callaghan, 'We see no prospect in the next five years of any political change which would remove PIRA's *raison d'etre*.' Seamus Twomey had considered calling off the IRA campaign at the start of 1976; within two years, Martin McGuinness had dramatically reversed their decline. Reorganisation had been an outstanding success; the time had come to publicly announce the new policy. In a statement at the end of November claiming responsibility for bomb attacks in 14 towns, the IRA admitted for the first time that it was 'preparing for a long war'.

In the run up to Christmas, the IRA escalated their agenda when they launched an English bombing campaign with explosions in Liverpool, Manchester, Bristol, Coventry and Southampton. Police leave was cancelled in London, and more than 2,000 uniformed officers were drafted into the West End to prevent a pre-Christmas IRA bombing campaign. Similarly, as a British Army patrol walked through the small border town of Crossmaglen, shoppers looking for last minute bargains four days before Christmas dived for cover when the back doors of a red Post Office van were thrown open and an IRA unit fired a hail of bullets from an M60 into the crowds, killing three soldiers. There would be no Christmas ceasefire as the IRA's long war strategy began to bite.

CHAPTER EIGHT

18 Paras and Mountbatten

In the early winter of 1980, passengers queuing to board the plane bound for Ireland noticed nothing unusual about the young, curly-haired man who stood among them on the icy runway. As his New York host had observed, he looked like any other young Irishman, returning home after visiting relatives who had emigrated years earlier, perhaps. Few would have suspected that their fresh-faced fellow passenger was the IRA Chief of Staff on his way back to Ireland after another successful arms-buying trip to America. As he forced his legs into the cramped space provided in economy long-haul seating, he might have looked back on his time in the IRA. Since he became the first OC of the Northern Command in 1976, he had reorganised the IRA along cellular lines. McGuinness was pleased with the results, which were designed to make the IRA less vulnerable to penetration by agents. The new political approach pioneered by Gerry

Adams had by and large been accepted by the membership, with a significant reduction of the bloody splits which had erupted from time to time since he had joined the IRA at the age of 20 in 1970. Ten years later, McGuinness was Chief of Staff, with Gerry Adams as his Adjutant General along with several other Northerners who now dominated the Army Council. Under his stewardship, the republican movement had gone from strength to strength. The long war strategy, McGuinness believed, was weakening the Brits. They hoped to bleed the economy dry, a strategy they planned to exploit to the full with the new Prime Minister, Margaret Thatcher. If there was one thing that troubled McGuinness as his flight took off, it was the fear of betrayal. McGuinness was well aware that informers had been ordered by the RUC and the Brits to target him; so far, none had managed to penetrate the hand-picked coterie of close comrades who surrounded him. But no one knew how recruits would react when they were faced with seven days detention and constant questioning – many had already broken. As Brian Keenan's arrest the year before had shown, no amount of IRA counter-surveillance could undermine the sophisticated electronic monitoring available to the British. Notwithstanding, McGuinness believed the men he would report to on his return to Ireland could be trusted. Many were former prisoners, like Kevin McKenna, from Aughnacloy. He had been in Portlaoise with McGuinness on a second charge of membership of the IRA and had resumed command of East Tyrone when he was released in August 1977, directing operations from his house in Smithborough, Co. Monaghan. South Armagh was in the safe hands of Tom 'Slab' Murphy, the millionaire pig smuggler whose farm at Ballybinaby straddled the border. Like McKenna, Murphy lived in the Irish Republic, safe from questioning by the RUC and the British Army. McGuinness was surrounded by men like Joe McCallion of Lisfannon, Co. Donegal who had been in prison with him in 1973; Joe McColgan, married to his sister, Geraldine; and Martin's brother Willie, six years his junior at 24, and already known to the security forces for his ruthlessness. These men were the backbone of Northern Command, where they were augmented by a handful of other volunteers with similar backgrounds. McGuinness' close friend and ally, Pat Doherty from Donegal, was OC for Southern Command, where he had just taken over from Daithi O Conaill.

McGuinness had been lodging with George Harrison, the Irish-American who had been sending guns to the IRA since the '50s. His first visit to

Harrison's three-storey house at 465 East 9th Street had been in the spring of 1977, where he stayed in the top storey apartment vacated for him by one of Harrison's two sisters. As Harrison remembers, McGuinness fitted in well. 'He was a very nice young fellow with a small family and he was very easy to put up with – curly red hair, dressed very simply in working-man's clothes, a very down-to-earth man and I remember he had two children at the time. He didn't smoke, didn't drink, very easy to feed. He was very soft spoken, and a very gentlemanly sort of a fellow. My sister Agnes was still alive then and he made himself very well liked.'

McGuinness had come to New York to collect the money that had been raised for the struggle by supporters across the US and would disappear for days on end to meet them. Harrison had been responsible for most of the weaponry that had been supplied through America, and had already met Joe Cahill and Brian Keenan.

> Joe and Brian were like Martin, very quiet, thorough people, with nothing of the braggart about them. When he was with me, he came and went and suited himself. He would stay for two or three days, then would go off again and come back for another two or three days. Later in the visit he inspected some rifles, AR15s, M16s and so on, and it was quite obvious that he knew one part from another – I was a pretty good mechanic and I had a pretty good knowledge myself. His trip was more or less to set up the machinery to ensure supply of the wherewithal to continue the armed struggle.

As the two men got to know each other, McGuinness told Harrison of his plans to reorganise the IRA and that they needed greater firepower. McGuinness' commitment to the intensity of the armed struggle impressed Harrison greatly, as he recalls. 'My memory is him saying "the only language the Brits understand comes out of the barrel of a gun. The more guns we send, the quicker we get the Brits out." Words to that effect, and that is my own opinion to this day.'

A criminal gang from Boston, known as the Roxbury Rats, had earlier approached Harrison, offering to sell him seven M60 heavy machine guns that they had stolen from an armoury of the US National Guard at Danvers, near Boston. The M60 is a heavy calibre machine gun, powerful enough to bring down a helicopter. McGuinness was delighted when Harrison bought them for the knock down price of six hundred and sixty-seven pounds each.

Ruairi O Bradaigh shared the top floor apartment of Harrison's house when McGuinness returned to New York in 1978. He had accompanied McGuinness to reassure supporters that the leadership was united behind the new strategy. When O Bradaigh was at meetings, McGuinness and Harrison practised aiming with some Armalites, which were stored in the house. McGuinness was determined to bring Harrison's network of fundraisers and arms dealers under his control and used one of these sessions with the Armalites to ask Harrison to formally join the IRA and take charge of North America as OC. Harrison refused, telling McGuinness that he was uninterested in rank, but his reluctance had its roots in an internal IRA dispute linked to the death of a former President of Sinn Féin in 1964. When McGuinness returned to Ireland, he began to send his own people to New York. Harrison was unimpressed with those he met. 'Some of the people he sent over were very definitely out to take control of supply lines and that wasn't the way myself and my old comrades wanted it at all. It takes a certain type of person to become involved in supplying the wherewithal, and there is one thing above all else you need, and that is people who can do their thing and keep their mouths shut about it.' The man McGuinness chose to replace Harrison was Belfast IRA man Gabriel Megahey. Despite his misgivings, Harrison cooperated with Megahey, whose nickname was 'Skinny Legs', and who worked in a bar. He and Harrison put together a consignment of weapons ordered by McGuinness, who had gone through arms catalogues with Harrison during his stay. He had constantly stressed to the older man that the IRA needed more and better weapons to respond to the strengthened British Army presence in Northern Ireland. Harrison remembers that he always praised his efforts. 'He always said he was very pleased with the guns. The only thing was, like myself, he'd have liked a lot more of them.'

When the first M60s arrived in Ireland in September 1977, the IRA was eager to show off their new firepower. McGuinness looked on when two masked volunteers held an M60 aloft at the seventh anniversary of Bloody Sunday in January 1978, as a watching crowd cheered. Small elite groups of volunteers were dispatched to training camps in Co. Kerry where a former captain in the Irish army drilled them in their use. Two months later, the IRA brought them up to the North, where they were used for the first time in the murder of Gunner Paul Sheppard in North Belfast. Five days later the IRA used another M60 when they engaged soldiers in Crossmaglen in a half-hour gun battle. The Provos withdrew the M60s after losing some weapons in security force searches, only bringing them out to murder three British soldiers in Crossmaglen at the end of the year.

By the beginning of 1979, Northern Ireland's new Commander of Land Forces (CLF), Major General Jimmy Glover, had arrived at army headquarters in Lisburn. Glover had written a report called *Future Terrorist Trends* when he was a Brigadier in the Ministry of Defence, which was to prove influential. He had already noted, 'One of the weaknesses of the Provisionals' organisation is its communications . . . we suspect that the terrorists fear to pass explicit information on the telephone. The main system of communication is therefore probably by courier, though meetings of leaders are held both North and South of the border and some members of the leadership travel widely themselves . . . Indeed the Provisionals' communications will probably remain vulnerable to interdiction by the security forces for many years yet.' There was such distrust of communications, in fact, that Tom Hartley, a Belfast Sinn Féin member who later became a councillor, would patiently travel by train between Belfast and Derry to exchange messages between Gerry Adams and Martin McGuinness.

Operation Hawk had already begun by the time Glover arrived in Lisburn. It was developed by the security forces to target what Roy Mason had termed the 'Provo godfathers' who headed up the IRA and it made full use of the most sophisticated surveillance devices available. A dedicated team of over 70 RUC Special Branch officers had been channelled into Operation Hawk, which was based at Castlereagh Holding Station. Each target changed frequently, and was given the code-name of a bird. By the end of February, Martin McGuinness had become their focus. Keen young army recruits were eager to arrest McGuinness, and RUC officers at one liaison meeting had been amused to hear how one soldier had failed to recognise McGuinness at a roadblock, freeing him after 20 minutes when he gave a false name. By the time a senior officer had radioed through that the name given by McGuinness was in fact his alias, he had fled across the border. The soldier was beside himself with rage – officers had spread a rumour that the first man to arrest McGuinness would get ten cases of beer and an extra week's leave.

By the beginning of March, 'Parrot', as McGuinness had been code-named, was unaware that he was being watched. Little of any significance had so far emerged from his surveillance and the watchers in Ladas Drive police station were just about to turn the spotlight on another target when one alert officer spotted Brian Keenan at McGuinness' side. Keenan was unaware that a warrant had been issued for his arrest when his fingerprints were found in a flat used by the London bombers, and had thought he was safe as long as he avoided his New Barnsley Park home. It was a stupid mistake, and it would prove disastrous. The self-confidence that gave Keenan such edgy brilliance as Director of Operations and Chief of Staff had developed unchecked into arrogance – some IRA volunteers had already recognised this tendency, changing his IRA *nom de guerre* from 'Dog' to 'God'. The RUC went on full alert after Keenan's appearance and the small, wiry man was quickly given the alias 'Budgie'. An informer had told police that Keenan had come to Belfast to watch an IRA 'spectacular' modelled on a guerrilla attack on an oil refinery in Salisbury, Rhodesia, which had resulted in a fire that took a week to put out. A 420 lb cache of explosives had been driven into Belfast from the Republic, where an IRA team planned to scale the perimeter fence that surrounded BP's giant oil refinery two miles from Belfast city centre to plant 42 bombs on top of the 14 storage tanks. Once fire caught hold in the refinery, the IRA hoped that it would spread to the nearby Harland & Wolff shipyard. Just an hour before the attack was due to start, an Andersonstown IRA man who had been code-named 'Bald Eagle' by Operation Hawk – tipped off the bombers. The operation was off, he warned them, 'Get off-side – the Brits are on to you.'

On 20 March, police watched as Keenan and McGuinness drove in separate cars towards the border. The RUC decided to intervene, and set up a roadblock just outside the mainly Protestant town of Banbridge, which, at 17 miles from the border, was the last safe place for them to intervene. The first car stopped, a brown Honda Civic, contained Keenan. He was with a woman from Ballymurphy. McGuinness was following Keenan in a yellow Toyota with Joe Deery. They were all detained under the Prevention of Terrorism Act although they tried to bluff their way through, with Keenan claiming to be married to the woman. After a few days, McGuinness, Deery and the woman were released with no charge. However, three days later Keenan, still detained, was in an army helicopter with anti-terrorist squad detectives from Scotland Yard, who had a warrant for his arrest under the

Explosive Substances Act. As they crossed the English coastline, Keenan claimed that two RAF jets buzzed them. 'It was an exciting trip,' he told prisoners in Brixton jail, where he awaited trial.

In his pockets, police found three bank notes, one Libyan and two Irish, all roughly torn in half. The other halves were never found. They also found a diary, with the entry, 'Hallo, Brian, my brother. Here is some money.' This was a code that had been used frequently in the past as a recognition signal between IRA emissaries and contacts in Libya. The signal was completed only on receipt of both the diary entry and the missing halves of the notes. This discovery compromised a major weapons shipment from Libya, and in August 1979, a pilot, Sadiq Baahri, disappeared after his plane was forced down at Benghazi in Libya. It was rumoured that he was subsequently jailed on Gadaffi's orders after refusing to fly weapons to Ireland, where he feared that Keenan's arrest had compromised him.

For years after his arrest, rumours persisted that Keenan blamed McGuinness for setting him up, and he was said to have told fellow prisoners that McGuinness had signalled to the RUC at a previous roadblock. Conspiracy theorists claimed that McGuinness' rigid Catholic doctrine had influenced him to dump the Marxist Keenan on ideological grounds; for others, it was simply a victory for the new strategy over the armed struggle. It was common knowledge among fellow republicans that their relationship was strained at times, but it was Keenan's carelessness that led to his being seen with McGuinness, who was the RUC's prime target. McGuinness was too shrewd to let his guard drop for a moment, but nevertheless he and Adams were certainly the main beneficiaries of Keenan's detention. Keenan would undoubtedly have opposed their embryonic plans to engage in political activity in the Irish Republic without an accompanying military strategy, and his absence gave McGuinness a free hand as sole Chief of Staff.

During the months after Keenan's arrest, the RUC laboriously sifted the reports of Keenan's movements collated by Operation Hawk. By June 1979 they were ready to move against the occupants of four houses Keenan had visited regularly. One of them was a communications command post, filled with radios, unscrambling equipment, sophisticated monitors, military-style transmitters, and telephone taps rerouted through the telephone network. Most worrying, they found evidence that the IRA had intercepted calls to British Army HQ and had access to the private lines of GOC Sir Timothy Creasey. At the end of June 1980, Keenan was jailed at the Old

Bailey, receiving a 21-year sentence for masterminding 18 terrorist atrocities, including the murders of Ross McWhirter and the cancer expert, Gordon Hamilton Fairley; the murder of a bomb disposal expert who died trying to defuse a device in West London and various explosions. What clinched the case against him was an uncompleted crossword in his handwriting, which he had carelessly left behind after he visited an IRA bomb factory.

Cryptologists called in by Scotland Yard pored over Keenan's diary in a desperate race against time to decode the entries, suspecting that the most prestigious IRA operations were listed. Two days after Keenan's arrest, a floating IRA unit in the Low Countries killed the British Ambassador to the Netherlands, Sir Richard Sykes and his Dutch valet, Krel Straub, in a gun attack in Den Haag. Keenan had extensive international contacts, particularly with Libya and the PLO, where the East Germans and GRU, Soviet military intelligence, also had an interest. At one of his meetings, Keenan had heard that Sykes had been responsible for the internal inquiry into the murder of Sir Christopher Ewart Biggs and had made several recommendations about future security measures. This sealed his fate. The Ambassador was shot as he sat in the back seat of his silver-grey Rolls Royce, which was taking him from his residence to the embassy. The IRA did not claim responsibility for Sykes' killing until after Keenan's conviction in 1980. The Provisionals' statement claimed that Sykes had been 'intelligence gathering against our organisation . . . [and] was also a leading propagandist'. They added that Sykes had also been conducting the investigation into the attack on Sir Christopher Ewart Biggs, 'What that and other attacks have shown is the IRA's capability to operate abroad and against the enemy, not the host country, and gained our struggle attention there.' Later that same day a Belgian businessman was shot dead after the IRA mistook him for the British envoy to NATO. There was another blow for the British when the INLA assassinated Airey Neave, Conservative Party spokesperson on Northern Ireland and a close confidant of Margaret Thatcher.

In August, the IRA unit in Europe detonated a bomb as a British military band played at the Grand Place in Brussels, injuring 16 people, including four members of the band. Shortly afterwards, West German intelligence notified the British of surveillance reports they had received to show that the murder of Sir Christopher Sykes and the bomb in Brussels were jointly carried out by the IRA and the Palestine Liberation Organisation (PLO). The British took this seriously. Israeli intelligence had already passed them documents identifying IRA men who had exchanged bomb-making techniques with Black September (the terrorist arm of Al Fatah, disbanded in the '70s) and the PLO at a training camp south of Beirut. According to the documents, some of the men had then moved on to a Syrian-sponsored training camp in the Bekaa Valley in the Lebanon. Among the techniques they learned there was how to pack milk churns with home-made napalm, which produced a hail of shrapnel as the containers were blasted apart. Already the army had defused a number of these bombs after McGuinness had introduced the technique to Derry. But the real jewel in the crown as far as the IRA was concerned came at a training camp where the Libyan instructor introduced them to Semtex, the odourless, virtually undetectable plastic explosive manufactured in Czechoslovakia, which has ten times the blast effect of commercial explosives.

By this time McGuinness had devised a strategy for a 'liberated zone' along part of the meandering border between Northern Ireland and the Irish Republic and was working closely with the local commanders, Kevin McKenna in Tyrone and Tom 'Slab' Murphy in South Armagh. Following a series of massive van-bomb attacks, the area was already effectively a no-go zone for the RUC. The British Army were reluctant to travel by road through parts of South Armagh and had occupied part of a GAA pitch in the IRA heartland of Crossmaglen to use as a helipad. In February 1978 the Commanding Officer and the Platoon Commander of the Second Battalion Royal Green Jackets had been killed when the IRA fired at their helicopter at Jonesborough. Three officers were injured when a Scout helicopter came under automatic fire in March 1979, but the pilot managed to fly the helicopter back to the pad at Crossmaglen.

Major General Jimmy Glover's report had mentioned 'the possibility that some SAM7s may reach PIRA's hands', which he said were easily available on the black market for seven thousand pounds. Now McGuinness was to tell Gabriel Megahey that his top priority in New York was to obtain as many Red-Eyes as he could. Red-Eyes, or surface-to-air missiles (SAMs) were easy to operate and, when aimed at a helicopter or plane, will zero in on the heat from the motor and bring it down. McGuinness was eager to shake off his Catholic country boy image and prove that he was as capable of mingling with the international revolutionary underground as Keenan had been.

Keenan himself had promised to introduce McGuinness to the 26-year-old Arab woman who was liaison officer between the PLO and the IRA. She lived in Dublin, and had rebuffed an earlier approach from McGuinness. Now she had disappeared, worried that her cover as a student might be blown and she would be expelled from Ireland if her name were found in any of Keenan's diaries. The IRA already had some Soviet manufactured RPG-7 rocket launchers, but a second consignment of RPG-7s, which included 106 SKS/AK rifles, had been seized at Schipol Airport, Amsterdam, in October 1977.

McGuinness turned to an old and trusted friend of George Harrison for help. Phil Kent was already in his late 40s when McGuinness got in touch with him. His contacts with Palestinian groups were a result of his friendship with some members of EOKA, the Cypriot movement fighting for independence from Britain. Kent had met them when they were in Wormwood Scrubs prison with Sean MacStiofain and Manus Canning in 1956. Kent became involved in supplying weapons after an approach from one of the IRA's top weapons experts, 35-year-old Eamon Doherty, who had been Chief of Staff for a few months in 1973. He had also directed Northern operations in 1972, the bloodiest year of the Troubles: 'After Eamon Doherty from Carrick on Suir was ousted as Chief of Staff in 1973, he was put in charge of all this business. Doherty knew me and of course naturally enough he asked me if I would work with him. "Of course," I said, "My God, there is no question."' Kent remains critical of the international operation, which was under the overall control of Joe Cahill at that time. 'Richard Behal [a veteran Republican] was in charge in France. He didn't get on too well with Cahill because Cahill was too fucking thick, he didn't know a whole lot, so he tried to starve him to death. Cahill only gave Behal 10 francs a week to live on in France. He is mean with other people but he told me one time, "the only thing I drink is Remy Martin."' Gerry Adams once made a similar joke when Cahill bawled out another IRA man for over-spending, 'I think Joe still has his confirmation money.' Behal was a flamboyant figure who had escaped from Limerick prison in 1966 where he was serving a jail sentence for firing on a British torpedo boat, the *Brave Borderer* in a protest against a visit to the Irish Republic by Princess Margaret the previous year. He later lived in France for some time and was Foreign Affairs spokesman for Sinn Féin for a period.

Phil Kent says, 'I was all over the world with Martin McGuinness, not only in North Africa.' They spent some time in Milan, where two million pounds worth of IRA arsenal was later hidden in a secret bunker. From Milan they travelled to Rome for a flight to Tripoli, where they lazed around for days waiting to meet their military intelligence contacts. According to one man who claimed he was in Italy with McGuinness, 'We sent him out to buy meat for the dinner. He was the butcher's boy, wasn't he?' When McGuinness returned they discovered he had bought horsemeat, but cooked it anyway.

McGuinness returned to Derry for the general election on 3 May 1979. The IRA were supporting Sinn Féin's campaign to burn polling cards and boycott the elections and, on the night of the election McGuinness looked on as a riot broke out at the close of polling. Pat Devine was the SDLP Deputy Mayor of Derry at the time and was in the Holy Child School in Creggan when the trouble started. 'The IRA had big bins up in Creggan, where they encouraged people to burn their polling cards in big braziers. Things got very nasty when a crowd of young thugs – Provo supporters – broke into the back of the school when the cops were trying to take out the ballot boxes for the count. Martin McGuinness was part of the crowd and did nothing at all to calm things down. There were milk bottles flying round our ears and it was a miracle people weren't brained with them. It was ironic. People were being attacked just for trying to use their vote.' The IRA later burnt out Councillor Devine's car on two separate occasions.

The IRA set out to give Margaret Thatcher, who had just been returned as Prime Minister, a long hot summer in her first term of office. In June, NATO Chief, General Alexander Haig, narrowly escaped an IRA assassination bid in Belgium when he was caught in a land-mine explosion near Mons which was meant for a senior British Army officer. Two explosions in July at the British Army barracks in Dortmund followed this attack. By the end of August, Martin McGuinness' dream of a liberated zone along the border came a step nearer when the IRA struck at the very heart of the British establishment.

Earl Mountbatten had spent every August in Sligo since 1969. For ten years the 79-year-old Earl had defied warnings from security experts, who had told him that he was a prime target for the IRA. The most recent warning had come from Sir Maurice Oldfield, who had just retired from his post as 'C' – the Director General of MI6, the government security arm responsible for international espionage. The writer John Le Carré based the character 'Smiley' on Oldfield, who had been told about a possible attempt on Mountbatten's life as he secretly prepared for his new job as overall security coordinator in Northern Ireland, at the request of Margaret Thatcher. He was powerless to intervene when Mountbatten chose to ignore his advice. To the IRA, Mountbatten was a symbol of British imperialism. As a cousin to the Queen and adviser to the Royal Family, his death would give the IRA the propaganda victory over the British that they craved. Since Mountbatten's first visit to Classiebawn ten years earlier, the IRA had been watching him. The previous year an IRA unit had carried out a dry run, and McGuinness gave his assent to the operation after Thatcher's victory. Slab Murphy had acted as Intelligence Officer for the operation and had selected his best men for the attack. McGuinness knew the man who would plant the bomb, Tommy McMahon from Carrickmacross, a close friend of Murphy's. McGuinness had been worried during the RUC raids in Andersonstown after Operation Hawk when police arrested a member of a sub-aqua club. However, although they had found evidence that he had been on a diving expedition at Mullaghmore, near the spot where Mountbatten moored his boat, they failed to make the connection to Mountbatten and the man was released.

On the night of 26 August 1979, the assassin placed a 50 lb bomb in the bottom of *Shadow V*, Mountbatten's boat. Mountbatten hated the attentions of the Garda Siochana officers sent to protect him, and kept them at a distance. On the morning of 27 August, two plain-clothes officers were watching through binoculars as the *Shadow* silently sailed past them. Suddenly the silence was shattered when a massive explosion ripped the boat to pieces. The dead included Lord Mountbatten, his nephew Nicholas Knatchbull, Paul Maxwell, a 15-year-old schoolboy who was helping out as boatman, and the Dowager Lady Brabourne. Nicholas Knatchbull's twin brother, mother and father survived with serious injuries.

Security forces in the North were put on the highest possible alert following the attack. That afternoon, a convoy of two army trucks led by a Land-Rover drove from an army base at Ballykinler, Co. Down, to another at Newry. Its route took it past Narrow Water, on the shore of Carlingford Lough, which marks the boundary between Northern Ireland and the Republic. As the rear vehicle of the convoy passed by a trailer at the side of the road, a watching IRA team detonated an 800 lb bomb. Simultaneously, an IRA unit on the southern side of the border opened up on the troops, who returned fire. A civilian, Michael Hudson, was killed in the crossfire. Six soldiers were killed in this explosion. During the next half-hour, several more Land-Rovers and two helicopters arrived to help in the rescue effort. As a Wessex helicopter took off to ferry injured soldiers to hospital, a second 800 lb bomb was detonated, killing 12 more soldiers. The commander of the second contingent of troops, Lieutenant Colonel David Blair, was among the dead. With the exception of the radio operator and Blair, who was the most senior officer killed in Northern Ireland at that point, all the military casualties belonged to the Second Battalion of the Parachute Regiment. It was their highest death toll since Arnhem in World War II. When Margaret Thatcher visited the scene two days after the attack, the reality of the situation was brought home to her in the words of Brigadier Thorne as he took an epaulette from his pocket, 'Madam Prime Minister, this is all I have left of a very brave officer, David Blair.'

The IRA's strategic use of 'armed propaganda' was underlined by the press treatment of the two atrocities. The death of the 18 soldiers was pushed into second place, while the murder of Lord Mountbatten of Burma held the front pages for days, described in headlines like, 'Those murdering bastards killed the man who was loved by all.' One journalist rang the Sinn Féin press office to ask why the IRA had killed a harmless old man. With chilling economy, the Sinn Féin aide replied, 'Why are you ringing me from New Zealand?'

In a libel action brought against the *Sunday Times* by Tom Murphy, Sean O'Callaghan revealed that Mountbatten's murder had been set up by the IRA in return for a payment of two million pounds by Syria. O'Callaghan claimed that Pat Doherty, McGuinness' close associate who was OC of Southern Command at the time, confirmed it in 1981. The money had been paid through the Syrians, and arranged by a mutual PLO contact in Cyprus. At the same time a major weapons and explosive cache had been hidden in a consignment of electronic transformers that was on its way to Ireland. The IRA's statement boasted that Mountbatten's killing was, 'A discriminate operation to bring to the attention of the English people the continuing occupation of our country. We will tear out their sentimental imperialist heart. The execution was a way of bringing emotionally home to the English ruling class and its working-class slaves that their government's war on us is going to cost them as well.' Tommy McMahon was later convicted of Mountbatten's murder and served 19 years in an Irish prison. Martin

McGuinness was one of those who applauded and cheered him at the party to celebrate his release, which was held in a Co. Louth hotel in October 1998.

At the end of 1980, McGuinness made his final visit to New York, where he looked bored as he listened to George Harrison's complaints. McGuinness had sent over some more IRA men to join Megahey, and in Harrison's opinion they would jeopardise operations. A consignment dispatched by Harrison had been intercepted at Dublin docks in the autumn of 1979. It was one of the largest shipments he had put together, and included two more M60s, fourteen M16s, and a Soviet made AK47, an unusual find for Harrison. McGuinness seemed unconcerned that the Irish police had intercepted the haul. 'All that concerned him was to get more guns in and to keep them coming,' he remembers. By the end of 1981, McGuinness was concerned at Megahey's consistent failure to come up with any gear and decided to send some more experienced IRA men out to join him. The team included the man responsible for the murder of Ewart Biggs, and another by two men named by Mounties as chief suspects in the killing of Lord Mountbatten. Dessie Ellis, an electronics expert who later became a Sinn Féin councillor, was said to have made the bomb, while the other, Ted Howell, was described as the brains behind the plot. McGuinness had given the men a 'shopping list' of 200,000 rounds of ammunition, remote-control detonation devices and remote-control model aeroplanes capable of carrying 20 lbs of explosives as far as five miles. The gang were arrested as they tried to cross the border from Canada at Whirlpool Bridge near Niagara Falls; when they were searched, police found Gabriel Megahey's phone number in an address book, along with casting dies similar to those used by the Irish government to validate passports.

Two men watched from a distance as the FBI moved in for the kill and the IRA's gun-running network collapsed like a house of cards. George Harrison had already decided to call it a day after McGuinness had ignored his warnings about Megahey, but he had left it too late to escape the FBI raid on his home, where Joe Cahill's passport was among the items taken by the police. Harrison was acquitted on charges of exporting weapons without a licence in 1982. Gabriel Megahey was arrested at work in Manhattan where he was sentenced to 11 years. One man got away: Gerry McGeough – one of 'Slab' Murphy's top men – and went on the run in America before being caught in Germany with two AK47 rifles. He was extradited to America where he received a three-year sentence. Dessie Ellis, who was wanted by the Irish government for jumping bail on explosives offences, remained in jail to await extradition. Ted Howell was deported from Montreal, where he had to change planes at Orly Airport, Paris, en route to Ireland. Telling the immigration officer escorting him that he needed to go to the toilet, Howell gave him the slip, abandoning his passport, coat and luggage. Shortly afterwards, Howell turned up in Dublin.

The second man who kept a close eye on the messy denouement was Phil Kent. Shortly after Howell had slipped secretly back into Ireland, Kent had met Joe Cahill and Martin McGuinness in a Dublin restaurant. McGuinness was still obsessed with getting the SAM7s, and his judgement was getting clouded. Ted Howell was the last person who should have been considered to return to America to buy weapons, but McGuinness did not agree. He left the restaurant briefly to phone Howell, telling him to meet them. As Cahill handed over a bag with eighty thousand dollars in cash, a blank driving licence, and a passport, Irish Special Branch detectives arrested Howell. There was little evidence against him. After all, it was not a crime to give someone a present of cash, and Howell denied IRA membership in court, saying the money was for election expenses incurred by Sinn Féin. In the absence of any concrete evidence to the contrary, he was acquitted. Ironically, McGuinness repeated these mistakes in 1990 when he sent his former brother-in-law, Joe McColgan (whose marriage to McGuinness' sister Geraldine had broken up in the mid-70s), to Florida to buy Stinger and Red-Eye missiles. McColgan received a four-year sentence after he joined the growing list of IRA gunrunners who became the victims of an FBI sting. Phil Kent was also later arrested and charged with exporting weapons to Ireland illegally in 1983 after being watched for some time. 'When I was arrested down there, the guy says to me "at last we have got the scarlet pimpernel."'

As the perceptive Major General Glover had warned, 'A new campaign may well erupt in the years ahead.' As McGuinness tried to forget about the comedy of errors that had unfolded in 1980, the stage was being set for a tragedy.

CHAPTER NINE

The Hunger Strike

By their suffering and deaths on hunger strike, they ensured that things will never be the same again.

Martin McGuinness, *Iris Magazine*, 1982

When Kieran Nugent's mother visited him in prison on 16 September 1976, she was unaware it would be the last time she would see him for almost three years. Two days previously, he had received a three-year jail sentence for possession of weapons and hijacking a car. His first day in the Maze Prison, as Long Kesh had just been renamed, was spent naked. On the morning of his second day, the prison guards gave him a blanket, which he draped around his shoulders to take exercise. Later in the day, he surprised the guards by asking for a prison uniform to take a visit from his mother. As his mother walked into the visiting area where Nugent was waiting for her, he got to his feet and stripped off his uniform as he told her, 'You will not be seeing me for three years because to have a visit I have to wear uniform. If they want me to wear a uniform they'll have to nail it on my back.' When puzzled staff bundled the naked man out, he was still shouting.

Nugent was reacting to the decision taken several months earlier by the British authorities end Special Category Status, a privilege that allowed republican and loyalist prisoners to wear their own clothes and maintain their own command structures within paramilitary compounds. A Colditz-style regime grew up with the creation of a 'camp council', escape committees and a code of paramilitary discipline maintained by elected

Officers Commanding (OCs) in each wing. The guards were referred to as 'the Huns'. Increased remission, improved educational facilities and individual cells in the modern H-Blocks at the Maze were the carrots offered by the government for giving all this up, but for offenders who considered themselves prisoners of war, it was anathema. Nugent's protest was one of hundreds more made by inmates as the dispute escalated. Since the protesters would not wear uniform they were allowed no clothes at all. Rather than go naked, they wrapped themselves in prison issue blankets but were told they couldn't remove them from their cells when they went to wash or slop out. It ended with the prisoners refusing to wash at all, getting rid of their excreta by plastering it over the walls and pouring their urine under the doors. By 1980, the 'dirty protest' involved 360 male blanketmen and 33 women in Armagh jail, who joined in solidarity even though they could already wear their own clothes. However, more prisoners were abandoning it than were joining and cells were regularly steam cleaned by conforming orderlies. Despite the grim conditions, there seemed little prospect of the issue being brought to a head by an outbreak of epidemic disease as had been widely predicted a couple of years earlier.

McGuinness was naturally sympathetic to the plight of the inmates, who included several personal friends, but it was a minefield. A defeat would be a blow to the moral of the entire movement and the flagging public interest was an ominous sign that the IRA, with its elitist cell structures and minimal political presence, could be easily marginalised. The IRA was standing clear of the whole affair, hoping that the struggle would be broadened into a human rights issue. The prisoners had formulated a list of five demands, originally devised by Adams, which were pitched as rights for all inmates. A case was going through the European Commission of Human Rights (ECHR) and the Provos also looked to Cardinal Tomas O Fiaich (now Archbishop of Armagh), Father Denis Faul, Father Alec Reid and a number of other Catholic clerics to pressurise the British on the issue.

The Link in Derry was also engaged and Father Reid, a Redemptorist based at Clonard monastery who had won the trust of Gerry Adams through mediating in feuds between rival republican paramilitary organisations, had made contacts with Michael Oatley of MI6. Reid would later suffer a nervous collapse because of the stress; however, another Redemptorist from Dublin maintained contact. 'My idea all along,' Reid later said, 'was to substitute the moral authority of the Catholic Church for the pressure that might be brought by a hunger strike or by violence.' The spectre of a hunger strike had been raised in the jail on several occasions as a means of ending the blanket protest and lifting the campaign for political status onto a new level. The leadership, including McGuinness, opposed it because of the risk of failure and in February the prisoners were persuaded to delay a hunger strike in order to give O Fiaich time to negotiate. Thatcher took their hesitation for weakness and proceeded to remove Special Category Status even for offences committed before 1976. In June the options narrowed further when the ECHR rejected the five demands, saying that political status was not a right under international law. By August, a note of desperation was creeping in. An IRA spokesman told *Magill* magazine, 'We want the H-Blocks settled, we don't want to see the warders killed, and the H-Blocks are of no propaganda purpose to us. Our people in jail are suffering real deprivation and we want that resolved.' For most of 1980 the prison situation, which would later have such a decisive effect on McGuinness' career, was only a background worry. Still a traditional militarist, he was beginning to sense that the republican movement was getting hemmed in. One straw in the wind was the funeral of Kevin 'Dee' Delaney, who became the first volunteer to die in the new decade when the bomb he was transporting detonated aboard a train to Lisburn in January, killing two civilians. Three chapels refused his remains and the funeral mass had, in the end, to be conducted at his home by Father Des Wilson, a local curate of radical views.

The tighter cell structure needed to sustain the campaign was making the IRA less accessible to the community. In addition, military successes tended to produce concessions from the British to the SDLP, a tactic specifically aimed at undermining republican support. Rather than talking victory, the IRA now told *Magill* magazine it aimed 'to maintain a certain level of armed activity to effect political change within the Six Counties. We have to be able to make "political progress" impossible.' This they were able to do, and talks with Humphrey Atkins, the Secretary of State, collapsed, but isolation was the flip-side of such negative and reactive strategy. McGuinness was trying to improve matters. The England Department of the organisation was being restructured and a new Active Service Unit had been inserted into Britain to replace Keenan's ruined network. After the suspicion surrounding Keenan's arrest McGuinness could afford no failures of security.

On the British side, Major General James Glover, the Commander of

Land Forces, was developing the surveillance capacity of the 14 Intelligence Company (the Det), scaling down SAS involvement and developing a dedicated agent handling unit, the Force Research Unit, to penetrate the paramilitaries. It would be up and running later in the year. Sir Maurice Oldfield, former head of MI6, was also in the province to overhaul the intelligence apparatus and to encourage the use of informants, particularly by the RUC. In the short term, the MI5 effort against the IRA in Derry was directed by a somewhat eccentric officer, code-named 'Ben', who wandered around the city in a pipe and tweeds, frequently drunk. Willie Carlin, one of Ben's agents, was a Derry man who had been allowed to leave the British Army early in order to return home as a salaried mole within Sinn Féin. Carlin later learned that Ben was Michael Bettaney, the rogue MI5 officer, who was jailed a few years later for trying to pass documents to Arkadi Gouk, a KGB agent in London. Before his posting to Northern Ireland, Bettaney had warned his superiors that he was not suited to the job. Carlin heartily concurs. He found Bettaney 'a weird character who always wanted to meet Martin McGuinness, he kept saying he and McGuinness could do business. I was at the building stage and he wanted to cut to the chase.' Carlin was never asked to join the IRA but was instead encouraged to operate within Sinn Féin, to get close to McGuinness and Mitchell McLaughlin, who was one of his most senior aides. Carlin took it for madness, but Bettaney's enthusiasm to meet the Chief of Staff may have been a sign of ambition; he knew that McGuinness was someone his bosses wanted to cultivate.

Carlin was amazed that Bettaney was not killed. He said, 'Ben could walk about with his pipe and his shoes, the very thing that would get you noticed in Derry. As time went on and I went to meet him to give him documents, he would be drunk, half a bottle of Bushmills before the meeting.' Anxiety about his handler's behaviour affected Carlin's work as an agent. He started withdrawing into his shell in the presence of other Sinn Féin members and soon McGuinness was commenting on how quiet he had become. After Bettaney rang him, his voice thick with whisky, to say he was outside McGuinness' home, Carlin complained to a more senior MI5 official who arranged a meeting at the Ballygally Hotel on the Antrim Coast Road. Bettaney cleaned up his act for a while but 'two months later I was in the Londonderry Hotel [in Portrush], and Bettaney's pissed out of his mind, and he's going to drive to Derry, to the Brandywell, to see McGuinness. So

I went down to reception, phoned the London number, and I said this guy's going to get me killed, I want out. I'm not having it. He was my handler but he had no cover at all, he just wandered around like an idiot. Literally wandered about like an idiot. An Englishman with a pipe and tweed jacket wandering round Derry.' Carlin was flown to London where it was agreed that he could stop reporting and he was given two thousand five hundred pounds to settle his affairs. Carlin continued as a member of Sinn Féin. He had come to agree with their policies, but later, after Bettaney was recalled to MI5's Soviet desk in 1982, he again offered his services to British intelligence. He still wonders whether Bettaney did make contact with McGuinness and whether that was the secret of his survival.

MI5 was not the only force monitoring republican activity in Derry. In October 1980, a new recruit was sworn into the IRA, a former member of the INLA. He said he wanted revenge on the Brits for shooting a friend three years earlier and that he regarded the smaller organisation as ineffective. He didn't mention that the INLA's disarray was largely down to him or that he was an RUC agent who, now that he had smashed up and demoralised the INLA was being tasked to clean up the Provos. Like most volunteers at this period, Raymond Gilmour was inducted into the Provos by Stubby Wall, a close associate of McGuinness since his footballing days, after being instructed in the *Green Book*, the IRA training manual, in a local school.

As Gilmour dug in, the pressures for a hunger strike mounted and McGuinness was involved in meetings with his local bishop, Edward Daly, the former Father Daly who had tried to rescue Jackie Duddy on Bloody Sunday, in a bid to defuse the crisis. When seven prisoners, including his old friend Raymond McCartney, began refusing food, McGuinness ordered pickets on the home of John Hume in protest at alleged 'SDLP inactivity'. According to the SDLP leader, however, 'I was the go-between in the hunger strikes, to get them stopped. I was arguing with the British to let them wear their own clothes and I also spoke to Thatcher about it.' Hume took the view, 'What did it matter what they wore, after all, as long as they were in prison?' Things came to a head when Sean McKenna, a hunger striker who had been injured as a result of being kidnapped in the Republic by the SAS and taken to the North, deteriorated quicker than the rest. On 17 December, the prisoners were shown the draft of a speech by Atkins promising them civilian clothes and were told that a senior British official would be in the jail in the morning to explain. They had received medical advice that McKenna was likely to die overnight. They ended the strike at midnight to save his life but it quickly became apparent that they would be required to wear 'civilian' prison issue slacks and shirts before being allowed to bring in their own clothes. On the outside the IRA tried to step up the pressure. Before the end of February, the Derry Brigade bombed and sank a British coal boat, the *Nellie M*, off the coast of Donegal, firebombed three shops in Derry City and destroyed the centre of Limavady with a van bomb. On the inside the prisoners negotiated, but to no avail.

A second hunger strike, this time led by Bobby 'Sass' Sands, began on 1 March 1981, with the result that next day the failing blanket protest was ended. Sands advocated using the prison issue to open up new avenues for republicanism. In one communication smuggled out of the prison in August 1979, he wrote, 'when we do move, we can move in all directions at the one time. Personally I envisage creating an atmosphere of mass emotion, trying to use it as best we can and as soon as we can to assert pressure from all angles on the Brits.' He also suggested putting forward prisoners for election. There must, he said, be 'no opponents, we need to do it right. We must have it I/O'd [checked out] right beforehand. We want at least 70 or 80 per cent of each area turning out.' Just four days after Sands refused food, the opportunity arose when Frank Maguire MP, who held the Fermanagh and South Tyrone seat as an Independent Nationalist, died. Maguire, a wing OC of republican internees in the 1950s, had been a supporter of the blanketmen. The constituency had a nationalist majority of almost 5,000. The Provos dithered. At one meeting they voted against contesting the seat but, partly as a result of backing from McGuinness as Chief of Staff, the decision was reversed. McGuinness argued that victory would create an opportunity for the prisoners to end the protest if they wished. Once the IRA's mind was made up, it brooked no opposition. A variety of other nationalist candidates, ranging from Bernadette McAliskey, who had been shot by loyalists the previous year, to Maguire's brother Noel, were dissuaded from standing and urged instead to give their support publicly to Sands. Noel Maguire had appeared close to tears when he withdrew but in the end Sands' only opponent was Harry West, the former Ulster Unionist Party leader who had lost the seat to Maguire in 1974.

Sands' campaign was based entirely around the H-Block issue, with no mention of local affairs. The canvass literature promoted the notion that Sinn Féin merely wanted to 'borrow' the seat, stressing that a vote for

Sands would save his life, whereas failing to turn out for him was 'a vote for West and Paisley'. Meanwhile, McGuinness and the rest of the leadership had ordered a boycott campaign against the census, which they regarded as an intelligence trawl on the part of the British government. In Derry, a gunman from the Waterside area murdered Joanna Mathers, one of the census workers, in the Gobnascale area. The last house she had been at before she was shot was the Anderson Crescent home of Willie Carlin's mother. Carlin, still a member of Sinn Féin, was there at the time, 'She said she was scared because of the campaign against the census and we told her not to worry, she only had a few more houses to finish and then she would be out of the republican streets. I told her I was a republican and I was sure she would be all right.' Her murder was one of the determining factors in his decision to make contact with the army once more and start working for FRU. At Gilmour's IRA unit meeting the members expressed disgust, but were told, 'So what, she's dead, bleating about it now is just a waste of breath.'

McGuinness, as so often after embarrassing deaths, ordered a denial and an IRA statement was issued putting the shooting down to an attempt to discredit Bobby Sands' election campaign. Few believed the comments and the statement had no credibility. Elsewhere in the Derry Brigade area, census-takers had been robbed of their forms and later forensic tests showed that Joanna Mathers' murder weapon had been used in two additional IRA kneecappings. Sands won by 30,492 votes to West's 29,046, but far from caving in to his victory, the British government went on to amend the Representation of the People Act to make it impossible for prisoners to stand in the future. The victorious candidate, who had by now lost two stone in weight, declined a suggestion from the IRA leadership that the hunger strike could be ended at this point without loss of face.

On Easter Sunday two young men, Gary English (19) and James Brown (18) died in Derry when an army Land-Rover ploughed into them at speed. When the soldier driving it was acquitted of reckless driving, there was uproar and further rioting. The *Derry Journal* described the killing as resulting in effects similar to those caused by the earlier deaths of Seamus Cusack and Desmond Beatty, who were shot during riot in 1971 and whose deaths led to an upsurge in IRA recruitment. It is undeniable that Gary English's younger brother, Charles, went on to join the IRA. He was killed four years later when a bomb he was carrying detonated prematurely. In the continued disorder that followed the deaths, a plastic bullet killed a 15-year-old schoolboy from the Bogside, Paul Whitters, as he led other youths in an attempt to hijack a lorry. He was wearing a green balaclava at the time and at his funeral his distraught family appealed to young people not to allow themselves to be used in further violence. The advice went unheeded. Sands' death on 7 May, after 66 days, was greeted with rioting on an unprecedented scale and the largest security operation since internment was launched to contain it. 100,000 attended his funeral and a street in Tehran, where the British Embassy was situated, was renamed Bobby Sands Corner as a gesture of Iran's solidarity with the Irish against the hated Thatcher. Two days later, the new deep penetration units in the mainland showed their teeth by exploding a 7 lb gelignite bomb in Sullom Voe oil terminal in the Shetland Islands while the Queen was on an official visit there. 'While the British occupation in England continues, then members of the British ruling class and administration will continue to be the subject of IRA attacks,' the IRA stated.

The next hunger striker to die was Frank Hughes, McGuinness' old comrade from South Derry. At his funeral in Bellaghy, the Chief of Staff himself gave the oration after a volley of shots had been fired over the coffin, despite RUC efforts to divert the cortège and take control of the funeral arrangements. McGuinness described Hughes as 'one of Ireland's noblest sons', and compared him to James Connolly, on the anniversary of whose execution in 1916 the hunger striker had died. He then took the opportunity to condemn the leaders of constitutional nationalism for not doing enough to support it. 'In frank terms, John Hume and Charles Haughey [the Taoiseach] have been whipped into line by Thatcher and instead of standing on their own they have wilted. The question must be posed: why don't they publicly support the five demands? And the only answer to that is that their, and the British, long-term interests are one and the same and they are not prepared to jeopardise those interests.'

Two more hunger strike deaths, one of them Patsy O'Hara, the Derry INLA man, occurred a few days later. In the subsequent rioting, Harry Duffy, a 44-year-old widower with seven children, died when his skull was fractured by a plastic bullet. 'It was mayhem in Derry during that nine-month period of the hunger strike,' according to a detective who was serving at the time. The IRA had two main Active Service Units. During the hunger strike the units were, according to Gilmour, allowed to operate at will: hijacking cars and attacking the security forces on an opportunity basis, often under cover of the rioting.

Throughout the hunger strike McGuinness allowed Adams to take the lead publicly and also in private, partly because the Maze was in the Belfast Brigade area, and partly because he failed to see its full potential. No Derry City members of the IRA joined the 1981 strike, though two members of the INLA, Patsy O'Hara and Mickey Devine, did. There was considerable anger at the lack of direction from the local leadership during the hunger strike period. At one stage, Peter Doherty and another IRA man met Martin McGuinness outside the Bogside Inn, where they had an argument with him. 'We were tackling him about the lack of activity, saying that we should be taking the initiative against the Brits, not sending wains out to throw stones. He just stood there, looking at us. We told him, if you get us the weapons, we'd guarantee you one dead Brit within twenty-four hours. McGuinness just said, "what's the point?", and walked away.'

By this time, Martin McGuinness had moved again, this time to a house at 1 Glendara, in the Brandywell, close to the Bogside. Bernie was expecting their third child, who was born in Altnagelvin Hospital on 21 August. The child was a boy, and Martin McGuinness named his first son Fiachra Mairtin.

On 28 May, George McBrearty's unit was carrying a bugged M16 rifle, which had been given to them the previous day by Gilmour. They were also under both helicopter and ground surveillance. The four-strong unit were in a hijacked Ford Escort, driven by Paddy Lawlor, and were looking for a second vehicle to steal, settling on a brown Opel Ascona. Lawlor pulled in ahead of the car and forced it to halt. Charles Maguire, McBrearty and Eamon 'Peggy' McCourt were masked and carrying rifles when they approached the driver, who put his hands above his head. McBrearty's weapon was on fully-automatic. As he turned for an instant the driver whipped a pistol from under the sunshade and shot him dead. The driver, part of a Det surveillance detail fired a total of 11 shots and, as McBrearty fell, his rifle went off. In seconds Maguire lay dead, McCourt was seriously injured and there were six bullet holes in the Ascona. Lawlor ducked down in the Escort to avoid being seen and when he put his head up the Opel was gone. Lawlor later burnt the Escort and sent McCourt to hospital in a taxi. These were the only IRA members killed by undercover soldiers between 1978 and 1983. It was a shattering blow to morale in Derry and was only one of several planned attacks which were sabotaged with Gilmour's help. He

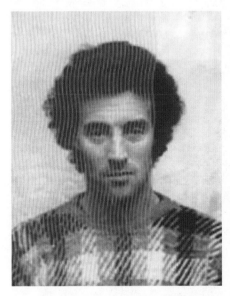

ABOVE: Martin McGuinness as goalie for a local team in the early '70s. (Private Collection)

LEFT: Paddy Ward.
(Private Collection)

ABOVE: Martin McGuinness smiles as British soldiers dismantle barricades in the Bogside during Operation Motorman, July 1972. (Private Collection)

RIGHT: Martin McGuinness, with hair and moustache dyed black, is handcuffed to a Garda at the Special Criminal Court, Dublin, 1 January 1973. (Private Collection)

ABOVE LEFT: Martin McGuinness in a
police photograph, 1972. (Private Collection)

ABOVE RIGHT: Martin McGuinness rushes for a taxi after walking free from a
Belfast court on 2 March 1976. (*Belfast Telegraph*)

BELOW: Martin McGuinness (2nd left) and Daithi O Conaill at a press
conference in 1972. (Private Collection)

ABOVE: Bernie McGuinness (far left) joins husband Martin McGuinness as he is congratulated by Barney McFadden and Liam McCartney (far right) after his election to the Northern Ireland Assembly, 20 October 1982. (*Belfast Telegraph*)

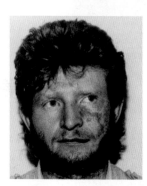

Willie McGuinness, Martin's younger brother, in a police photograph, 1982. (Private Collection)

'If you allow yourselves to be led out of this hall today, the only place you will be going is home.' – Martin McGuinness appeals for unity at the Sinn Fein Ard Fheis 1986. (Photocall Ireland)

ABOVE: Martin McGuinness and Gerry Adams at a meeting at the GPO in
O'Connell Street, Dublin, 1986. (Photocall Ireland)

BELOW: McGuinness stands by as a masked colour party carry the coffin of
IRA man Brendan Burns on 5 March 1988. Burns detonated the Narrow Water
bomb on 27 August 1979, which killed 18 soldiers. (Pacemaker Press)

ABOVE: Martin McGuinness salutes supporters with his sons Fiachra and Emmet in Omagh after winning the Mid-Ulster seat in the Westminster general election, 2 May 1997. (Pacemaker Press)

BELOW: Martin McGuinness and Gerry Adams embrace Hugh Doherty of the Balcombe Street Gang, at Sinn Fein's special conference on the peace agreement in Dublin, 10 May 1998. (Photocall Ireland)

TRAITORS TO THE REPUBLIC

SHAME FEIN

ANTI REPUBLICAN - FACIST - THUG
- IF YOU VOTED SHAME FEIN -
YOU VOTED FOR CHILD BEATERS
YOU VOTED FOR THUGS
YOU VOTED FOR IRELAND'S NAZI PARTY
YOU VOTED FOR TRAITORS
ASK MARTIN
ABOUT HIS 30 PIECES OF SILVER
JUDAS GOAT!

LEFT: Poster which appeared in Derry Sinn Fein strongholds during the June 1998 Assembly elections, put up by disillusioned republicans mocking Martin McGuinness for 'betraying' IRA principles. (Private Collection)

ABOVE: Martin McGuinness, with Pat Doherty (left) and Caoimhghín Ó Caoláin (right), after fracturing his thigh while playing football for the 'Exiles' in Derry, October 1998. (Photocall Ireland)

ABOVE: Dessie Ellis (far left), with Martin McGuinness, Mick Kehoe and Larry O'Toole (far right), at the local government elections in Dublin, 12 June 1999. (Photocall Ireland)

RIGHT: 'Trust me to be the first one to make a mistake.' Martin McGuinness, first member of Sinn Fein to join the Stormont government takes a seat reserved for a Unionist, 2 December 1999. (Photocall Ireland)

MR MICHAEL McGIMPSEY
MINISTER FOR CULTURE, ARTS & LEISURE

tells of one incident around March 1981 when he attended an IRA meeting with Eddie McSheffrey and three other volunteers, one of them a woman, at which McGuinness was scheduled to give a lecture on anti-interrogation techniques. However, army surveillance was spotted and the meeting was called off. Afterwards Cathal 'Drummer' Crumley, an IRA man whom Gilmour plied with drink to gather information, told him, 'Martin McGuinness was a member of the Provisional Irish Republican Army Council in Dublin and he was one of the top men in the Northern Command of the Provisional IRA.' Gilmour said, 'When Drummer asked me where I got the money to buy him drink I bluffed it and told him I worked for the Branch in Strand Road. He took it as a joke and assumed I'd been lucky with the horses.' In 2001 Crumley became Derry's first Sinn Féin Lord Mayor. Gilmour added, 'Most members of the Provos in Derry knew about Martin McGuinness' position in the movement and from my involvement in the Provisional IRA in Derry, I know that he was on the Northern Command of the Provisional IRA.'

Planned attacks at Magee College were aborted when Gilmour tipped off the police who sent armoured vehicles into the area. In further RUC operations acting on Gilmour's information, arms were lifted from dumps securely buried under slabs of concrete beneath kitchen sinks and, on one occasion, a gun attack on Strand Road Police station was aborted when Gilmour, who was the driver, braked and clutched to stall the car and make the shots fly wild. When suspicions were raised about Gilmour's behaviour, he talked his way out of it. If the military campaign under Chief of Staff McGuinness was faltering, the hunger strike was going no better. On a visit to Belfast, Thatcher described it as the IRA's 'last card'. As the year wore on, it became plain that the impact of each succeeding death was diminishing and the families of the prisoners began to take their loved ones off the strike once they became unconscious. Limited offers were being made through the Catholic Church's Irish Commission for Justice and Peace but, to complicate matters, Michael Oatley, the MI6 officer known as 'Mountain Climber', was also in secret contact with the IRA and had convinced Adams and McGuinness that he could secure them something in advance of what was officially on the table provided they did not disclose his involvement. Dennis Bradley, who had left the priesthood and married by this time, was not personally involved in the issue but spoke to other mediators. He said:

My other partners in the Link got very annoyed because they thought a deal was on the table long before it was on the table and the reason it didn't happen was because the Provos gave away their authority to the hunger strikers themselves – they were far too emotionally involved and in no position to make any judgements because the Provos appeared to hand the whole thing over to them. As far as I can make out from our guys, Thatcher would have made a deal quite early on despite what she said in public.

In a 1993 statement McGuinness described the hunger strikes as a period of 'frenzied contact', and added, 'We were assured during this period that Margaret Thatcher had authorised the line of communication with us and with the political prisoners.' Whatever the truth of this, it seems likely that the fact that negotiations were going on at two levels prolonged the hunger strike by holding out false hope. Certainly in her memoirs Thatcher gives no hint that her attitude had softened and instead spoke of her hope that the families would intervene to end it. This is what finally happened as the year wore on and on 3 October, after ten deaths, the six remaining hunger strikers called off their protest saying it had been undermined by Father Denis Faul, a priest who supported the five demands but encouraged the families to intervene to end the increasingly futile sacrifice. In fact Sinn Féin, who invited him to address a meeting of relatives knowing his intention, used Faul as a scapegoat. It was, he believed, a way for them to end the strike without compromising. Within days Jim Prior, the Secretary of State, granted the central demand – that prisoners be allowed to wear their own clothes – and the other demands were granted over a period of years, until the point where paramilitary regalia was openly displayed on the segregated wings of the Maze and prison officers patrolled only with the permission of wing OCs. The real importance of the hunger strike was, however, the political opportunities it opened up for Sinn Féin. In June the blanketmen won two seats in the Irish general election, contributing to the fall of Charles Haughey's government, and on 20 August, just over a fortnight after the funeral of Kieran Doherty, the last hunger striker to die, Owen Carron, a Sinn Féin member, won the Fermanagh and South Tyrone by-election following Sands' death. In a new departure that was to change the nature of Irish politics Sinn Féin announced that in future it would contest all Northern Ireland elections, though it would refuse to take seats if elected. There were other consequences. In her memoirs, *The Downing Street Years*, Margaret Thatcher said of Tuesday, 5 May 1981, the day Bobby Sands died, that 'the date was of some significance to me personally, though I did not know it at the time. From this time forward I became the IRA's number one target for assassination.'

Under cover of the hunger strike, when the security forces had been stretched to the limit, McGuinness and the Army Council had taken the opportunity to reorganise the movement. It now not only had political options but also the means to escalate its campaign, particularly on the British mainland. Within days the first bombs went off at Chelsea barracks, where two civilians were killed, and Oxford Street, where a police explosives expert died. Sir Steurt Pringle, the Commandant General of the Royal Marines, was also badly injured by a bomb under his car.

At the Sinn Féin Ard Fheis at the end of October, Danny Morrison, editor of *An Phoblacht*, found a soundbite to sum up the new policy which had been discussed among the leadership, 'Who really believes we can win the war through the ballot box? But will anyone here object,' he asked, 'if, with a ballot paper in one hand and the Armalite in the other, we take power in Ireland?' The comment hadn't been cleared and, sitting behind Morrison, McGuinness looked shocked, 'What the fuck's going on?', he hissed.

CHAPTER TEN

The Armalite and the Ballot Box

I saw young people committed to supporting the Irish freedom struggle here today. But I also saw young people in a drunken state running behind the bands. This is not what Irish republicanism is about. These young people had better realise we will never free Ireland with an Armalite in one hand and a pint of beer in the other.

Martin McGuinness, 18 March 1983, at an independent
St Patrick's Day parade in Dungiven, Co. Londonderry

Martin McGuinness had been shocked at Morrison's unscripted and unsanctioned outburst at the 1981 Ard Fheis, when he had blurted out the 'Armalite and ballot box strategy' the leadership had already discussed at an unofficial caucus. McGuinness had first heard the idea discussed at 'The Think Tank', which he joined in 1981 and which was later formalised as the 'Revolutionary Council'. It had a floating attendance – core members included Adams and Morrison, latterly joined by McGuinness and Pat Doherty. Their initial premise was that a long armed struggle by a tightly focused IRA could go hand in hand with a revitalised Sinn Féin. It drew on the ideas of the 1978 Staff Report and worked very closely with the prison leadership, men of the same generation as those in the Think Tank.

The results of the battle fought in the jails were starting to emerge. In September 1981 Sinn Féin had tasted the first fruits of the hunger strike when the British Labour Party's annual debate on Northern Ireland passed a motion committing the party to campaign actively for a united Ireland by consent. It was a pledge made in opposition, which rang hollow for some supporters, but by 10 November, the battle lines were firmly drawn when Margaret Thatcher announced in the House of Commons, 'Northern Ireland is part of the United Kingdom; as much as my constituency is.' Her words were later shortened to 'Northern Ireland is as British as Finchley.' Sinn Féin were keen to test out the benefits of the ballot box, and on 22 March 1982, Martin McGuinness had been selected by Sinn Féin as the candidate for the Foyle constituency. Around the same time he met Cardinal Basil Hume; and the press began to note that he went to mass every Sunday. Eager to impress their friends in the Labour Party, on 3 May, both McGuinness and Adams addressed the first ever May Day Parade in Derry.

By this time, there were signs of cooperation between the Gardaï Siochana and the RUC. In 1982, for example, intelligence reports from IRA informer O'Callaghan about a GHQ meeting in Mayo were later passed to the RUC. O'Callaghan noted that Gerry Adams was still Adjutant General and McGuinness was Chief of Staff. Pat Doherty was OC, Southern Command, with Smithborough man, Kevin McKenna, now replacing McGuinness as OC Northern Command. Seamus Twomey was Director of Security. At the meeting, McGuinness reported that the IRA needed 'gear and cortex'. It was bad news for the IRA, and on Thursday, 23 September it was compounded when RUC Chief Constable John Hermon said that the IRA and INLA were both 'reeling' from the evidence given by informers.

Around this time, his closest friends and family began to notice that McGuinness was prone to attacks of depression, which were sometimes severe, when 'he would get very low'. They were followed by fits of elation. This was to be the pattern at the Assembly elections, where he was convinced he would lose the seat, and damage Sinn Féin. When the opposite happened he reacted enthusiastically, becoming even more involved in the political arena. At the 1982 Sinn Féin Ard Fheis, he declared in his speech that 99.9 per cent of the volunteers he represented were against federalism. He was trying, he declared, to organise 'his people' to fight.

On 20 October 1982, McGuinness won a seat in the first election in Northern Ireland since the beginning of the Troubles to be contested by Sinn Féin. However, McGuinness did not 'recognise British authority in this part of Ireland', and did not take up his seat, a stance, he claimed, which was followed by John Hume and the SDLP. 'If Sinn Féin had not been so successful', McGuinness said at the time, 'the SDLP would have taken up their seats. As it stands . . . the assembly is a talking shop now, with no power whatsoever.' Quoting Danny Morrison, he underlined his point, 'It is an Orange Hall, with the Alliance Party washing the floors and cleaning the windows to make it more respectable.' Certainly there were many ready to embarrass McGuinness. One RUC man remembers, 'After he was elected to the Assembly, some of the boys met him in an early morning search. It was a particularly cold day, and one of the boys asked him what he was going to do about the heating in Strand Road police station.' The contradictions of electoral and military office were irreconcilable for McGuinness and Adams, who had been forced to resign as Chief of Staff and Adjutant on the Army Council respectively before putting themselves forward for election. Ivor Bell, Adams' Belfast crony, took over from McGuinness as Chief of Staff. Shortly before the Northern Ireland Assembly elections on 20 October 1982 McGuinness met Sean O'Callaghan, the IRA man secretly passing information to the Irish police. McGuinness was at a dinner dance in Tralee, where he briefed O'Callaghan on plans to kidnap Patrick Gilmour, father of the supergrass Raymond Gilmour. McGuinness had come to Kerry to meet a local businessman who was involved in arms importation, as well as Richard Behal, then current Sinn Féin head of Foreign Affairs, and a man with extensive international contacts. O'Callaghan told McGuinness about two men who could be of use in arranging arms shipments. The first was a cattle dealer who regularly exported cattle to Libya; the other was a coach driver who was willing to hide explosives or weapons on his bus on one of his regular weekly trips to England. McGuinness was delighted and asked O'Callaghan, he claims, to contact a man called Mick Hayes, the Quartermaster for the England Department, and introduce him to the coach driver. O'Callaghan also claimed to have introduced McGuinness to the skipper of the *Marita Ann*, which was later caught by Gardai off the Co. Kerry coast with four tons of arms and explosives in 1984.

On Thursday, 18 November 1982, the IRA kidnapped Patrick Gilmour, the father of supergrass Raymond Gilmour, from his home in Derry. Raymond Gilmour had penetrated the Derry Brigade's Active Service Unit, the IRA's local elite. He had secretly been passing information to his RUC Special Branch handler for years, compromising IRA operations and ensuring the detention of many top terrorists. In the words of his handler, 'he really kept the city clean for us.' When his cover had finally been blown by the seizure of one of Martin McGuinness' prized M60 super guns, he had pressed the RUC to let him give supergrass evidence against his erstwhile comrades. Although his testimony was rejected in the end by the courts, hundreds of suspects were taken off the streets for lengthy periods of detention. There were enough activists among them to paralyse the IRA and cause debilitating hunts for more informers. Gilmour's penetration had been so skilful that McGuinness himself now feared arrest. It was a turning point for him. From this point on, he would surround himself with trusted friends and family members and would rarely involve himself in the minutiae of IRA operations.

The Derry journalist Nell McCafferty, who has known Martin McGuinness since he was a child, described the scene as Gilmour gave evidence. 'His halting evidence,' McCafferty said, 'was like a slow and gentle journey round the town. First he went to Hugh Duffy's house in Lislane Drive – of course you mentally nod, there's Hugh sitting over there, know that street well, know his mother too, a widow woman, worked as a cleaner for a while in the schools, what's she doing now, you wonder – and then Raymond says Hugh sent him over to Ducksie Doherty's house . . . hello Ducksie, instinctively your head nods in greeting to him, grand nickname that, terrific smile Ducksie, he's all teeth.' Another IRA man, Robert Quigley, had turned supergrass after being named on Gilmour's evidence. Police were pleased when he told them that in 1972, when he had been living at 9 Cromore Gardens in the Creggan, he had seen Martin McGuinness outside changing rooms used by footballers at the Bishop's Field, where the Bloody Sunday marchers had assembled. There were rifles, hand-guns and Thomson sub-machine guns lying against the walls. McGuinness was issuing instructions to armed men, asking them which barricade they were performing duty at. At one drill session he saw 200 men obeying orders shouted in Irish by McGuinness. Quigley said McGuinness punished IRA slackers at Central Drive, where he made some sweep the streets and others walk around the Creggan with rifles held above their heads. He saw McGuinness himself many times carrying rifles and sometimes a Thomson, coming out of the changing rooms with other armed men who would all then get into a car. At barricades, McGuinness was always armed. Quigley told the RUC it was obvious that McGuinness was one of the leaders of the IRA during the time of the No-Go areas. He often wore a combat jacket with a wide army type belt around the outside of the coat, topped off by a bush hat.

By 29 November, Martin McGuinness had applied to the RUC for permission to carry a firearm for personal protection and was refused. He claimed, 'The RUC don't want to give me a gun licence. It creates a political problem for them, in that all unionist politicians have licensed firearms. Why should nationalist and republican politicians not have firearms?'

On the night of Monday, 6 December 1982, the INLA exploded a bomb at the Droppin' Well Bar and Disco in Ballykelly, Co. Derry, and killed 17 people: 11 British soldiers and 6 civilians. On 8 December British Home Secretary William Whitelaw imposed a banning order on Martin McGuinness, Gerry Adams and Danny Morrison under the Prevention of Terrorism Act (PTA) when Ken Livingstone, the GLC leader invited them to visit Britain. Whitelaw's decision was taken under sub-section 'A' of the Act, which allowed him to exclude person(s) if he was satisfied 'that they are or have been concerned, in Great Britain or elsewhere in the commission, in the preparation or instigation of acts of terrorism.' The exclusion order was delivered by hand through the letterbox of the Republican Press Centre on Belfast's Falls Road. Livingstone declared that Whitelaw's decision was 'the biggest propaganda coup they [the British government] have had in ten years', and announced that he would travel to Northern Ireland in the New Year, 'after the GLC budget and the London Transport fares have been settled'.

On 10 December 1982, Post Office workers at Belfast sorting office intercepted three envelopes containing live bullets addressed to the three Sinn Féin Assembly men. Head Office, Donegall Quay. An RUC spokesman confirmed that they had started an immediate investigation into the finds. McGuinness commented that he believed 'agents on behalf of British rule in Ireland', had sent the bullets. On Saturday, 26 February 1983, Ken Livingstone made good his pledge by travelling to Belfast for a two-day visit at the invitation of Sinn Féin. Nine days earlier, McGuinness claimed soldiers on Cable Street assaulted him, ripping his coat, when he tried to stop them entering the premises. He claimed they had later threatened him with arrest. Livingstone's visit was uncontroversial, but on 18 March, at an independent St Patrick's Day parade in Dungiven, McGuinness said, 'We in the IRA and the Irish Republican Movement and Sinn Féin have put Britain to the test. There is growing support from the people for us. The people are realising that the SDLP will never solve the problems of Ireland.' McGuinness added that the members of Oglaigh Na hEireann needed the support of the people because they were prepared to lay down their lives and die for the Irish people. 'We must arm ourselves politically and any other way we see fit to remove Britain from this country,' McGuiness added. He concluded, 'I saw young people committed to supporting the Irish freedom struggle here today. But I also saw young people in a drunken state running behind the bands. This is not what Irish republicanism is about. These young people had better realise we will never free Ireland with an Armalite in one hand and a pint of beer in the other.' An RUC spokesman confirmed that they were studying a newspaper report of the speech but refused to comment any further. The British media were beginning to realise that the fiery and inexperienced Derry man could provide good copy for them, and shrewdly cultivated his press aides. The results were perhaps not what a more mature and sober IRA spin-doctor would have desired. On 17 April, for instance, McGuinness told *The Observer* newspaper that the IRA had 'a legal and moral right to kill a British soldier at any time', and in April he told an Easter commemoration that the British establishment was under pressure from IRA attacks and Sinn Féin electoral successes.

The IRA had been badly damaged in Derry by the death of a young man after a knee-capping had gone wrong, and McGuinness had been deeply embarrassed by the personal references made to him at the time. Twenty-six-year old Colm Carey had died from loss of blood after being shot in the knee in the Gobnascale area of Derry on 16 July the previous year. McGuinness told marchers that, 'The IRA accepts that punishment shootings of young offenders had outlived its usefulness and favours a socially involved solution to the problem.' He went on to say that the SDLP had no support from the young and was 'probably becoming non-existent'. After a group of masked men and women in combat gear led marchers, joined by more than ten bands, to the Republican Plot, a volley of shots was fired. A masked man then told the crowd that the IRA were 'sapping the will of imperialist rule in Ireland', and would, 'set an example for the nationally oppressed and dispossessed of the world'.

In the *Sunday Times* on 8 May 1983, he was quoted as the man who had been in charge of 'Free Derry', and who had claimed that the only reason he was not interned was because the government couldn't catch him. During McGuinness' election campaign, the *Sunday Times* article went on, 'one enthusiastic [Sinn Féin] helper was heard to observe, 'and this is better crack than stripping an Armalite'.

He was increasingly willing to take on the Catholic Church and the SDLP, whom he saw as the alternative leadership. At an H-Block hunger strike commemoration on 9 May, he said that Britain needed only one thing – an Irishman or woman pointing a weapon at its head. 'That and the united opposition of the Nationalist people through principled leadership are the only way in which the socialist Ireland can be won. All the SDLP possess are deceit, dishonesty and discredited politicians.' He called Bishop Cahal Daly 'the front man for anti-republican outbursts. According to him it is nearly a sin to vote for Sinn Féin. However, while Bobby Sands and his comrades slowly starved to death there was no condemnation of the intransigence and inhumanity of the British government.'

On 30 May 1983, McGuinness, Mitchell McLaughlin and Seamus Keenan, were arrested by RUC while electioneering. Police held them for an hour after two police constables were assaulted while attempting to remove a tricolour from a car, but no charges were brought against them.

McGuinness was worried about losing the election, and, safe in the knowledge that it would not be taken up, challenged John Hume on 1 June to a public debate in any hall in any nationalist area of Derry to discuss the root causes of violence in Ireland. Hume responded two days later, saying, 'There is nothing new about the Provisionals. They have filled the graveyards, the jails and the dole queues. Their target has been the destruction of the economy and Sinn Féin is now trying to exploit that. The contradiction is an insult to the electorate's intelligence.' McGuinness was incensed by Hume's attack, saying, 'It's very easy for people to put the blame on to the shoulders of the IRA. I think the people who do that are making a very serious mistake and are failing to understand the sensitivities of people who feel very strongly and are very angry about what the British government has done here.' However, he also recognised the folly of needlessly antagonising the electorate, adding:

> I think at the same time we have a responsibility to understand the feelings of the people who support the SDLP. Many of them are frightened, they don't want to stand up to the British Army and the RUC; they are afraid of losing their jobs, they are afraid of their children becoming involved. I understand all those things and criticise nobody. I think that's a tragedy, but at the end of the day I am still of the opinion

that the only hope for peace in this country is for the British to face up to their responsibilities and disengage and tell the unionists that they must find a new future for themselves within the context of a 32-county republic of whatever description.

On the day of the election, 9 June 1983, McGuinness only managed to get 10,607 votes. It was a poor showing after his Assembly victory, and rang all the more hollow to those who had been bussed in to his constituency to steal votes. One man remembers, 'There were two bus loads from Strabane went to help out at the 1983 election to vote for McGuinness. On average they would have done over 30 votes each.' Willie Carlin, the FRU agent within Sinn Féin, remembers organising impersonation, as vote stealing was known, on a massive scale. He also organised an incident to close a polling station where he believed that only SDLP supporters had still to vote. 'There was even a competition, with a prize of a bottle of whisky, for the person who could register the most votes. The winner, who later became a Sinn Féin politician, claimed she had stolen 57 votes.' Although McGuinness could not have seriously hoped to beat John Hume of the SDLP in the election, he was painfully aware of the high proportion of stolen votes. He was said to be 'extremely depressed' at losing the election, and was reported to be dreading his next meeting with Adams. Adams was more resilient, however, and McGuinness' spirits rose when he reminded him that he was still a member of the Assembly. McGuinness, in buoyant mood, agreed, pointing to the 13- and 14-year-olds who would soon be voters for Sinn Féin in the next election.

In the General Election of Thursday, 9 June 1983, the Conservative Party romped home with an increased majority. In Northern Ireland, the election was marked by the success of both SDLP and Sinn Féin holding one seat each, with John Hume and Gerry Adams achieving a 17.9 per cent and 13.4 per cent share of the vote respectively. The election gave Sinn Féin the first real sense that they might eventually replace the SDLP as the main voice of nationalism in Northern Ireland.

On Monday, 26 September, the IRA released Patrick Gilmour, the father of supergrass informer Raymond Gilmour, after holding him hostage for ten months. Chillingly, when an IRA spokesman was asked during an interview with *Magill* magazine in July 1983, what would happen to Gilmour, the IRA replied, 'The fate of Raymond Gilmour's father rests in Raymond Gilmour's hands. It all rests with him.' The informer, Sean O'Callaghan, later revealed in the *Sunday Times* that Patrick Gilmour had been living quietly in Co. Kerry all the time, following a request from McGuinness that comfortable lodging be found for him. Gilmour had gone along with his 'abduction', but if he had not, he might well have been forced. When Raymond Gilmour had been in protective custody waiting to give evidence as a supergrass, he had rung home to find McGuinness on the other end of the line. McGuinness asked him to think about what he was doing to all the families in Derry and urged him to come home. When asked if McGuiness offered him immunity from the Provisionals, Gilmour replied, 'No, he just said I would be OK.' Gilmour was later asked if McGuinness identified himself as being in the IRA. 'He did not,' stated Gilmour, and he said it left him cold. He claimed that knew McGuinness only wanted him back to have him killed.

By the end of November 1983, relations between Sinn Féin and the INLA had broken down, and McGuinness had sanctioned statements like, 'While Sinn Féin supports the right of the Irish people to wage war on Crown Forces, we believe that Friday night's no-warning INLA car bomb in Strabane is both militarily and politically indefensible. No-warning car bombs in residential areas do not distinguish between civilian and legitimate military targets. The INLA should recognise that actions of this nature pose an unacceptable risk to civilians and suit the British military and political administration in Ireland.' The IRSP countered, claiming 'shock and dismay' at his statement, pointing out that the IRA had carried out a no-warning bomb at the Ulster Polytechnic a few hours earlier that Friday. Relations had deteriorated to such an extent that around this time, Martin McGuinness was forced to intervene in a dispute that threatened to spill blood on the streets of Derry. This time, it was the brother of a very senior IRA man in Derry and in the North who was involved, and the dispute centred on one of Martin McGuinness' main contacts in the IRA. Paddy Ward had joined the INLA after becoming, disillusioned with the IRA under Martin McGuinness' leadership. He later left the INLA following his involvement in the kidnapping of the wife of an INLA supergrass, Harry Kirkpatrick, which went disastrously wrong during 1983. Paddy Ward's brother, William, had been in an argument with the doorman at a bar he claimed was controlled by the IRA and which paid them protection money. His sister had been in the house when two IRA men came round looking for

William. She was about six months pregnant at the time when the senior IRA man's brother threatened her with a gun, sticking it under her chin. Frightened, she miscarried, but had been able to identify one of the IRA men. When Paddy Ward visited a Derry bar a few weeks later, the IRA man's brother was there, working as a part-time barman. 'I told him. "I am not paying for that". He insisted, and we argued. I told him, "My sister lost a child because of you, you bastard." I was carrying a .38 special and I stood up on the rail at the bar, and aimed it across the bar at him. He went sheet white. I told him, "the next time you do anything on our family, I am going to come here and shoot you." He was a bit brave in the chat then after I put the weapon away but that was my run in with him.' Ward's brother was subsequently shot in a punishment attack. Soon afterwards, Ward was in his house one morning and opened a bedroom window when he heard a knock at the door, at which point a man pretending to be the postman claimed to have a parcel for him. Suspecting it was an IRA ruse to gain entry to the house and attack him, Ward armed himself with a small .32 automatic pistol he kept under the floorboards in his bedroom, before climbing out a back bedroom window and walking round an alley at the side of his house. He crept round behind the man – a member of the IRA from the Waterside. 'They had obviously sent him to whack me over this bar incident, so I took the weapon and gave him a bit of a thumping.' At this point, Ward suspects, McGuinness feared that events would escalate into a feud, and he suggested a meeting between all concerned to clear the air. Ward warned him, 'We will meet in my house, because that is the only way I trust you'. He added 'no weapons'. The following Saturday, Martin McGuinness and another IRA man came to Paddy Ward's house around three o'clock in the afternoon. Ward closed the living-room blinds. Secretly, two INLA volunteers had hidden in the kitchen with two Ruger carbines. They were there, Ward says, 'In case things went wrong. I expected to be stitched up.' McGuinness, Ward says, wanted him to return the PPK automatic he had taken from the 'postman', but he refused to return it until he had an assurance that neither himself nor any of his family would be attacked. Ward became angry when McGuinness brought up the subject of his sister's miscarriage. 'At that point I saw a figure going past the window to knock the front door. I said to McGuinness, "I think that is for you at the door." He asked, "How would it be for me?" I called the two guys out of the kitchen who were tooled-up, one held a gun on the IRA man, while McGuinness opened the door. I was behind McGuinness so I reached around him to pull the guy into the house. I knew him, he was from Shantallow, where I lived.' The man was armed. Ward ordered McGuinness and the two men to sit on the sofa. '"I thought you said no weapons, Martin," I told him. "I've a good mind to do the three of youse – the only reason I haven't done it is that I don't want to ruin my new sofa. What do you suggest I do?' The Shantallow IRA man replied, "there are more of us than there is of you." To which Ward responded, "It will be no odds to you how many there are, you'll be gone anyway." At that point, still holding on to the 'postman's' PPK automatic and the Shantallow man's weapon – an M1 Carbine, 'a pretty lethal little weapon'– Ward says he told McGuinness and the others to leave. It was clear to him that the Shantallow man's arrival with the M1 Carbine was a preparation to exact retribution on him and he realised that McGuinness was determined to force the issue. McGuinness' first port of call was to the Derry INLA leadership, one of whom had already been tarred and feathered on McGuinness' orders. The man still remembered how McGuinness had ordered Raymond McCartney to beat up Patsy O'Hara, the INLA man who had died in the 1981 hunger strike, McGuinness had called a 'hood' and a 'scumbag'. The INLA contact had been reluctant to intervene, seeing the dispute as a personal issue and not one that both organisations should get enmeshed in. However, he reported what had happened to Dominic 'Mad Dog' McGlinchey, who still retained close links with McGuinness despite switching allegiance from the IRA to the INLA when he had been released from Portlaoise Prison in 1982. 'McGlinchey called me up,' Ward remembered. 'I met him in Dundalk. He basically said, "look the weapons have to go back," and I told him I would give the weapons back. He said he had an assurance from the IRA Army Council that there would be no retaliation taken; the family would be left alone. That was the last run-in I had with McGuinness.'

On 1 December 1983, IRA gunmen shot and seriously wounded Sergeant Ivor Semple. The IRA boasted, 'This follow-up attack on the elite RUC task group in this city demonstrates our continued ability to penetrate at will the security accorded to these individuals.' The gunmen had worn the uniforms of pupils at a local school, carrying schoolbags and wearing black blazers and grey flannel trousers. The police officer had been in his own silver Datsun in civilian clothes at the time of the attack and witnesses said that it was a miracle he had managed to steer the car safely to the kerb with such grievous injuries, and in so doing, avoided running into a group of children.

Later that same month, the IRA killed three civilians and three police officers in an IRA bomb attack on Harrods store in London on 17 December 1983. Margaret Thatcher took the opportunity to condemn Noraid for their fundraising, 'We condemn very strongly . . . money given to Noraid. It is given to those who reject democracy and pursue their ends by violence, and death, and destruction of innocent people.' The Harrods bomb was deeply embarrassing for Sinn Féin in the wake of the interest and support they were beginning to attract internationally. In PR terms it was a disaster and was perceived to have had such a negative effect stability within the IRA that McGuinness and Adams actually rejoined the Army Council 'to steady things' with McGuiness agreeing, in effect, to oversee all operations. McGuinness panicked at the flood of media inquiries he received and with a politician's instinct, moved to distance him, saying, 'All Active Service Units in Britain, as in Ireland, are aware of the need to avoid civilian casualties, and, indeed, as at Harrods, we do not believe that the IRA set out to cause casualties.' Such was the reaction to the Harrods bomb the IRA was forced to issue a lengthy statement clarifying their policy:

> If the British people really knew what was going on in their name, they would support the right of the Irish people to self-determination . . . In the absence of anything else, bombs in Britain provoke debate, however initially hysterical and racist.
>
> All active service units in Britain, as in Ireland, are aware of the need to avoid civilian casualties, and, indeed, at Harrods a 40-minute warning showed that there was no intention to kill or injure civilians. The British government has attempted to project the Harrods operations as a civilian bombing, despite the fact that they know that if the IRA wanted to kill British civilians, it could do so in hundreds.
>
> The Irish Republican Army does not abdicate responsibility for actions carried out by its Volunteers. We are comrades in arms who work at all levels in this army under tremendous pressures. While the Army Council did not authorise this specific operation at Harrods, we do not believe

that the Volunteers involved set out to deliberately kill civilians.

The statement concluded by saying that, despite British apathy towards Ireland, 'which is extremely frustrating, and because of British atrocities in Ireland, some oppressed Irish people and republican supporters, out of desperation, would view no-warning bombs as a way of shaking up the British public and their government . . .

However, regardless of these emotional tendencies and reactions, the republican leadership did not advocate or support such a strategy. Unfortunately, the IRA concluded, 'Despite all the logistical difficulties, we will continue to bomb the targets I have described as long as Britain continues its policy of terrorism in Ireland. This war is to the end.' They were chilling words for the British Prime Minister who had belatedly realised that events in Ireland had made her 'the IRA's number one target for assassination'.

Martin McGuinness, who had opposed the hunger strikers, now laid claim to their memory, stating that they had gone to their death, not just for the five demands, but also 'against the illegal British occupation of Ireland – the reason why they were in Long Kesh in the first place. By their suffering and deaths on hunger strike, they ensured that things would never be the same again. Tiocfaidh ar la, Bobby, our day will come.'

CHAPTER ELEVEN

The Cutting Edge

We Republicans don't believe winning elections will bring freedom in Ireland. At the end of the day it will be the cutting edge of the IRA that will bring freedom.

Martin McGuinness, *Real Lives:*
Edge of the Union, BBC, August 1985

The IRA in the mid-1980s was not the mass organisation of a decade earlier. Where it was once a broad movement of a thousand or more, it was now a tight military elite of 200–300 active volunteers. The emphasis was on maintaining efficiency and restricting the amount of information that any member could betray.

The reinvigorated Sinn Féin now surrounded the smaller IRA like a permeable membrane, protecting it from scrutiny but still allowing interaction with the community. In Derry, commercial bombings were largely abandoned because of an increasing feeling of civic pride and ownership among nationalists. In January 1984, McGuinness intervened to stop sectarian rioting around the Fountain estate, a Protestant enclave in the overwhelmingly Catholic West Bank. His wife Bernadette had just told him she was expecting their fourth child and he worried about what would happen to his young family if loyalists killed him.

Bogside Republican Youth (BRY), a loose grouping that acted as cannon fodder in the hope of progressing to the IRA proper, was formed around this time. McGuinness was a role model for these teenage boys and he played a

Fagin-like role, selecting youngsters for risks from which he was now able to protect his own growing family. Charlie Coogan recalled, 'Martin would see us and he would give us the auld wink. Then he introduced us to other people and got us to run wee errands. I think half the time he was only testing us out. This was exciting, this was my hero Martin McGuinness, the first person I ever wanted to be like. Martin was always on about education, about getting good grades in school and getting a better job. He told us he needed people in offices and businesses.' Entering the Fianna meant learning to use guns and was looked on as an honour. Induction lectures for young recruits were carried out by a teacher friend of McGuinness', but before that point the youngsters had to prove themselves by ferrying bags containing explosives around the city. In Coogan's case, 'Martin passed us on to an old guy who taught us how to do bags. Number one test for a bag when you are moving gelly is to hold it to your mouth and suck in and out to see if there is an air vent where the smell could get out. We used holdalls and to begin with there would only be margarine in them, but they wouldn't tell you that. You would get rounds of ammunition in boxes and be asked to hide them but you weren't allowed to hide them in your house. You'd find an outside dump and retrieve it when we were asked.' Coogan explained, 'In BRY you did petrol-bombing. In the Fianna you got to see guns. You were shown how to strip them down but you never got to fire them. We beat people for doing muggings, one guy for being a granny-basher. We ended up beating his girlfriend as well and we shot him in the leg. He called out our names when we were beating him so we came back for him and shot him.'

The youngsters in Bogside Republican Youth worked closely with the IRA, organising street disorder to drive troops into attack positions for the volunteers. One early success that Coogan remembers is an attack on a two-vehicle British Army mobile patrol in Bishop Street on Easter Monday, 1984. The BRY contingent pelted the Land-Rovers with petrol bombs made from gallon sweet jars which swathed them in flames and made them stall by cutting off the air supply to the engine.

Private Neil Clarke, a 20-year-old member of the Second Battalion of the Queen's Regiment, jumped out onto the street with his flak jacket ablaze. As Clarke landed, Paddy 'Nelson' Deery put his one good eye to the sites of his automatic rifle. Deery, who had lost his other eye to a British Army rubber bullet when he was a boy, hit Clarke in the back of the head, killing him instantly. Several BRY foot-soldiers were jailed but Deery escaped. Clarke's life was snuffed out largely because FRU's North Det, which controlled military intelligence informants in the city, had decided to preserve the cover of their agent 3018 at all costs. The agent, a man named Frank Hegarty, had gained the trust of Martin McGuinness who had personally given him the task of hiding a number of rifles – the one that was used to kill Clarke was among them.

Hegarty, a small-time smuggler originally associated with the Official IRA, was originally recruited in 1977 because of his love of greyhounds – the dogs were often used as a cover for smuggling and IRA activity. Weapons and contraband were often moved back and forth across the border in vans with dogs that were entered for races in the stadium at Lifford, Co. Donegal. Hegarty was approached as he walked his own dog along the Hollyhall Road at the back of the Creggan estate. A plain-clothes soldier, ostensibly alone but in fact with helicopter back up, strolled along beside him chatting about the races for weeks before making his pitch. Martin Ingram, a FRU handler at the time, said, 'In these circumstances you don't rush things. If the target is willing to make the running you let it gradually dawn on him over a few meetings what the situation really is.'

By early 1984 Hegarty voluntarily contacted the FRU after being dormant for a couple of years. He told them that McGuinness, an old friend, had asked him to hide guns as part of the reorganisation that followed the Gilmour arrests. As head of North Det it fell to John Tobias, a 31-year-old officer who later died in the Chinook helicopter crash that killed the elite of Northern Ireland intelligence officers in 1994, to decide how to proceed. Tobias had a number of options. He could confiscate the weapons, but that could draw suspicion on Hegarty before he was properly established. He could also order that they be 'jarked', army argot for rendering them inoperable or placing tracing devices in them. However that would have meant involving the RUC who did not know that Hegarty had been re-activated. Instead Tobias opted to have the guns brought in, registered and then returned to an IRA dump that Hegarty had established in the cemetery. The need to develop the agent and to build on his links to McGuinness were uppermost in Tobias's mind when Hegarty reported, shortly before Clarke's death, that he had been asked to provide a rifle for an attack on the army. FRU decided to let it ride. The rifle was later moved to a dump in Shantallow where, on 1 January 1986, it was seized with a number of others by the RUC. The guns were found to have been used in the murder of Clarke, of Private Martin Patten (18) killed as he walked a local girl home in 1985 and of Kurt Konig, a father of five who had a contract to run the catering department of Ebrington barracks.

By June, Bernadette was seven months pregnant and McGuinness took a back seat in the June 1984 European elections to be with her. Danny Morrison, the Sinn Féin candidate increased the party's vote by 50,000 to 91,476 or 13.3 per cent of the total. Their second son, Emmet Ruadhan, was born on 15 August. It was the week after the anniversary of internment, when BRY tore the city apart with rioting staged partly for the benefit of a visiting Noraid delegation. Martin Galvin, the Noraid leader, was barred from entering the UK and when he slipped in McGuinness could only spare him 30 minutes of his time.

McGuinness was becoming increasingly involved in community politics. A BBC *Brass Tacks* documentary screened in July showed him sitting on a committee comprising priests, social workers and an SDLP councillor to work out a strategy for dealing with petty crime. McGuinness advocated a policy of naming and shaming offenders before adding, 'now the very last resort has to be that you resort to violence of any description whatsoever'. Pressed by the interviewer, McGuinness told him, 'I am not a member of the IRA,' and condemned punishment attacks. He later turned up after a huge police and army raid on Rossville Flats where a terrorist command centre, complete with radio equipment, masks and documents, was discovered, to claim that there had been widespread damage to property and leakage of asbestos from radiators as a result of the search.

In September, after Morrison's success, Adams began to publicly set Sinn Féin the objective of overtaking the SDLP. The scale of the IRA's ambitions became apparent a few days later when the *Marita Ann* was arrested off the coast of Kerry with seven tons of guns and ammunition supplied to the IRA by organised crime in Boston. Informants at both ends had compromised the operation: Sean O'Callaghan in Ireland and in the US, James 'Whitey' Bulger, an Irish–American gangster who reported to the FBI. O'Callaghan was a dangerous agent who had met McGuinness at a number of high-level meetings. He had also penetrated the holy of holies, the IRA's England Department. However, he could not prevent the most stunning coup of the England Department's history, the bombing of the Grand Hotel in Brighton during the Tory Party conference on 12 October. The bomb came close to killing Thatcher and did in fact kill five other party members. As overseer of operations and a member of the Army Council, McGuinness would have had to approve an operation to target the cabinet, in principle at least, if not in detail.

The paranoia about informers remained rife on his own doorstep in Derry until well after Gilmour's evidence was thrown out of court in December. One victim of the purges was Paul McGavigan, a genuine but low-level police informant who had been involved, partly for himself and partly for the organisation, in stolen car rackets since 1979. McGavigan, who lived in Creggan's Central Drive, had promised to keep an eye on local Provos after being arrested for the theft of a milk-float but was never paid by the RUC because he never had anything of interest to tell them. In November 1984 McGavigan was held hostage and beaten for three days by an IRA unit to whom he admitted his role as an informer, but denied being paid. After his release, he was walking along the street, when a leading Derry republican pulled up beside him and told him to get into his car. This time McGavigan was taken to Sinn Féin's Cable Street Office where he met Martin McGuinness, whom he had known for most of his life, along with three other senior IRA men. His interrogators insisted that, despite his denial, the police had paid him and when one of them called him a tout and a liar, McGuinness walked out as if abandoning him to his fate. 'They were holding me there and I was again very afraid,' McGavigan told police. He was questioned by the IRA for a whole day before he eventually gave in and pretended the police had paid him three hundred pounds. He was again released, but that night at his home he was abducted once more by an armed gang who blindfolded him and took him to a house, which, judging by the smell in it, was near the gas yard. When his armed and hooded interrogators took a break, they left him tied to a chair, near a half-open door through which he could see them in the next room as they took off their masks to take tea and talk. McGavigan later told police that one of them was Martin McGuinness. Next day he was taken to a top room in the Telstar bar where McGuinness asked him to sign an affidavit admitting to being an informer before introducing him to a press conference and eventually releasing him. His ordeal was still not over. The next Sunday night, he opened his door to find two masked men who told him that he had forty-eight hours to get out, or risk being shot dead. McGavigan left town, but he had never been a serious informer and, even as Gilmour's evidence was dismissed and the accused freed in December, there were continuing signs that the IRA had been penetrated.

When William Fleming and Danny Doherty turned up on a motorbike to ambush a worker at Derry's Gransha hospital as he changed shift on 6 December, the SAS were waiting for them. The intended target was a part-time member of the UDR, but it was the two young IRA men themselves who were cut down in a hail of 59 bullets. McGuinness claimed that Fleming was struck 38 times and Doherty 30 times, mainly in the back. Two loaded hand-guns were found nearby but they had not been fired and there was widespread criticism of the shooting within the nationalist community.

Speaking at the funeral, McGuinness drew the moral that 'only the freedom fighters of the IRA could bring Britain to the negotiating table', but in the unionist community there was nothing but praise for the security forces. Gregory Campbell, a DUP Assembly representative from Fleming's home area of Waterside was the target of nationalist anger for his statement that 'Christmas had come early.' Campbell and McGuinness, two Assembly members of similar age who were increasingly seen as the two leaders of extreme opinion in the city, were about to be united in an unfolding drama.

According to Willie Carlin, the FRU agent within Sinn Féin, McGuinness now became seriously intent on building his political profile and Carlin helped him pick out a new tweed jacket in Donegal, which he wore on several television shows. There was concern that, despite its rising vote, Sinn Féin would be ignored because of the violence. For instance, McGuinness was enraged, and openly bitter, at Hume's ascendancy in local politics, when a November 1984 delegation from the US-based Committee for a New Ireland visited Derry to meet Hume but refused to see Sinn Féin. McGuinness had also been cold-shouldered by US Bishops who had visited the city a month earlier. Carlin said, 'We were reaching a situation where the IRA had to be fine-tuned to help political progress. We could ask them to take it easy for a while and in turn they would count on us to defend and explain any actions they did take.' Carlin claimed he had been privately briefing Northern Ireland Office officials on Sinn Féin personation tactics to help them draft new legislation, requiring the use of identity documents for voting, a measure announced in the Queen's speech that month. Carlin believed impersonation helped the political development of Sinn Féin. He said, 'We needed personation to get Martin elected but the task now was to use his position to turn the stolen votes into real votes.'

Carlin remained undetected in McGuinness' circle as the hunt for touts continued. In 1981 McGuinness had been warned by the INLA that a previous member, Kevin Coyle, had been caught passing information to the Gardai while on the run in Dublin. McGuinness chose to ignore the warning and allowed him to join BRY. In the wake of the paranoia following Gilmour's appearance as a supergrass, Coyle was subsequently pulled in by the IRA and confessed to passing low-level information to the RUC. Like McGavigan, he appeared at a Sinn Féin press conference and was released but on 21 February he was hooded and abducted from his home in Brandywell. McGuinness, who lived nearby, visited the family, offering to act as a mediator. It had the effect of calming them down for the two days it took for Coyle to be interrogated before he was murdered and dumped on Corporation Street. The family were given a taped confession and there was, the inquest heard, signs of bruising on his arms. Coyle's murder was an unpopular killing that attracted a lot of media attention – Coyle's father-in-law, Paddy 'Bogside' Doherty, was a leading community development worker.

Overall the IRA campaign was going through a bad patch and as the man in overall charge of operations, McGuinness was the target of criticism. Between December 1984 and April 1985, for instance, thirteen IRA members were killed in action, nine at SAS stakeouts, two by explosions and another, Sean McIlvenna, Director of Operations on Northern Command was shot by the RUC at the scene of a land-mine attack. A hawkish IRA faction, led by the former Chief of Staff, Ivor Bell, was convinced that the IRA was being hamstrung by electoral considerations and was pushing for an Army Convention at which to challenge the leadership head-on. However, McGuinness accused them of factionalism and in March he persuaded the Army Council to expel the four members from the IRA. Still, their criticisms carried enough weight to halt a proposed IRA grant of £250,000 to Sinn Féin for the local government election campaign, which had a knock-on effect on the 'fine tuning' of the IRA campaign for political considerations. In the run-up to polling in May, the South Armagh Brigade struck with a land-mine attack which killed four police officers and a less successful attack on a helicopter with three machine guns. The attack did not affect Sinn Féin support at the polls. In May the party received 11.8 per cent of the popular vote and succeeded in getting 59 councillors elected. Gerry 'Mad Dog' Doherty, who had been convicted of planting explosives contained in dustbins outside Derry City Council's Guildhall headquarters in 1971, was one of five Sinn Féin councillors elected in Derry. After the count there were wild scenes of jubilation as McGuinness was captured on camera in the throng carrying Doherty shoulder high down the Guildhall's ornate staircase chanting 'I, I, IRA', and, 'Up the 'RA, Up the 'RA . . . ' At a reception afterwards McGuinness presented the new councillor with a dustbin.

The next month in the Irish Republic elections, Sinn Féin put in a creditable performance, increasing its local government representation from 28 to 39 seats, which still left them on the margins of politics but somewhat ahead of the other minor parties.

In order to damp down sympathy for the dissidents, McGuinness approved a series of major operations proposed by local commands, effectively letting the IRA campaign rip. The biggest bomb so far detonated in Belfast – 1,000 lbs – was ignited in June and a few days later a similar sized device killed a police officer in Kinawley, Co. Fermanagh. On 2 July a prototype 50 lb ground, as opposed to lorry, launched mortar, newly developed by Jim 'Mortar' Monaghan, was test-fired against the army base known as Fort Pegasus in Belfast. It caused extensive damage and gave the IRA, 'a greater flexibility than ever before in operating against Crown forces'. Other attacks were thwarted, including a plan to destroy Newry with a 1,800 lb device which was captured by police.

McGuinness was now an iconic figure and appeared as the cultured and chivalrous IRA hero of a thriller novel called *Confessional* by Jack Higgins. Higgins was perhaps closer to the mark than he realised when he depicted McGuinness in regular contact with British intelligence as they collaborated in an attempt to foil a KGB plot to assassinate the Pope. Less plausible was a sub plot in which McGuinness spared the life of a British soldier, only to meet up with him, years later. 'Ah, Captain Fox,' McGuinness greets him, 'Nice to see you again . . . Derry, 1972. There was a bomb in a pub in Prior Street . . . The whole street was ablaze. You ran into a house next to the grocer's shop and brought out a woman and two kids. I was on the flat roof opposite with a man with an Armalite rifle who wanted to put a hole in your head. I wouldn't let him. It didn't seem right in the circumstances'. It was fame of a kind, but McGuinness' biggest publicity triumph and the event which would put him on the world stage was a BBC documentary in the *Real Lives* series entitled 'At the Edge of the Union' which was scheduled for Wednesday, 7 August. It featured Martin McGuinness and Gregory Campbell, the DUP Assemblyman who had exulted in the deaths of William

Fleming and Danny Doherty, the IRA volunteers shot by undercover troops at Gransha eight months earlier. The commentary described them as 'Both young, working class, teetotal, church-going, elected representatives.' Paul Hamann, the producer, was apprehensive that his programme might not attract high viewing figures, so contacted Barrie Penrose, a *Sunday Times* staff reporter at the time, to try to drum up some publicity for the weekend before broadcast. Penrose raised the issue with Bernard Ingham, Thatcher's Chief Press Secretary, Home Secretary Leon Brittan, and Douglas Hurd, Secretary of State for Northern Ireland, who pronounced himself 'alarmed'. The big quote, however, was to come from Thatcher who had, two weeks earlier, told the American Bar Association in a speech coloured by the recent hijacking of a TWA airplane by Middle Eastern extremists that terrorists must be starved of 'the oxygen of publicity'.

On Friday evening Thatcher was holding a press conference in the British Embassy when Mark Hosenball, a *Sunday Times* correspondent, asked her how she would react if she learned that British television were to broadcast an interview with a leading terrorist, for example, the IRA Chief of Staff. Thatcher said she would 'condemn them utterly'. She added, 'The IRA is proscribed in Britain and in the Republic of Ireland. We have lost between 2,000 and 2,500 people in the past 16 years. I feel very strongly about it and so would many other people.' On Saturday, Downing Street told the *Sunday Times* that Thatcher would be demanding an explanation about the film from the BBC. This was the story that the paper splashed with that Sunday, starting a bigger publicity firestorm than Hamann could ever have dreamed of. The next day the BBC Board of Management, who are in charge of the day-to-day running of the Corporation, passed the film for broadcast, but as they were doing so, Leon Brittan, the Home Secretary, wrote to Stuart Young, Chairman of the BBC's Board of Governors, requesting that the film should not be broadcast. On Tuesday, the Board of Governors decided to view the film, a decision that was outside their normal remit and arguably infringed on editorial independence. Having done so they decided to ban it.

BBC and ITN journalists promptly went on a one-day strike and there was an international furore about the affront to BBC editorial independence with bootleg tapes of the show being screened at radical meetings across the country. McGuinness himself turned up on the picket-line at BBC Radio Foyle. He later told the *Sunday Press*, 'I wasn't surprised the programme was banned', and that the film had tried to 'look at the situation through the eyes of Campbell and myself, showing the fact that we were family men, who had children and enjoyed playing with them . . . all that sort of thing. In other words that we don't have ten heads.'

Willie Carlin remembers that before the show, Sinn Féin were determined that McGuinness should appear mainly in soft focus and in this they were successful. He was shown as an active and law-abiding constituency politician, stopping patiently at roadblocks while Bernie and his mother expressed fears for his safety. Footage of Campbell, on the other hand, featured close-ups of his legally-held revolver as he crammed bullets into it, while he made incendiary speeches. 'The only way to deal with the IRA is to kill them,' said Campbell, who had no actual paramilitary past. McGuinness, on the other hand, admitted to playing 'a full role in attempting to bring about what I believe was the only solution to the particular problem and that is that the British must leave'. He went on, 'The fact of the matter is that we are strongly convinced that the responsibility for every death in Ireland, whether it be the death of a British soldier or IRA man or RUC man or UDR man or innocent civilians, at the end of the day the responsibility for all that lies at the feet of the British government because they partitioned this country against the overwhelming wishes of the Irish people. They are the people who must pick up the tab for that, not the Irish people.' His most intriguing statement came after a defence of 'armed struggle', when he added, 'If someone could tell me a peaceful way to do it then I would gladly support that, but then no one has yet done that.' In her first ever television interview, Bernie was visibly nervous, saying that she did not like to see anybody getting shot, 'but then they should not be here, you know. This is our country.' She believed, 'We will only get to freedom through the ballot box,' but added, 'I do not think they should give up the Armalite either.'

He was shown at a republican commemoration surrounded by masked men but the abiding memory of McGuinness was of a family man who walked on the beach with his children and took the time to spoon-feed baby Emmet. The programme was screened in a slightly amended form in October but the political repercussions rolled on for years. Alasdair Milne, the BBC Director General, later said that the programme led to his removal and the episode was credited with fatally damaging Leon Brittan as Home Secretary.

The most perspicacious comments about *Real Lives* were those of Byron

Rogers, whose review in the *Sunday Times* put the programme in its political context:

> If you see a man on television looking like a Sunday School teacher, you come to believe he is a Sunday School teacher; it is the images which linger in television. Yasser Arafat has never understood this. Whatever he says, you remember only the three-days' growth of beard, and the pistol in the belt on the rostrum of the UN. The IRA understands television only too well. Now thrive the barbers.
>
> *Real Lives: At the Edge of the Union* showed an extreme Protestant; he had a gun which he obligingly loaded for the cameras; he lived in a cage and talked with some enthusiasm about killing ('I will do such things/What they are yet I know not'). But there was another man, a mild blue-eyed man, neat as a shop-walker, seen with his family and in committee. He had no guns and made no threats, even expressing sadness about the killings, which he seemed to see as natural disasters. After the rantings of the other, you began to fear for his safety.
>
> This was the most remarkable achievement of Paul Hamann's film, that it made you worry about nice Martin McGuinness, believed to be the Chief of Staff of the IRA.

IRA business continued as normal. Between May and August 1985 the IRA claimed to have used 6,000 lbs of explosives in a concerted blitz on border security force installations. The province's 151 police stations were also undergoing a £150 million rebuilding programme. For a time the IRA's tactic had been to 'tax' or claim protection from builders working on these lucrative security force contracts some of whom they had also intimidated into providing plans of security force bases. In July and August that all changed, largely thanks to pressure from McGuinness. Derry Brigade had, in early July, issued a statement warning contractors working on the city multi-million pound Lisnagelvin RUC station that they had been identified and would be attacked if they continued. Work stopped immediately. That same month Charles English, who had had escaped narrowly when Eddie McSheffrey died, was killed when a grenade he was firing at the RUC exploded prematurely. McGuinness personally placed the black beret and gloves of the IRA on the coffin before linking arms with Martin Galvin of Noraid to carry it.

The next move against the builders came around 7 August when McGuinness, in his capacity as OC Northern Command and de facto head of the IRA, attended a meeting in Dublin with Sean O'Callaghan, then joint OC of Southern Command, Kevin Mallon, the nominal Chief of Staff, Kevin McKenna and another man whom we shall refer to as Burke. They discussed the fate of Seamus McAvoy, a wealthy builder originally from Coalisland in Co. Tyrone, who lived in Dublin and was supplying Portacabins to the RUC. McAvoy had been approached by Kevin Mallon and asked to cooperate by contributing money and intelligence to the IRA but had refused. O'Callaghan said, 'At that meeting Martin McGuinness ordered McAvoy's murder.' On 20 August the order was carried out under the direction of Burke, the OC of the IRA in Dublin, and McAvoy was shot dead at his home in Eglinton Road, Donnybrook, Dublin. O'Callaghan, who was the Irish government's most highly-placed agent within the IRA, had reported the plot to his handler. It was, after all, the first time it had happened, but it was not to be the last. McGuinness was determined to stamp out 'collaboration' and to ensure that police bases damaged in IRA attacks were not easily rebuilt.

In September the arrival of Tom King as Secretary of State to replace Hurd was greeted with a concerted mortaring campaign against such bases – 18 shells rained down on Enniskillen RUC training depot alone, and in Derry a British soldier was gunned down in the Waterside. There was also a brief return to commercial bombing in Derry, all part of an attempt to assert the IRA's profile as Margaret Thatcher and Garret Fitzgerald, the Taoiseach, finalised their negotiations on the Anglo-Irish Agreement. The British intended the pact, which was concluded in December, as a means of rewarding constitutional nationalism and isolating Sinn Féin. McGuinness believed that the Agreement, which gave the Irish Republic consultative powers in Northern Ireland and established a joint secretariat of British and Irish civil servants at Maryfield outside Belfast, had been helped along by the continued pressure of IRA violence. The Unionists, who had a similar analysis, were maddened and proclaimed it a staging post to a united Ireland, a proposition that Sinn Féin found intriguing. On 15 December all 15 Unionist MPs resigned their seats in protest intending to turn the by-elections into a referendum on the pact.

Sinn Féin desperately needed to put itself in a position to capitalise on the pressure that IRA violence created instead of seeing it contribute to concessions like these for Hume. Adams and McGuinness wanted to modernise the party by dropping abstentionism, the principle of not recognising or taking seats in any elected assemblies apart from the councils. However, O Bradaigh, O Conaill and the rest of the old guard jealously guarded the principle. They defeated a motion to have it removed at that year's Ard Fheis but in the coming year the Adams/McGuinness leadership were determined to change the policy. Making progress against them would mean keeping the IRA hardliners happy and plans were already afoot to equip the organisation with the means to escalate its campaign.

CHAPTER TWELVE

Trials

Don't worry, it will all be worked out, the Provos are not as bad as the Brits.'
Martin McGuinness to Rose Hegarty

As 1985 closed, Martin McGuinness was held on a seven-day detention order in Castlereagh interrogation centre where he was questioned about the murder of Kurt Konig and other serious crimes. 'He never said a word, he seldom does,' recalls one officer who dealt with him on that occasion. As usual, the officer tried every technique he could: expressing sympathy for the position of Catholics in Derry, talking about the hardships of families without a father, dead or in prison, and commenting on McGuinness' political achievements. 'The main thing was to evoke a reaction, to try to get a point of contact,' he said.

McGuinness was at his disingenuous best a few days later when he expressed surprise that interviews concentrated on his status in the republican movement and his position as an elected representative. This he said, was a tactic to disrupt the Sinn Féin effort in the 15 Westminster by-elections caused when Unionists resigned their seats in protest at the Anglo-Irish Agreement. In fact, the elections, from which Sinn Féin emerged with a low vote, were far from the minds of his interrogators who were focused instead on the efforts of the IRA to escalate its campaign in the run up to the 1986 Sinn Féin Ard Fheis and the first IRA Army Convention in 17 years.

McGuinness personally supervised the Derry IRA's first major success of

1987 when, on 23 March, they gunned down Leslie Jarvis, in Magee College car park. A soft and unsuspecting target, Jarvis was shot to bait a trap – he had taught leatherwork to inmates in Magilligan prison and the IRA claimed they killed him because of the 'violent and inhumane regime at Magilligan'.

Charlie Coogan, an IRA volunteer, takes up the story. 'Two brothers from the Waterside went in and killed him – they took his briefcase and put another one there with a bomb in it. When the cops came, two of them were blown up. Everybody was on the other side of the road watching as the bomb went off. Two cops standing against the wall and soldiers running around, they didn't know if they were coming or going. McGuinness was in the house opposite watching everything.' Coogan added, 'He quite often liked to be close when things went off to watch and see how they react, it was part of his strategy, his way of refining operations.' McGuinness was well satisfied. The two men who died examining the briefcase were Austin Wilson and John Bennison, a Detective-Inspector and a Detective-Sergeant. At IRA meetings in Derry, volunteers were encouraged to come up with ideas for operations. Coogan recalls, 'When you came up with something you would get the plan back with a lot of changes in it. That would be from what Martin had seen on previous occasions.'

At Easter, McGuinness organised a paramilitary stunt. As journalists left a press conference in the Creggan, where he had briefed them on plans for the banned Easter Parade, they were greeted by eleven hooded men and one woman brandishing weapons including a grenade launcher. They announced 'We will attack, as and when we wish, each and every manifestation of British rule in our country.' Afterwards, two bombs were hurled, to little effect, at Rosemount police station. A Noraid delegation was in the city at the time.

The Army Convention, a representative conference of IRA members and leaders, was called to consider allowing Sinn Féin to take seats in the Dail, the Irish Republic's Parliament. The Sinn Féin Ard Fheis would, a short time later, have to consider the same issue and much of McGuinness' year was spent travelling around the country trying to ensure that the proposal got the required two-thirds majority without producing a major split. IRA rules forbade members even to discuss the taking of seats and this issue, abstentionism, had been the stated reason for the earlier split from the Officials. When McGuinness attended preparatory conventions held throughout the country to select delegates, he took the opportunity to convince the key figures that the armed struggle would not suffer as a result of the new focus on politics. The Libyan supply route allowed him to counter criticisms that Sinn Féin was leaching resources away from the IRA and that the leadership was going soft.

Kevin McKenna was titular Chief of Staff but, his health problems compounded by alcoholism, left McGuinness in practical control as OC Northern Command and overseer of operations. McKenna provided cover for McGuinness, whose position allowed him to approve operations and then supply brigades with the means to carry them out. Criticism of the political direction would be muted as long as he could continue to deliver.

The Libyan weapons were McGuinness' ace in the hole and he entrusted Frank Hegarty, the FRU agent, with the task of establishing transit dumps along the border with which to supply Fermanagh, Tyrone, Derry and other areas in the west of the Province. McGuinness himself took Hegarty on a tour of supporters in the Sligo/Leitrim area who would help establish hiding places. In doing so, he ignored warnings from other republicans about the agent. An Official IRA leader said, 'I personally told McGuinness that he was an informer as far back as 1975. We had caught him meeting his handler and beat him up'.

When Hegarty told Brian, his handler, where the first 100 rifles were hidden, the FRU planned to monitor the weapons, trace them to their intended users and eventually make arrests in Northern Ireland. This would divert suspicion from Hegarty and, if the IRA resupplied, the cycle might be repeated indefinitely. It was what Special Branch refers to as 'turning a few tricks'.

Things might have proceeded according to plan if the dumps had been in Northern Ireland where covert observation posts, laser devices or hidden cameras could have been set up. Individual weapons could even have been fitted with tracking devices and 'jarked' to make them misfire. The difficulty was that the dumps were in the Republic where the British intelligence services could not deploy, and where the local security forces did not have the capacity to carry out such ambitious monitoring operations.

The matter was considered by a cabinet sub-committee. The danger of losing control of the weapons was obvious, and clear benefits were seen in tipping off the Irish authorities. The fact that Thatcher was secretly preparing to back Ronald Reagan in the bombing of Tripoli made it a golden opportunity to produce hard evidence of Libyan sponsorship for terror. It also strengthened the Anglo-Irish Agreement by providing a practical instance of Anglo-Irish security cooperation. The final decision to lift the transit dumps and expose Hegarty was taken by Thatcher herself.

On Sunday, 26 January the Gardai moved in and made their biggest ever arms haul: 95 rifles, including 87 Kalashnikovs, a box of Taurus pistols and 21,560 rounds of assorted ammunition. One ammunition pack bore the inscription 'Libyan Armed Forces – cartridges for weapons'. Tom King, then Northern Ireland Secretary, praised the Gardai, and the find provided the ideal backdrop for the Republic's decision, a few weeks later, to sign the European Convention on the Suppression of Terrorism.

The night before the Garda raid, Hegarty was with his widowed mother Rose when he received a call and left in a hurry. Rose assumed it was something to do with greyhounds but, instead, it was his handlers who picked him up a short distance away and took him to their debriefing suite at Ebrington barracks. From the start he expressed a deep sense of betrayal that the weapons were to be lifted and resisted the idea of leaving Derry, his mother and his familiar surroundings. He had little choice, however, and that evening Hegarty told Dorothy Robb, his partner, that he would have to leave Derry for a while. He slipped out quietly at first light so as not to wake her. After a pick-up on the Foyle bridge, he left from Aldergrove military airport aboard the Secretary of State's jet to England where he stayed initially at naval accommodation in Chatham and later at a house in Sittingbourne, Kent.

Ingram, who had finished his tour of duty in Derry, was briefly appointed to guard Hegarty. He found him to be 'quite a likeable guy who was set in his ways' and recalls 'we talked about Derry and how much he missed it. I asked him if he would return and he said he would at some stage. I reported this, of course, and he seemed convinced he could talk his way out of it. He was also resentful of Brian, his handler, who he felt had done the dirty on him by letting the weapons be lifted.' In a bid to calm him, it was agreed that Robb should join Hegarty in Sittingbourne and the couple were offered a new home, plus one hundred thousand pounds to help them resettle permanently in England. When she turned down the offer and returned to Derry, Hegarty was moved to Brighton for fear he would be compromised. He was already ringing his mother every few days to test the water for a return home. He offered Rose little explanation, saying he didn't know where he was or who he was with.

By now McGuinness suspected that he had another supergrass on his hands and he started visiting Rose, who lived with her unmarried daughter Martina. He soon persuaded Rose to allow him to talk to her son and at least one of the calls was recorded in Brighton with Frank's agreement. As he had done with Gilmour, McGuinness claimed that everything could be sorted out if Frank would only come home and talk. He accepted Hegarty's explanation that he had nothing to do with the arms find and had moved away because he was worried he might be blamed for it and was now under pressure from British agents. In reality his FRU minders were unarmed and had no power to hold him. After just a week in Brighton, on Friday, 24 April 1986, Hegarty walked out on them, giving the excuse that he was going to place a bet. He arrived at his mother's home the following evening. McGuinness soon appeared, saying he had heard Hegarty was back and he would like to speak to him. The family were suspicious and kept Frank hidden in an upstairs bedroom, but, after about four days of discussions, they became convinced of McGuinness' goodwill. When Frank signed an affidavit pledging never to give evidence in court and asserting that any information he had given was under duress, McGuinness appeared convinced the IRA would accept it.

In order to tie up the deal, Martina agreed to drive Frank across the border and drop him at a pub car park in Buncrana, Co. Donegal to straighten things out with the Provos. Next day McGuinness visited Rose and assured her that her son was safe. He said he had just left Frank making short work of a Chinese carry-out in Donegal. They all smiled. 'Don't worry,' McGuinness assured her, 'I will bring him home to you.' It was a ruse. On 25 May Frank's body was found on Cavanagh Road, Castlederg. He was wearing a fawn jacket, grey sweater, blue shirt, blue jeans and sports shoes. His hands were bound behind his back, his eyes were taped and there were bullet wounds in the back of his head. According to police and republican sources, Hegarty had been interrogated by Thomas 'Slab' Murphy and Kevin McKenna, but was killed with the approval of McGuinness. On the anniversary of Hegarty's death his family still place a notice in the *Derry Journal* saying that Frank was 'betrayed by the Judas goat'. The reference is to goats kept in Middle Eastern abattoirs for the purpose of leading sheep to the slaughter pen.

McGuinness commented in *The Long War*, a BBC film, 'if a republican activist who knows what the repercussions are for going over to the other side, in fact goes over to the other side, then they, more than anybody else, are totally and absolutely aware of what the penalty for doing that is.' 'Death?' asked the interviewer. 'Death certainly,' replied McGuinness. He later denied making any promises to the family or giving them false comfort.

The Provos could not tolerate dissent. In May 1987 they published a pamphlet entitled *A Scenario for Peace*, which called for British withdrawal followed by an all-Ireland conference and suggested that 'anyone unwilling to accept a united Ireland and wishing to leave would be offered resettlement grants'. They also launched another attack on the Hume family. Pat Hume, the SDLP leader's wife, remembers that 'all the windows were simultaneously hit and the front door was hit and my car was destroyed with petrol bombs. They tried first to shatter the windows with ball bearings, which we found in the garden the following day, but because the windows were security windows, the ball bearings didn't penetrate.'

Hegarty was not the only agent who McGuinness trusted. Another was Declan 'Beano' Casey, a Strabane man who was the IRA's quartermaster in West Tyrone and who remembers McGuinness regularly coming down to sanction operations and bring money for men on the run. Local sources put the figure at about four hundred pounds a week. Casey, who counted bomb-making among his skills, remembers being brought to a barn in Donegal and shown up to 500 rifles in cases which bore Libyan stamps, as well as rocket launchers, grenades and ammunition waiting to be dispersed.

Donegal was also used for strategy meetings which McGuinness used to flush out opposition. One republican recalls a series of meetings which McGuinness superintended in the run up to the Sinn Féin Ard Fheis. He said, 'the meetings were held in houses which were more like barns. People met in different rooms to discuss documents and McGuinness would have walked around the different rooms to hear what people were saying but no vote was taken. Both issues were discussed – elections and the campaign – and what would happen if there was a conflict. Most people felt we would not have got so far without the military strategy.'

One area McGuinness cultivated was East Tyrone where, under the leadership of Paddy Kelly, the IRA was cooperating with South Armagh in a 'war-winning strategy'. They aimed to create a 'liberated zone' between the border to the Clogher Valley in which crown personnel could not operate and where the IRA could develop new weapons and create bases from which to strike outwards.

In April, South Armagh asserted their control by blowing up Sir Maurice Gibson, the Chief Justice, and his wife, Lady Cecily, as they travelled along the main Dublin to Belfast road.

Another arm of the strategy was the destruction of RUC bases and the assassination of building contractors who attempted to reconstruct them. A recent victim was Harry Henry, whose brother's firm carried out work for the security forces. He was put up against a wall outside his home in Magherafelt and shot by an IRA firing squad.

Unknown to the terrorists, the Det, acting under RUC instruction, had launched a 'tech attack' by placing a listening device in premises used by Gerard Harte, OC of Mid Tyrone. As a result, it was learned that an assault, similar to one that had been launched on a police base in the Birches the previous year, was planned against Loughgall RUC station and Jim Lynagh, a top assassin who ran cross-border operations from Monaghan, was placed under surveillance.

Lynagh and Kelly's plan was to neutralise perimeter security by dropping a bomb over the fence from the claws of a digger and then to open fire on those inside. After consultation with Tom King, the Secretary of State, Operation Judy was launched to foil the attack. When the IRA unit, including Kelly and Lynagh, arrived at 7.20 p.m. on 8 May, 24 SAS soldiers opened up from all sides with machine guns, rifles and pistols. In all, eight IRA men were killed along with one civilian, Anthony Hughes, who happened to be driving through the killing ground wearing a boiler suit. The volunteers who perished were regarded as being among the most militant members of the IRA and the weapons recovered on the scene had been used in at least nineteen attacks, including seven murders. McGuinness is still, at the time of writing, supporting their relatives in their call for a public enquiry.

It was a devastating blow, particularly since there were damaging, though erroneous, suggestions from some of the bereaved that the 'Loughgall Martyrs', as they became known, had been sacrificed by the Adams/McGuinness leadership to facilitate the move into politics. The impact on the campaign, and on McGuinness' credibility as the man who directed it, was potentially severe. The IRA had suffered its worst casualties in any single incident since 1921 and for the rest of the year their operations would have a note of ruthless desperation.

In Derry, McGuinness' old adversary John Hume came under renewed pressure. He recalls 'They burned the brakes on my car. I didn't know it had happened but by sheer chance the first time I had to use my brakes was when I was going down my own street. I went on and hit the car in front of me. Had I been driving on a main road and tried to work my brakes, I would have been driving at 50 or 60 miles an hour instead of going down the street. When I took it into the garage, they said, "oh your brakes have been burned." I believe they [the IRA] were trying to get me to move out of the area.'

All summer, there were loyalist protests against the Anglo-Irish Agreement and the Assembly collapsed in June, with the UUP, SDLP and Sinn Féin all boycotting it. These were favourable circumstances for the IRA convention, suggesting, as they did, that Northern Ireland was still ungovernable and could be further destabilised. McGuinness talked tough, 'Freedom can only be gained at the point of an IRA rifle and I apologise to no one for saying that we support and admire the freedom fighters of the IRA,' he told the *Irish News* in June, while the IRA searched out soft targets and issued renewed threats against contractors working for the security forces. In Derry, professionals, such as clergy or doctors, who visited security bases, were warned that they should place signs on their vehicles to avoid attack. Next day the IRA shot dead an electrician, Mervyn Bell, who they claimed had been working on a UDR base.

The IRA had larger ambitions. Tom Murphy met Al Ashour, his Libyan contact, at least seven times after the bombing of Tripoli took place on 28 April. After giving the Libyan a gift of a German-Shepherd dog on behalf of Joe Cahill, and transporting furniture for Al Ashour he had secured the most significant arms shipment yet – 150 tons. It was to include 20 surface-to-air missiles. Hopkins, the skipper, later stated, 'I transmitted a message to Tom [Murphy] via a shipping company in London. I used a code word which indicated the unloading date, 29 October 1987.'

The Army Convention was held under the cover of an Irish language gathering in Co. Meath on 14 October and, against this background, McGuinness' proposal sailed through with, as an IRA statement trumpeted, 'more than the required two-thirds majority'. As part of the price for the support of the hardliners, there would be no restrictions placed on local units, and McGuinness was given overall charge of the military campaign at both Northern Command and Army Council. Now McGuinness and other

IRA members were free to advocate the taking of seats in any parliament and to support any Sinn Féin candidates who won seats in the Dail.

The next day, two charges of conspiracy to murder against Willie McGuinness were dropped and a day later, in another minor victory for the McGuinness clan, *Real Lives*, the controversial 1985 BBC documentary profiling McGuinness and another Assembly member, Gregory Campbell of the Ulster Unionist Party, was shown for the first time. A couple of days later, on 20 October, McGuinness was arrested and held for two days by Gardai at Smithborough, Co. Monaghan near McKenna's home. He was on his way back from the first meeting of the new Army Council which had confirmed his position.

At the Ard Fheis, McGuinness could now speak for the IRA. The old O Bradaigh leadership had been rallying opposition and, while Adams spoke of flexibility, he went on the attack, accusing them of refusing to 'come to terms with this leadership's criticisms of the disgraceful attitude adopted by them during the disastrous 18-month ceasefire in the mid 1970s'. In a final contemptuous thrust he spat, 'if you allow yourselves to be led out of the hall today the only place you are going is home. You will be walking away from the struggle.' Joe Cahill supported him, admitting he had been wrong to oppose abstentionism before, and McGuinness easily carried the day. O Conaill and O Bradaigh, however, led a walkout to form their own Republican Sinn Féin Party. Sean Keenan, who joined them, later said McGuinness had tried to win him over by asking, 'do you really think I would take a seat in Stormont?' With the organisation firmly in the hands of Adams (the Sinn Féin President) and McGuinness (Vice President), the new leadership began to scale down expectations. On 10 December, Adams launched *The Politics of Irish Freedom*, a book setting out his political strategy, which McGuinness now broadly shared. He spoke of pulling the republican movement out of 'many years of stagnation' and stopping the SDLP from reaping the political rewards of IRA pressure on the British. The key phrases were a description of the IRA campaign as 'armed propaganda' and an assertion that 'the armed struggle is itself a tactic . . . one cannot shoot or bomb a United Ireland into existence.' The campaign was no longer the be-all and end-all, it was more a means of keeping the Brits' attention and vetoing change which did not have Sinn Féin's approval.

Adams had warned that electoral gains were not automatic: He was proved correct in January 1987, when Sinn Féin fielded 29 candidates in the

Irish general election but lost 24 deposits, emerging with 1.7 per cent of the vote and no seats. Dropping abstentionism was not enough – Sinn Féin was still seen as a 'Brits Out' party and the violence imposed a low ceiling on their support in the Republic.

McGuinness involved himself in a year-long running battle with the RUC and the Catholic hierarchy over paramilitary displays, such as the presence of masked volunteers and the firing of shots, at republican funerals.

In March the Provos put down a marker by detonating a no-warning 100 lb car bomb at Roselawn cemetery as the cortège of Reserve Constable Peter Nesbitt, who had been murdered by an earlier bomb in Ardoyne, passed by. Two officers were injured in the blast and the IRA issued a statement warning police, 'if you want to bury your dead in peace then keep a dignified distance from the funerals of nationalists and republicans.'

McGuinness was involved in angry stand-offs at the funerals of Larry Marley, dubbed 'Papillon' from his days in the Maze, who was shot by loyalists, and Finbar McKenna, an IRA volunteer who died when a blast-bomb he had thrown at a Belfast RUC station bounced back on top of him. Marley's funeral was postponed twice as mourners clashed with police and McGuinness used the oration to make a scathing attack on Cahal Daly, the Bishop of Down and Connor, and Cardinal Thomas O Fiaich both of whom he compared to Pontius Pilate for refusing to back him. However there was to be one more funeral clash that year, and this time it was one that McGuinness would win.

The occasion was the burial, in November, of two of his most experienced volunteers – Paddy 'Nelson' Deery and Eddie McSheffrey, who died when a bomb they were transporting exploded prematurely. McGuinness pressurised the church to hold a requiem mass against the directions of Bishop Edward Daly whom he accused of 'colluding with the British government against the IRA'. To avoid trouble, the coffins, complete with paramilitary trappings, were admitted to the church to prevent a scene. A priest then asked police to pull back to allow the cortege to leave but when they did so the IRA broke its undertaking and fired a volley outside the church.

Within months the whole question of funerals would reach a dreadful denouement, but there were more immediate problems. In October, the long awaited shipment from Libya carrying 150 tons of weapons, the largest consignment ever sent to the IRA, aboard the *Eksund*, was arrested by

French Customs. According to Adrian Hopkins, the Captain who made a full statement to the French, it was the fifth consignment he had taken to Ireland – the other four had carried 240 tons of weapons. His statement, when it was supplied to the British and Irish authorities, would provide the basis for all future estimates of the IRA arsenal. There was more than enough to supply the IRA for years to come, but the loss of the *Eksund* hit at the quality as well as the quantity of their weaponry. It had carried not only SAM missiles, but also the coded cards needed to fire those supplied in previous shipments.

Although the launchers and warheads were often put on display for publicity purposes they were largely useless. With the cards they would have lifted the IRA campaign onto an entirely new plane, enabling it to take down helicopters and aircraft, bringing the dream of a liberated zone along the border a step nearer to reality. By the end of the year up to four IRA units would be arrested in Belfast, many of them clearly on good pre-emptive intelligence. The deaths and the *Eksund* had already made 1987, which McGuinness had begun with such high ambitions, a year of disappointments.

The Gardai started an immediate search for the Libyan weapons and had early successes in turning up two purpose-built underground bunkers, one complete with a firing range and accommodation for volunteers, prepared in order to receive the weapons. The Irish government then amended its extradition legislation to close most of the loopholes the IRA had exploited in the past.

The IRA's growing desperation to strike was to produce still worse tragedy. Fermanagh units, seeking revenge for Loughgall and for the treatment of IRA funerals, were given permission by Martin McGuinness, who was in overall command of both the Army Council and Northern Command, to attack a number of Remembrance Day ceremonies in the hope of catching UDR or British Army personnel. Two were defused, but the third detonated, killing 11 civilians at the cenotaph in Enniskillen. The most damaging aspect of the massacre for the IRA was the televised statement by Gordon Wilson, a local draper whose daughter Marie had died holding his hand beneath the rubble. In his statement Wilson said that he forgave the killers and that he wanted no revenge. Wilson's magnanimity shamed the terrorists on both sides, making it impossible for loyalists to hit back at innocent Catholics and equally impossible for the IRA to justify the carnage.

McGuinness' first reaction was denial. An IRA statement, authorised by him, claimed that the bomb had been a radio device which was set off by British Army scanners. It was later shown to have been detonated by a simple timer. Sinn Féin's electoral hopes were dashed in Fermanagh for more than a decade and the wave of revulsion hit Provisional support everywhere. McGuinness later told the BBC, 'It was a total and absolute disaster. I felt absolutely gutted by it. I felt this would be damaging to our strategy in trying to build Sinn Féin as a political party.'

Enniskillen carried a personal price for McGuinness. Police raided his house on 26 November but did not find him at home, and the atrocity also spurred on a stalker. Michael Stone, a freelance loyalist assassin had been shown intelligence files by John McMichael of the UDA that named McGuinness as OC of Northern Command, the man with the final say on IRA operations. Stone was determined to kill him. The Provos had their own man in the UDA. Jimmy Craig, the organisation's head of racketeering was a career criminal who lined his pockets with protection money he extorted from builders for loyalist prisoners. He also had an IRA handler who lived in the Unity Flats area of Belfast to whom he reported regularly in return for favours.

McMichael was investigating Craig for corruption and Craig had told the IRA that McMichael was behind an unsuccessful attempt on Gerry Adams' life. Craig possibly passed on a warning about McGuinness too, or it may have come from McGuinness' own contacts. Either way, he changed his movements and the IRA murdered McMichael, using an under-car booby trap that went off as he left home for a UDA meeting on 22 December. Thanks to Craig, IRA intelligence had been precise, but eliminating McMichael did not remove the threat to McGuinness. Stone was now on autopilot.

CHAPTER THIRTEEN

Turning Point

I am not saying that the IRA have the ability to drive every last British soldier out of Derry, Armagh, Antrim, Down or anywhere else. But they have got the ability to sicken the British forces of occupation.

> Martin McGuinness at the first
> anniversary of the Loughgall Martyrs

The loyalist gunman had nursed his murder plans for months. He knew McGuinness lived near Derry City's grounds at Brandywell, so he wore a team scarf and kicked a football against the wall as he looked for a place to strike. He considered shooting through the bathroom window.

Michael Stone had already murdered three Catholics. The first, Paddy Brady, was a milkman and Sinn Féin member. He was blasted from a range of three feet with a shotgun in 1984. Stone also used a shotgun to murder Kevin McPolin, who was waiting in a parked car for his work to open when Stone emptied both barrels into him. His last victim was Dermot Hackett, who was driving a Mother's Pride bread van when Stone drew up alongside and sprayed it with a machine gun.

McGuinness was a tougher challenge than these unsuspecting victims; studying the files the UDA had given him, Stone worked up a visceral hatred of his new quarry. He explained how he felt to UTV, 'it was that tweed jacket with the leather elbow pads and his pathetic attempts at disguise, his black and white photographs in police custody and with the round glasses and the hair greased back, that wavy hair, and it sticking up all over the place, you know?'

He watched McGuinness as he walked his daughter Fionnuala, 'a wee blonde girl, really wee skinny kid', to school and honed his hatred as he thought of the children who had been injured in Enniskillen. He would have shot McGuinness there and then, he claimed, if his daughter had not been so close. The next place he tried was a paper shop near Bishop's Gate, where he saw McGuinness buying the *Sunday Times* and *The Observer*, but he dropped that idea when an unexpected army patrol passed.

Stone remembered the IRA's tactic of murdering Constable Peter Nesbitt, and then bombing his funeral. That gave him the idea to kill a republican in a rural area, to draw McGuinness and Adams to the funeral. 'Why should I chase them?' he reasoned. 'I'll make them come to me instead.' Councillor John Joe Davey, a 60-year-old from Magherafelt, was chosen as bait, but Stone conceded that 'It was a bit of a cock-up, you know, the man got away.' Davey, who was later assassinated by the UVF, spotted the gunmen standing in the lane, stalled his car, rolled out the door and ran away. His would-be killers fired a few shots before scattering. The UDA now doubted Stone's abilities.

Fate took a hand on 6 March, when the SAS shot dead three Belfast-born IRA members in Gibraltar. The dead were Mairead Farrell, former OC of women prisoners in the Maze; Dan McCann, the Belfast Brigade's Explosives Officer, and Sean Savage, one of his staff. A fourth member of the team, another Belfast bomber named Siobhan O'Hanlon, was not present but had earlier reconnoitred the changing of the guard ceremony in Gibraltar. All four were attached to GHQ staff and lived in the Republic before travelling as an ASU to southern Spain. There, McCann and Savage assembled a car bomb using 140 lb of Semtex to detonate at the ceremony. They then drove into Gibraltar with Farrell in another car which they left parked to reserve a place for the bomb. The three of them were walking, unarmed, towards Gibraltar's single border crossing when they were gunned down. SAS soldiers later said they had been briefed that the ASU might be carrying radio detonation devices and believed they were reaching for them before they opened fire. This briefing made no sense: if the bomb had been detonated by radio, the colony would have been sealed and the bombers trapped. A timer set to coincide with the ceremony would, on the other hand, have allowed the IRA members to cross safely to Spain before any hue and cry started.

Many nationalists in Northern Ireland believed that the Gibraltar Three had been murdered and could have been arrested, but in Britain public opinion was so strongly opposed to them that the bodies had to be flown in through Dublin and moved by road to Belfast. Stone told police 'I knew big funerals were coming up after Gibraltar, and top Provisionals – Adams, McGuinness and them boys – would all be at them. I decided to blow them away. I knew I might not make it.' In any case McGuinness's presence had been flagged up in advance by a media ruckus when Jenny McGeever, an RTE journalist, was suspended for breaching Section 31 of the Irish Broadcasting Act by including comments from McGuinness on a morning news package. He had been telling journalists about arrangements for the funeral.

The UDA refused to provide back-up and told Stone the funeral would be too crowded for a successful attack, so he went ahead on his own. Security was low-key because the RUC had agreed, following representations from Bishop Cahal Daly, to have a minimal police presence at the funeral to avoid a repeat of the undignified scenes at the interments of Marley and McKenna.

When 16 March dawned, Stone stuffed grenades and guns into a holster belt and stuck spare bullets in his pockets. He had a woollen 'monkey hat' which doubled as a balaclava, but he never used it. He later told police, 'I said bye-bye to the wife and kids and I kissed them,' before travelling by bus and taxi to the requiem service at St Agnes' church. There he had an opportunity to shoot Adams, but decided to wait for McGuinness. A number of people who had met him in city centre bars greeted him as he approached the Republican Plot but even these close shaves did not galvanise him into action. He was in a world of his own, wondering whether, if he was killed, his funeral would be like this one. It was only as McCann's coffin was lowered into the ground that, he later told Martin Dillon, 'I suddenly realised I had blown it and should have taken Adams and the others out as they walked into the cemetery.' He told police 'once they started the speeches, I got two grenades out. I threw them over the mourners on to the Republican Plot. I wanted to get the right ones, the ones with the berets and the flags.' Father Alec Reid, who was praying at the graveside, thought he was throwing stones. He hoped to scatter the IRA colour party to get a clear shot at Adams and McGuinness, and he shouted 'come on', challenging them to approach him. Instead, McGuinness dived for cover behind a tombstone. According to Stone, 'I pulled the Browning pistol. Straight in front of me was women and children. I aimed above them. I wanted to kill the main Republicans, not the women and the children.' The crowd gave chase shouting 'Orange Bastard' and 'I, I, IRA' as Stone ran downhill along the perimeter fence towards the M1 motorway. McGuinness wisely kept behind the hundreds of pursuers. He told the BBC, 'I saw him taking off, then I took off after him but I was behind the other people who themselves had charged after him. As they ran after him he was firing shots at them and he was throwing hand grenades.' Towards the front of the pursuers was Paddy Flood, a tall gangling man known as 'Camel' Flood, one of McGuinness' main bomb-makers in Derry. Unlike his leader, he was wounded by shrapnel from a grenade.

On the motorway, the last of Stone's seven Russian-made fragmentation grenades slipped out of his hands and exploded on the ground as he vainly attempted to stop passing cars. When the mourners caught up with him he was felled and bundled into a car but, luckily for him, proceedings were being monitored from Andersonstown police station and an RUC Land-Rover was shortly on the scene to arrest him. When the police told him he had killed at least two mourners he replied 'Brilliant', adding that he would have done more damage if his pistol hadn't jammed. In fact there were three deaths: Thomas McErlean (20), John Murray (26), and Caoimhin MacBradaigh (30). They left four orphans. There were two widows, one of them pregnant.

The funeral of MacBradaigh, the only IRA member to die, provided a glimpse of what might have lain in store for Stone. Derek Wood and Robert Howes, both off-duty corporals of the Royal Signals Regiment, drove into the massive cortège and, assuming that it was another loyalist attack, the crowd dragged them from their car, stripped them and beat them. After the initial panic, the IRA identified them, beat them again, took them to waste-ground and shot them dead. In a statement it was claimed that the two young men, who had produced their personal protection weapons and fired a single shot in the air, were working undercover. Howes had just arrived in Northern Ireland and it seems likely that Wood was taking him on a tour of the trouble spots when they blundered into the path of the funeral.

Amidst all the anger and fear that day, Father Alec Reid knelt, weeping, beside a naked and bleeding soldier on the Andersonstown Road. A friend of Adams, Reid had for some time been trying to draw the Provos into the

Catholic nationalist mainstream. He had arranged talks between Adams and Cardinal O Fiaich and he briefed Charles Haughey, the Taoiseach, on progress. In January he wrote to Hume and Adams suggesting that they meet to develop 'an overall political strategy to establish peace and justice in Ireland'. It was a lot to ask Hume. Over the years he had been treated as an enemy by McGuinness' IRA followers in Derry and even his children had been harassed at school. His wife Pat recalled, 'there were various years in the '80s that the house was petrol-bombed and the walls were daubed and car paint put on the windows. We usually didn't publicise it because you were only giving it attention. When John would make statements criticising violence they wrote up things like "Hume Traitor."'

Hume nevertheless agreed to the meetings which involved delegations from Sinn Féin and the SDLP. McGuinness, whose presence would have been a liability, chaired a monitoring committee, while Mitchell McLaughlin joined the Sinn Féin talks team. Hume's position was that violence against the British was futile, it had failed to dislodge them and, in any case, they were now a neutral force who, as Article One of the Anglo-Irish Agreement specified, were willing to facilitate Irish unity if a majority in Northern Ireland ever wanted it. He argued that, since unilateral British withdrawal was likely to produce civil war, persuading the unionists was the only way to achieve republican objectives. While Hume accepted 'the right of the Irish people to self determination', by now a Sinn Féin mantra, he redefined it, saying that the Irish people were divided on how to exercise this right and that their divisions must be resolved by dialogue in a peaceful atmosphere. He refused to cooperate with Sinn Féin politically while violence continued, but he suggested that if it ended, Haughey would convene a conference of all parties to agree how self-determination could be implemented. Whether or not the unionists attended, this would provide Sinn Féin with an entrée to the political process.

Haughey backed Hume and even opened up his own tentative secret discussions with Sinn Féin, which were conducted by Dermot Ahern, a Co. Louth TD (Irish equivalent of MP), and Martin Mansergh, his special adviser on Northern Ireland. McLaughlin also attended these two meetings, which took place at the Redemptorist Monastery in Dundalk during March and June 1988. Like the SDLP contacts, they were predicated on the idea that real progress would follow a ceasefire and this was something which, McGuinness repeatedly spelt out, the IRA was not ready for.

Speaking in Milltown at Easter, McGuinness dashed the hopes of Austin Currie, a member of the SDLP team, that the talks might result in 'a permanent end of military and violent activity'. He told the annual 1916 commemoration, 'the IRA position on ceasefires has been on record for a long time: No more ceasefires. Talk can take place but the war will go on.' He then read out an IRA statement telling Britain, 'we will demoralise you. We will make your six counties into a millstone which will strangle you. We will eventually defeat you. Our strategy is clear. It is to sap the political will of the British government and British people to remain in Ireland. The means are by limited guerrilla warfare against crown forces.' McGuinness dismissed the SDLP as 'the linchpin of British government strategy' adding, 'our strategy has been to close down every option until the British realise they can do nothing else but leave. The SDLP has contrived to bale out the British by allowing them to believe that an internal solution may be possible.' He made it clear that the IRA did not regard the SDLP as an acceptable go-between with Tom King, the Secretary of State, 'The IRA is quite capable of talking with Tom King when withdrawal is on the agenda,' he said. At another rally, this time to mark the seventeenth anniversary of internment in August, he referred to the IRA's recent success in murdering three British soldiers in Europe and said, 'it shows the ability of the IRA to bring about a final victory in Ireland. We see the continental battalions in Holland, Germany, in Belgium and London as freedom fighters. They speak with one voice. It is the only voice the British understand.'

Although McGuinness denied rumours of a dispute between himself and Adams, there was a difference in emphasis. By now they both realised that outright military victory was impossible but, where Adams saw violence as 'armed propaganda' to push republican concerns up the political agenda until Britain was forced to negotiate in a peaceful atmosphere, McGuinness saw the continuing slaughter as the means of wearing down Britain's political will to remain in Ireland. For him, negotiation would come after the British conceded that they were going. McGuinness played a convincing hawk to Adams' dove.

IRA 'mistakes' were also getting harder and harder to explain away. 1987 ended with McGuinness being humiliated into denying IRA involvement in the murder of 68-year-old Gerry Doherty in Derry. In March, Gillian Johnston was shot by the IRA, who then issued a statement saying they had meant to kill her brother who, they wrongly claimed, was in the UDR. In

July, two passers-by had been killed by a bomb at Falls Road swimming baths and three members of a single family had been blown up on the Dublin to Belfast Road by a bomb intended for Judge Eoin Higgins. In August, McGuinness characteristically placed the 'fundamental responsibility' on the British, but expressed sympathy with the victims when his IRA men kidnapped a pensioner and placed a booby trap in his flat which killed three neighbours who came to investigate. Paddy Flood had made what became known as the 'Good Neighbours Bomb'. The IRA said it had gone 'tragically wrong' – they had meant to kill a British Army search squad. McGuinness stated solemnly that, 'While the freedom struggle goes on the IRA has a grave responsibility to ensure as much as humanly possible that civilians are not endangered.' The reality was that he and the IRA were prepared to risk civilian lives in order to continue to operate. That October a 70-year-old woman collapsed and died after a mortar attack on an RUC station and in November, a civilian pensioner and his teenage niece were the only fatalities in the van bombing of a Tyrone RUC station.

These 'mistakes' were, in any case, occurring at a time when McGuinness was widening the IRA's list of legitimate targets to take in large swathes of the population. Not only the security forces, but people working for them or supplying them with goods or services were on the list along with loyalist and collaborators. In September, civil servants were added and, to make the point, a bomb was placed at the home of Sir Ken Bloomfield, the head of the Northern Ireland civil service. Even before this addition the Irish Congress of Trades Unions had estimated the number of 'legitimate targets' at over 40,000, and still the IRA kept getting the wrong people.

It was a year in which McGuinness had hoped to make a big military push with the new Libyan weapons and perhaps political cooperation from he SDLP. There were successes, the most notable when eight soldiers travelling in a coach were killed in a land-mine attack in Tyrone in August, but even these tended to produce political isolation. The contacts with the Irish government had been broken off in the summer when it became clear that no ceasefire was on offer and in September the SDLP talks were also concluded without agreement though Hume privately kept in touch with Adams. Publicly Hume, speaking at his party conference, described the Provos as bearing 'all the hallmarks of undiluted fascism'.

The British were incensed when Sinn Féin went on television to publicly justify the Bloomfield bomb and they moved forward measures to ban Sinn

Féin, Republican Sinn Féin and the Ulster Defence Association from the airwaves. From now on their words would have to be read by actors, a restriction which dramatically reduced media enquiries to Sinn Féin, according to Danny Morrison, its publicity director. A similar ban already applied in the republic.

1988 marked a turning point for the IRA and for McGuinness personally, though the implications took some time to become clear. For one thing it was the year in which his criminal record came abruptly to the fore with a forty-five pound fine for speeding in Limavady in May and a hundred pound fine in Derry for causing an obstruction in April. There was a flash of his wit in court in February when he asked a police witness, 'one more question – who gave you that awful haircut?' Since the end of 1984 he had been involved in a series of petty disputes with the police starting with a seventy-five pound fine for assaulting a police officer, when he stamped on his toe, and another forty pound fine for obstruction. There were three more assault charges for incidents in 1985 and two more obstruction convictions, all settled by the payment of fines. 1986,1987 and 1988, up until May, were much the same, with convictions for assault, obstruction and taking part in illegal marches. After that he wasn't as handy with his fists, not even when he was beaten by soldiers on the way to an anti-extradition march in August.

The IRA tried to combat attempts to isolate them with a statement in February 1989 in which they claimed that they had 'stood down' their Fermanagh Unit, responsible for the bombing of Enniskillen, following the murder of a former RUC officer whom they shot claiming he was still a member of the force. McGuinness then approved the text of a soul searching GHQ staff interview in *An Phoblacht Republican News*. It admitted that civilian casualties 'dented the confidence of our supporters' and wondered whether 'the armed struggle is contradicting and undermining the political struggle'. A partial answer came in the Irish general election where Sinn Féin was trashed, emerging with a derisory 1.2 per cent of the vote. The Northern Ireland council elections in May were better but the vote still slipped from 11.8 per cent to 11.2 per cent and the number of seats dropped by 16 to 43 while the SDLP hit an all-time high. This trend was confirmed in the elections to the European parliament in June when Danny Morrison talked of overtaking John Hume but saw the SDLP leader elected on the first count and his own support fall more than four points, or 40,000 votes, to 9.1 per cent. The signs were that the Provos were being pushed back politically and that, militarily, there was what some analysts referred to as a 'plateau of violence' which could continue for years to come.

The IRA continued to strike hard, for instance, murdering two very senior Special Branch officers in South Armagh in March, and, earlier the same month, one of Flood's bombs concealed behind a metal sheet killed two soldiers on the Buncrana Road. Charlie Coogan described the gossip and hype that still surrounded such operations in Derry, 'it was made in Bishop Street and people who were there told me about helping with the circuit testing and that it was under a big sheet of steel at the side of the road. I can remember coming into my uncle and saying, "wait till you hear this coming on the television, listen for a big bang tonight" and, wham, there were two soldiers dead. We all felt good about it, it was a success.'

The IRA responded to the scarcity of British troops on the ground by striking abroad. Their biggest success was the slaughter of 11 soldiers with a bomb in a military band school in Deal, and they mistakenly murdered the German wife of a British soldier in Dortmund. For the British this was punishing but could be contained. In this, the twentieth year since the deployment of troops, all sides were taking stock of the impasse, but for the British the paradigm was still one of security containment and a political settlement working outwards from the centre parties. The main priority was to implement the Anglo-Irish Agreement now that unionist resistance was waning. Gauging republican attitudes was still primarily a matter for the intelligence agencies.

When Adams spoke intriguingly of creating a 'non-armed political movement to work for self-determination', Special Branch started picking up talk of a rethink within republican ranks, particularly of concern on the part of McGuinness about the effect that an unending struggle would have on his daughters. Brian Fitzsimonns, then deputy head of Special Branch and the leading intelligence analyst in Northern Ireland, predicted privately that Adams would eventually end the campaign, but at the same time, Fitzsimmons reckoned that Adams was so cautious of splits that it could take years to work through. In the meantime the IRA would keep up the military pressure.

What was emerging was a search for a way to finish the struggle rather than continue it indefinitely. One communication from a Belfast IRA man on remand in Crumlin Road jail intercepted by Special Branch read, 'hoping that this talk of bringing the armed struggle to a conclusion that

McGuinness and co. are talking about bears fruit as I've thrown the hands up on at least two occasions. But I've an awful feeling this war is set for another decade. Whether we have the ability to break out of the containment the Brits are imposing on the war I think is crucial to the ultimate success/failure of the conflict. At the present I'm not optimistic of our ability to do so.'

In September, McGuinness spent much of his time getting filmed removing British Army barriers from restricted border roads and was arrested for three hours during a visit by Margaret Thatcher to Derry. A 100 lb bomb placed at the gates of the City Cemetery to disrupt the Prime Minister's visit wasn't noticed until the next day when Derry City was due to play a European Cup match against Benfica of Portugal. It was the most prestigious game in the club's history and the device was near Brandywell stadium so the Provos would clearly suffer politically if there was a cancellation. Club officials reached an arrangement with the police allowing McGuinness to defuse the beer keg device and pour the fertiliser mix down a manhole. It underlined the conflict between prosecuting the armed struggle and courting political popularity. Benfica won 2–0.

Northern Ireland Sir Peter Brooke, who read *An Phoblacht/Republican News* each week, as well as listening to security briefings from Sir Hugh Annesley, the new Chief Constable, had decided by September to try and push the debate along. He speculated that the IRA might some day find that, 'considering the lifestyle they have to adopt, the return which they are securing did not justify the costs that it was imposing in personal terms'. If such a debate opened up, he pledged that the government would be 'imaginative' and even compared Northern Ireland to Cyprus prior to British withdrawal.

At the relaunch of a toned-down version of *A Scenario for Peace* McGuinness responded, 'Republicans can take some encouragement from the fact that Brooke said what he did,' but Adams added that Brooke 'should drop any pretence of pre-conditions and he should talk now rather than later'. In a speech in February 1990 he called Brooke 'the first British Secretary of State with some understanding of Irish history' and asked him to specify 'what imaginative steps he would be prepared to take if the armed struggle ceased'. Even after the order excluding him from the mainland UK was extended for three years McGuinness continued to throw bait to the British. He told the *Sunday Correspondent*,'We are prepared to take part in a peace process.'

Boiled down, this was not much different to the three points he laid down in 1972, but the mood music was softer. It was clear that McGuinness was now looking for a peace process that would end the armed struggle, but his price was still high and he was bound to push all the harder militarily to try and force the British to meet it.

A taste of his ruthlessness emerged that month in Derry. Michael Williams, an Englishman who lived with his Derry-born wife Mavis and their 12 children in Creggan, heard screaming. He said, 'At first I thought it was young kids playing so I looked around, but there was nobody on the street . . . I listened a bit more and realised it was coming from my neighbour's living room. She was screaming "get out", "get out". I could hear screaming "don't shoot me, don't shoot me" and I thought "Oh Jesus, this is getting a bit serious."' He concluded she was being robbed and went to a neighbour's house and called the RUC. Instead, the IRA were holding Rose Garnon, an elderly widow, hostage while they hijacked her car. When police caught one member of the gang and recovered an RPG-7 launcher, a warhead and an automatic rifle in the car the IRA responded by branding Williams an informer and demanded an explanation. He agreed to meet them, taking two witnesses, and after they had questioned him for 20 minutes in a fairly friendly way they told him to go. He thought the matter was at an end but Mavis, who remembered Frank Hegarty and Kevin Coyle, persuaded him to leave Derry until the position became clear. Three days later, an IRA punishment squad arrived at her door to shoot him. Bishop Daly took up the case, describing Williams as a Good Samaritan and McGuinness was forced to intervene. He told Mavis flatly, 'I do not in the foreseeable future believe that circumstances will change so dramatically that the IRA could change their position.'

At this stage McGuinness was gaining some leeway in mainstream society. On the strength of his overtures to Brooke, Channel Four used sophisticated lip sync technology to seamlessly dub his words in an April documentary. He was seated amongst the VIPs, yards from Brooke and Annesley, at the funeral of Cardinal Tomas O Fiaich in Armagh Cathedral in June. The celebrant, Bishop Cahal Daly quoted O Fiaich as saying 'Our first step must be to secure an end to the violence,' and urged, 'May those committed to violence listen at last in death to the words of that great Irishman who was Cardinal Tomas O Fiaich.'

That June, at the Easter Commemoration in Creggan cemetery, Williams was still in exile and McGuinness took the opportunity to attack those who campaigned for his return to his family, including the Bishop and the SDLP. He said, 'They don't give a tuppenny damn about Michael Williams. When their allegations that this man has been unfairly treated are decoded they are suggesting that nationalists should give information to the RUC.' He added that Williams had 'made himself an informer'.

On a more hopeful note, he pledged that if assembly elections were held, Sinn Féin would contest them. The quid pro quo was that he had backed proposals to put all necessary resources into the England campaign, which from now on would be handled from South Armagh instead of Dublin. It was the beginning of a strategic alliance with Thomas 'Slab' Murphy which would become increasingly important in the coming years.

CHAPTER FOURTEEN

Judge, Jury and Executioner

There are a lot of people who would like to see an end to the suffering and death, and I am one of them, but we need an honest settlement — and that means a real commitment from Britain to withdraw from this island — before people like me can stand up and call for a truce.

Martin McGuinness, Washington Post, 1 June 1991

Many people involved in terrorism develop the ability to shrug off the grievances of others without undue reflection. When republicans suffer an injury there is a requirement for closure and justice but once an action is taken by the IRA it is time to move on. One example of this is the death of Eoin 'Ta' Morley, from Newry, Co. Down who was shot by the IRA on 16 April 1991. Morley had left the IRA to join the Irish People's Liberation Organisation, a splinter group of the INLA. A republican familiar with the case said, 'If you leave the IRA you are not allowed to join another organisations. On a lot of occasions nobody ever pushed it but in Morley's case the OC did push it.' An armed ASU was sent to abduct him at his girlfriend's home in Newry's Derrybeg Crescent. After they battered down the front door there was a scuffle and Morley made a break for it. As he ran through the front door one of the gang, who was standing in the hall, thought he had grabbed a hand-gun and fired two shots into his back from a Belgian Cal FN rifle. The range was less than six feet and Morley died instantly. His father, David, was once OC of IRA prisoners in the Maze and his mother asked McGuinness to look into the killing, alleging that the unit involved had been drinking and had no reason to open fire. McGuinness promised a 'full enquiry'. It took place in Dundalk's Muirhevna Mor estate. A witness said: 'I happened to be in the bungalow at the time with the people who did the shooting. McGuinness came in and said he was holding an investigation into the death of Eoin Morley. He then asked the people who were involved "were youse drinking?" and the guys were saying "no we don't drink." One man got up to leave and McGuinness said, "sit down Patrick I am finished, I'm quite satisfied." The investigation took something less than ten minutes.' McGuinness told the family that the court of enquiry had uncovered no wrongdoing. A republican source said, 'it was the same story with the Fermanagh Unit who had been stood down for killing civilians, they were returned to active service within two months.' It was a measure of the priority that was attached to the deaths of outsiders and was in marked contrast to the treatment of Michael Williams or even Frank Hegarty who, when all is said and done, had only compromised arms dumps, not human beings.

Paddy Flood, who had come into the IRA via Bogside Republican Youth, was soon to see a tougher side of Provo 'justice'. BRY was a cat's-paw of the IRA but, like Direct Action Against Drugs, its activities were deniable and its members had no say in republican decision making. Instead, they provided a hard core of petrol bombers and rioters. Flood distinguished himself in the BRY, earning the nickname 'Warhead', and graduated to the IRA where he became a bomb-maker. His devices claimed lives and he was a major RUC target. *An Phoblacht/Republican News* carried stories on how he had been forced to delay his wedding and then abandon his honeymoon because of arrests under the Prevention of Terrorism Act. A born scapegoat, Flood craved approval. Charlie Coogan recalls, 'Paddy Flood was a big ugly bastard, nobody really liked him, he was one of them ones who, as soon as he walked away, we used to say "Camel Flood" and laugh. Liz, his wife, was good-looking then and we all wondered what she was doing with him. She was his only shot and he was very protective of her.' Liz found Paddy a devoted husband who shared everything with her, including details of his IRA activity.

On 11 August 1989 police seized a bomb he had just made and the two volunteers who were transporting it were arrested. Before the trial they were shown forensic reports on the device and noticed that a battery was not listed among the components. They concluded that Flood was an informer, that he had sabotaged the device by omitting the battery and that he had then set them up to be arrested. This theory has been dismissed by a senior police source: 'Paddy Flood was not an agent, there were other means of covering that unit. The battery was most likely a simple omission in the forensic report, we have less obvious ways than that to stop bombs going off.' In fact, at least three RUC informants were operating in the Derry IRA at that time. They included John Gerard Holmes in finance, Martin Hogan who was on Brigade Staff and Pat Moore who was in the Quartermaster's department and sometimes worked with Flood on bombs. FRU ran its own agents and listening devices were more widely employed than the IRA realised at the time. However, when the various failures and mistakes that occurred during IRA bombings were added together, Flood took the blame. Liz Flood said that in early June 1990, 'Paddy came home and told me he was going to a meeting and would be back at such and such a time the next day. He was hugging me and kissing me before he left.' The next morning two men from IRA internal security appeared at her door wondering if, since Paddy wasn't in, she would answer a few questions about his movements. Several days later they admitted that Paddy was in IRA custody and tape-recorded interviews with her to play back to him. At one stage she was told that she could visit him but the offer was withdrawn at the last moment. In desperation she went to the home of a 'senior Sinn Féin representative' who has been identified by locals as McGuinness. He told her that ten men were with Paddy and that they were all convinced he was not an informer and that he would be home soon. After seven and a half weeks Flood's body was found, dressed in a blue boiler suit, with a bin-bag over his head, on a South Armagh roadside. A taped confession was given to his family who noticed that the tape had been turned on and off several times during the confession. On the tape Flood said he had been a Special Branch informer because the police had threatened to implicate Liz in an explosives find and 'break her like a plate', if he did not work for them. Reliable sources in Derry say that Flood remained unbroken despite severe beatings and was held until the bruising went down. He was told that as he had been held for so long and had also seen his interrogators, he could now not be freed because – irrespective as to whether he was an informant or not, there was now a risk that he would become one. The IRA wanted a confession and if he did not give it, Liz would be taken, questioned and killed with him. They would be like Catherine and Gerard Mahon, a husband and wife murdered for informing in 1985. Their daughter, Aoibheann, would carry the shame into the orphanage with her. The Army Council, of which McGuinness was a member, sanctioned such executions.

For much of 1990, the Council's major attention was on the overseas campaign, which had been revived under South Armagh's direction. The campaign involved some PR disasters – the accidental murder of two Australian tourists in Roermond for instance – but the IRA focused more on its successes. A bomb detonated at the Carlton Club in London was claimed to have 'struck at the heart of Tory rule', in June. By the end of July the threat became a reality when extensive damage was caused at the London Stock Exchange and Ian Gow, a Tory MP and close friend of Margaret Thatcher, was murdered by an under-car booby-trap. Amid all this Michael Oatley, MI6's 'Mountain Climber', took matters into his own hands and made contact with the IRA through the Link. According to McGuinness, 'we received some general and occasional oral briefings on the British government position during this time.' Dennis Bradley, who had dropped out of the Link since the late '70s, had, by this time, rejoined and was intimately involved in what followed.

In September Brooke was attempting to re-launch his talks process with the constitutional parties and Hume was again in contact with Adams. At this point Oatley requested a face-to-face meeting. McGuinness said, 'Gerry Adams and I discussed this invitation with others on the officer board and decided to go ahead with the meeting. I was instructed to proceed on a listening brief.' At the meeting in October they talked for about three hours with McGuinness saying little. Oatley told him he planned to retire in the spring but that a new British representative would initiate a fresh round of contacts. The Provo leadership appeared non-committal outwardly but privately decided to respond to any further contact. John Deverell, the senior MI5 officer in Belfast, informed Brooke that a channel was now open to the republican leadership and Brooke gave him permission to proceed, provided the contacts would be deniable in the event of exposure. At this stage the Secretary of State saw it primarily as an intelligence exercise and did not keep day-to-day contact. Like McGuinness, his priorities lay elsewhere. As they gave their permission for the contacts to proceed Northern Command unveiled a new tactic, a wave of proxy bomb attacks, which would surpass the overseas department in their ruthlessness. Kathleen Gillespie was naturally frightened when her home was taken over by the IRA, she was held hostage and her husband Patsy, a cleaning worker at Fort George Army base, was made to drive the family car away. However, she accepted the assurances of the gunmen who made her tea that it would not take long. Patsy had been forced to drive a proxy bomb to the base before and, while it was a nerve-wracking experience, he had emerged unscathed. She was relieved when the phone rang and her captors took off assuring her that Patsy would soon be home. When she heard the explosion she thought resignedly, 'there is our car away.'

In fact the car was safe. The family's Nova had been too small for the IRA's purposes and had been abandoned. Instead Patsy Gillespie had been strapped into a van full of explosives and, with the IRA leading the way, was ordered to drive to Coshquin fixed checkpoint on the Donegal border. The IRA men watched from Donegal until soldiers of the King's Regiment stopped him. They then detonated the bomb by radio signal and opened fire with an assault rifle. The largest part of Gillespie's body to be recovered was his upper hand. Five soldiers also perished.

Shortly afterwards, Martin McGuinness' brother Willie and five other men, including his friend Anthony Heaney, a 30-year-old man from Crievesmith, Leterkenny, were arrested in a house in Burt, Co. Donegal, about three miles away from the site of the explosion,and charged with IRA membership and possession of an assault rifle and ammunition. Willie McGuinness, who refused to account for his movements, was described in court by Brian McArthur, an RUC Detective Chief Inspector as, 'the officer commanding the Provisional IRA in Derry and very important to that organisation'. Sean Ginty, a Garda Superintendent, also said he believed all six men to be IRA members. However they were all acquitted on both counts. The membership charge fell because they denied it and they also denied knowing that the rifle was in the house. After the trial the police had no further suspects for the attack.

Two other human bomb attacks were carried out that night: one in Omagh failed to detonate and in Newry one soldier was killed, though the driver, who had his leg broken, managed to escape. Security forces north and south believe the attacks were sanctioned personally by Martin McGuinness and were coordinated by Sean 'Spike' Murray, his Director of Operations on Northern Command. After Gillespie's death McGuinness said, 'Republicans want to see an end to a conflict which has claimed so many lives', while a statement from the IRA said, 'Until the British government ends its futile war in Ireland, attacks such as this morning's will continue.' It seemed as if, in a period without elections, the Provos were prepared to do anything to raise their profile and to force Britain into negotiations. Gillespie's death did not hurt their hard core support. Charlie Coogan recalls, 'I was a bit horrified when I saw the pictures, it was a bit gruesome, but the feeling about Patsy Gillespie was he worked for the soldiers so fuck him. You wouldn't see Martin gloating though, his attitude was "it is done, forget about it."'

Just over a fortnight later, on 9 November, Brooke made another overture to the Provos when he said, in a speech in his City of London constituency, 'If in the future a majority of the people of Northern Ireland clearly wish for and formally consent to the establishment of a united Ireland it [HMG] would introduce and support in parliament legislation to give effect to that wish. The British government has no selfish strategic or economic interest in Northern Ireland.' Hume had urged Brooke to use the phrase 'no selfish strategic or economic interest', which confirmed his 1988 analysis to the Provos and prepared the way for a new approach to Adams. In October Brooke had passed an advance copy of the speech to McGuinness through the Link and in it he pledged that 'an Irish republicanism seen to have finally renounced violence would be able, like other parties, to seek a role in the peaceful political life of the community. It is not the aspiration to a sovereign united Ireland against which we set our face, it is its violence expression.'

The next good news for Sinn Féin came on 27 November when Margaret Thatcher was replaced by John Major as Tory leader and Prime Minister. The IRA followed up with a three-day Christmas truce and the year ended well for McGuinness personally when he was awarded one thousand pounds in damages for unlawful arrest, false imprisonment and minor assault at an army checkpoint in 1987. 1991 was to be a year in which the UDA would restructure in a shake up which followed the arrest of Brian Nelson, a FRU agent in its ranks, and the ousting of much of the old leadership. They were replaced by younger and more militant characters, men like Johnny 'Mad Dog' Adair. As the year unfolded the loyalist paramilitaries would, for the first time in the Troubles, match the killing rate of the IRA and would create another pressure point for the war-weary Provos.

The first republican funeral of the year carried a still bleaker message. McGuinness travelled to Ballysteen, Co. Limerick, along with the rest of the leadership to attend the funeral of Patrick Sheehy, who had been on the run for two years, and was wanted for a string of bombings in Britain and arms raids in the republic. Sheehy had shot himself in the head with a Brazilian 9mm pistol that had been among the weapons imported from Libya. The funeral was held in gale force winds in the west of Ireland and many of those in attendance were struck by the human cost of the long war. Although the Provisionals were keen to open dialogue with the British, their terms were still high and they still used violence to underscore their message. In February, John Major received a letter of congratulation from Gerry Adams that invited him to secure his place in history by considering British withdrawal from Northern Ireland. Next day there were hopeful noises from the Sinn Féin Ard Fheis in Dublin.

McGuinness declared:

> Republicans want peace. We want an honourable peace, no papering over the cracks or brushing under the carpet the humiliations, degradation and injustices inflicted on us by a foreign power. Difficult though it may be, we will not let the murder of Fergal Caraher [a Sinn Féin member shot dead by the army just after Christmas] and the repression and discrimination inflicted on the nationalist community prevent discussions, which could lead to peace, from taking place. To do so would be infantile and immature.

He pledged further, 'It is time for that circle of violence to be broken. We are prepared to help break it.' Major was considering a reply to Adams, when, at a cabinet meeting to discuss the Gulf War, an IRA mortar, launched with two others from a transit van parked in Horseguards Parade, landed in the garden of Downing Street. Another 15 yards and it would have been in the cabinet room where the ministers were sent ducking under the table suspecting an Iraqi air strike. Major made no reply to Adams' letter after the mortar attack, but Oatley and Deverell were not so easily put off and in April McGuinness received another message through Bradley. It gave him prior notice of a ceasefire that was called on 17 April by the Combined Loyalist Military Command, an umbrella group for the UDA and UVF, to facilitate Brooke's political talks with the constitutional parties. In May the UDA found a loophole in its ceasefire undertaking, which covered only

Northern Ireland, and murdered Eddie Fullerton, a Sinn Féin councillor, in Donegal. Fullerton had been a close friend of McGuinness and a neighbour from the Illies, whom he later mentioned in one of his poems. The response was to shoot Cecil McKnight; a senior UDA man from Derry who McGuinness believed was responsible for authorising Fullerton's death. When McKnight was shot – through his front window – he was sitting discussing his security with two detectives who had warned him of the threat. As a result the IRA became suspicious of Martin Hogan, an RUC informer who had passed on the warning. After Hogan was invited to a 'meeting in Donegal', he reported to his handlers that his cover was blown and he was re-located to England by C14, a specialist unit for that purpose. It was one of the few occasions when the IRA's suspicions were correct. Earlier that month another man, Ruairi Finnis, had been blamed for more of Hogan's links and, after being held for five days, he was shot dead and dumped behind shops in Creggan. The families of people murdered by the IRA or ordered out of Derry on suspicion of informing were by now beginning to band together and to compare notes on their treatment. 'There were a small group of them meeting from time to time, we called it the Calvary Group,' aid Father Denis Faul, who advised the group.

Through all these tout hunts that McGuinness oversaw in 1991 he was still in regular contact with British intelligence. Indeed, shortly after Finnis' death he was contacted again by Oatley, who was now retired, and given the name of Deverell and another man who called himself 'Fred' as the new contacts. 'Fred', a Scot, told Bradley that his real name was Robert McLarnon and produced a letter of accreditation from Peter Brooke. From that point until Christmas 1991 he continued to brief Bradley and the other members of the Link, whom he met both in London and Northern Ireland. McGuinness said, 'The representative declared that it was his objective to ensure that republicans knew the thinking of the British government.' McGuinness fed little back through the Link but instead sent through to the press. In May he told the *Washington Post*: 'There are a lot of people who would like to see an end to the suffering and death, and I am one of them but we need an honest settlement – and that means a real commitment from Britain to withdraw from this island – before people like me can stand up and call for a truce.' Glenn Frankel, the journalist, spent several days in Derry and talked to McGuinness at length. He concluded that McGuinness was afraid to mention the word ceasefire for fear of internal opposition and came away from Derry with the impression that 'morale within the IRA and Sinn Féin appears at a low ebb. There are tensions between the movement's politicians and its commanders, as well as disagreements over IRA "mistakes" – civilian deaths.' McGuinness told him, 'People get tired, they do get weary, and there's a constant fear of what's going to happen next. It's been like that for 20 years.'

In August and September he received a request for clarification from the British who had heard, through Archbishop Robin Eames, that the IRA's coming Christmas ceasefire might be extended indefinitely – McGuinness denied the report. In October he received an advance copy of a speech Brooke intended to give in Enniskillen and in November there was a suggestion to set up a permanent point of contact in the home of a retired civil servant in Co. Londonderry. By the end of the year the loyalists, whose ceasefire had ended in the summer, had killed 41 people, compared to 45 murdered by the IRA, and there had been dozens of unsuccessful attacks. Many republicans who were targeted fled south of the border with their families and, after the killing of McKnight, McGuinness tried to halt the damage to morale by directing that a mutual non-aggression pact be offered to the loyalists. The offer was taken as a sign of weakness and the loyalist attacks continued. In 1992 they would claim 39 lives, a total higher than the IRA who killed 34.

The British Army, the IRA's prime target, was also becoming harder to hit: 21 soldiers had been killed in the province in 1988; it was 12 in 1989, 7 in 1990, 5 in 1991 and 4 in 1992. The diminishing total accounted for the IRA's attempts to attack troops abroad and their subsequent focus on military suppliers, a concept that, after the May 1991 murder of Wallace McVeigh, was extended to include the sale of fruit and vegetables to NAAFI. Commercial bombings were also a developing feature. They had caused two million pounds worth of damage in 1991 and there were plans for still more destruction. New weapons were also developed, including horizontal mortars that were dug into embankments and fired at point-blank range at passing vehicles but overall the tide was turning against the IRA. The organisation were pinning their hopes for a non-catastrophic way out of the campaign on a combination of military pressure and revived contacts between Gerry Adams and John Hume. They had engaged the interest of Hume and Brooke and this, together with the backdrop of violence, would probably be enough to prevent the inter-party talks succeeding in their absence. McGuinness and Adams continually asked to be admitted 'without preconditions' – which meant without a ceasefire, but it was implicit in their comments that a halt to violence, 'the right atmosphere', might occur once talks started.

Hume had been revisiting the documents exchanged between his party and Sinn Féin in 1988 and had also considering Father Reid's idea of a declaration of intent by the British as the key to ending IRA and then loyalist violence, which was justified by the loyalists as a reaction to IRA actions. In October 1991 Hume had drafted a declaration to be made by both the British and Irish Prime Ministers. Brooke's November statement on Britain's lack of a selfish interest had gone some way towards the declaration. An additional key point in the proposed declaration was introducing a clause regarding the agreement of the people of Northern Ireland, that is, the consent principle, a necessary condition for the exercise of Irish self-determination. It also specified the creating of cross-border institutions aimed at allowing the people of Ireland 'to work their substantial common ground together in order to build the necessary trust for an agreed future'. If the governments reached agreement on a declaration, it would undermine the republican justification for armed struggle but would not involve a British declaration of intent to withdraw. Hume first showed it to Haughey who got his advisers – Martin Mansergh, Sean O hUiginn and Dermot Nally – to redraft some points before giving it his approval. Haughey then informed Major while Hume passed it to Adams, who in turn consulted the IRA and Sinn Féin leadership. McGuinness decided to continue with the pressure before the IRA showed its hand politically and the only reply for some time was the continued roar of explosions.

The IRA started 1992 with a series of bombs in January designed to demonstrate their ability to strike at will. First came two large devices in two of Belfast's central shopping areas and then a smaller one, detonated about 300 yards from Downing Street. Within days, eight Protestant construction workers were murdered by a roadside bomb at Teebane crossroads near Cookstown as they travelled home in a bus from Lisanelly base in Co. Tyrone. The IRA claimed the atrocity branding them 'collaborators'. In early February an off-duty RUC officer entered a Belfast Sinn Féin advice centre and went berserk with a pump-action shotgun killing three people before shooting himself. The official loyalist response to

Teebane came next morning, 5 February, when five Catholics were murdered as Sean Graham's Bookmakers on Belfast's Ormeau Road was sprayed with gunfire. The SAS struck with more precision in Tyrone on 16 February when they shot dead four IRA volunteers shortly after they had launched a machine gun attack on Coalisland RUC station. This slaughter formed the backdrop as McLarnon continued to brief McGuinness who said of the period up to April 1992, 'the major part of these briefings was taken up by reports of the progress or lack of it which was being made in the inter-party talks. Peter Brooke made a number of keynote speeches at this time and we were advised of these in advance.' The carnage also occurred during a British General election campaign which saw further setbacks for Sinn Féin with Adams losing his West Belfast seat to Dr Joe Hendron of the SDLP and the party's overall vote falling from 11.4 per cent to 10 per cent, the fall being particularly apparent in Fermanagh/South Tyrone where the memory of Enniskillen, and now Teebane, blighted Sinn Féin's chances. McGuinness himself stood in Foyle, emerging with 9,149 votes, nowhere in sight of Hume's 26,710. It was becoming clear that, although Sinn Féin now had a more or less irreducible hard core of one in ten voters, they would be permanently behind the SDLP as long as the campaign continued.

In Britain, Major had retained power but with a reduced majority which left the Ulster Unionists in a powerful position in Westminster and made the Provos, especially McGuinness, suspicious of his government. Sir Patrick Mayhew, the new Secretary of State, was willing to maintain the dialogue with republicans but throughout the Major administration every overture was accompanied by bombing – the IRA's version of gunboat diplomacy. South of the border Haughey had fallen as a result of an internal dispute within Fianna Fail and been replaced by Albert Reynolds who made the development of the peace process an early priority. In McGuinness' account of the period from April to Christmas 1992 he was told that Mayhew was 'fully on board'. He added, 'We were given consistent reports from the British government representatives that the Brooke/Mayhew talks were going nowhere and the government's prediction was that they would end in failure. We were also told that there was friction between the senior civil servants [in London and Stormont] and Mayhew. In October, we were provided with a two-page document on the progress of the talks.' There were also friendly gestures from the republican camp. In June at Bodenstown Jim Gibney, one of the Adams/McGuinness circle, said Sinn Féin now accepted that any British withdrawal from Northern Ireland could come only after 'a sustained period of peace', opening the possibility of a ceasefire for talks. In July, during a discussion with Bishop Edward Daly, McGuinness said republicans now recognised that the Irish people could not be united by force and that the process of national reconciliation could not begin until there was complete demilitarisation. McGuinness' importance was now registering with the British public and he was listed in September by *Esquire* magazine as part of the 'ruling class', and 'one of the 25 men who really run the country'.

On 26 October McGuinness' importance was underlined when he met McLarnon and received an advance summary of a speech which Mayhew intended to make in Coleraine in which he planned to announce the ending of legal bans on street names in Irish and repeated the point that the British government would present 'no obstacle' to a united Ireland if that was the wish of the people in Northern Ireland. The speech pledged that if violence ended permanently, the army would be withdrawn to barracks and hinted that Sinn Féin would be admitted to talks. McLarnon asked Sinn Féin if, in future, they would send addresses and keynote speeches to the British and suggested that if this happened there might be meetings later. Instead, on 13 November, an IRA bomb destroyed the shopping centre of Coleraine, the mainly Protestant Co. Derry town, where the speech was due to be given. This was symptomatic of the type of messages that the IRA would send the Major government throughout its term in office and goes some way to foregrounding its suspicion of them. When Mayhew did deliver the speech, somewhat later than intended on 16 December the inter-party talks had collapsed and there had been several more bombs in Britain and Northern Ireland as well as unsuccessful UFF incendiary attacks south of the border. The IRA marked Mayhew's overture with two small bombs in London, their last before the three-day Christmas ceasefire.

CHAPTER FIFTEEN

Operation Taurus and the Ceasefire

I think the British Government is slowly but surely disengaging from Ireland.
Martin McGuinness, BBC's *On The Record*, 13 October 1994,

Rackets involving cars have remained a source of IRA finance ever since the days of Free Derry. By the '90s, IRA 'staff cars' were loaned by dealers as a form of protection payment and motor insurance fraud was an organised source of finance. The fraud usually depended upon the use of hire cars, for which insurance was purchased from the hire company. The vehicle might be driven at low speed into a skip and the hirer then say he had crashed into another car and admitted liability without calling the police. A string of 'passengers', and sometimes 'pedestrians', would later submit claims for injuries ranging from whiplash to broken bones. The IRA matched up injured people with 'crashes' and provided the necessary medical and legal documentation. In other cases the plates of a hire car would be swapped with those from a vehicle of the same make and model which had already been written-off and sold for scrap. The hire car would then be sold from the write-off's documentation which would be altered to indicated that it had been rebuilt. The wreck would be given to the hire company and personal injury claims for the 'crash' would follow. Another angle was to re-register English write-offs in Northern Ireland, claim that they had been rebuilt and then use their plates on stolen cars. John Gerard Holmes, a 35-year old car dealer from the Waterside area, was a vital figure in facilitating these rackets. He supplied vehicles to the IRA and had been working as a Special

Branch agent since the early '80s, giving his handlers access to the vehicles which they could then spray with markers visible from helicopters or fit with tracking devices. Through him, the Special Branch were able to track the movements of senior republicans, including McGuinness. Holmes came under suspicion after he was remanded in custody on motor fraud charges in Belfast Crumlin Road jail in August 1992. During his month in jail he was visited by his friend Harry Lynn, a republican with convictions for attempting to murder a policeman and making false insurance claims. Lynn agreed to carry a letter out of the jail to Holmes' girlfriend in which Holmes referred to his Special Branch handler. The page containing the name was not delivered with the rest of the letter. It was brought a few days later by the wife of another prisoner who claimed to have found it in her letter.

Holmes was bailed on 26 October 1992 and, soon after, he received a message through Lynn that Sinn Féin wanted to see him at their Waterside offices on Racecourse Road. He went there on 17 November and did not return. A few days later a family delegation visited McGuinness' home in Brandywell. McGuinness promised that they would have news of Gerry before the day was out. Around midnight Holmes' girlfriend received a call saying that a tape would be left at Gerry's father's home and that the body would follow shortly. Two shots had been heard in Creggan about the same time and next morning Holmes' body was found bound and shot twice through the head in an alleyway. According to a statement issued by the family, the taped 'confession' they were given, 'lasts approximately two minutes and contains nothing to suggest Gerry had been an informer at any time'.

By now McGuinness had been proved influential in a number of incidents that had resulted in dead bodies being abandoned by the roadside. People were beginning to talk. Local difficulties in Derry were not McGuinness' only priority at the end of 1992. For much of the year Gerry Adams had been suffering from hepatitis and, to help spread the burden of the peace process, McGuinness had brought in Gerry Kelly to help handle the contacts with the British. Tall, dark and conventionally handsome, Kelly was no intellectual but had, at 38, spent 13 out of the past 23 years in jail in Britain, Northern Ireland and Holland. From the Ballymurphy area, Kelly had joined the IRA in January 1972 at a time when Adams was OC in Belfast. He had gone to England with Marion and Dolours Price as part of the Provos first British bombing unit who had, in 1973 and 1974, hit targets ranging from Scotland Yard and the Old Bailey to British military installations. When they were arrested they went on a hunger strike for transfer to Ireland and, following 205 days of force-feeding, were moved to Belfast. After several breakout attempts in the Maze, Kelly finally succeeded in the mass escape of 1983 and immediately went to Holland, where he was subsequently arrested in an arms smuggling plot and deported to the UK. Kelly had travelled and trained widely in the years following his escape and was a close friend of Robert McBride, an ANC militant and bomber of Irish descent, whom he met at a training camp. Kelly was a man whose commitment could not be doubted. He made a valuable addition when it came to selling any new strategy.

As 1993 opened, the British Army had drawn up a 60-point plan for demilitarisation in case the IRA's Christmas ceasefire was extended. The ceasefire broke but the peace process continued to proceed on three fronts. Firstly, there was the three-stranded talks, presided over by Mayhew and Dick Spring – Spring went on to become Tanaiste and Foreign Minister in December after his Labour Party replaced the Progressive Democrats as Reynolds' coalition partners. Sinn Féin was excluded from the talks but felt no pressure because McLarnon was assuring them that the talks were likely to fail. Meanwhile Hume showed no great enthusiasm, focusing instead on his links with Adams and his idea for a joint declaration, which was being handled on the Irish side by Reynolds personally. Lastly there was the back channel communications through the Link. This was being controlled by intelligence agents with an interest in Ireland who were to some degree telling Sinn Féin what they wanted to hear, just as they had during the hunger strike. Oatley had held at least one unauthorised meeting with McGuinness and there were feelings in British circles that, as one Minister put it, 'he had bogged it a bit' and overstated the British position. Mayhew wrote to Oatley assuring him that, overall, his career remained a distinguished one. Dennis Bradley, who spoke frequently to McGuinness, was as enthusiastic as Oatley and, in February, they decided to send a message of their own using McGuinness' name in order to try and jump start direct talks. Bradley said, 'I made it up, but I made it up on the basis of what I knew their real position was. Any mediator worth his salt will push things along from time to time but you can't do it too often.' Later McLarnon, to whom he sent the message, added a few lines of his own to make it more intriguing. The finished version read:

> The conflict is over but we need your advice on how to bring
> it to a close. We wish to have an unannounced ceasefire in
> order to hold a dialogue leading to peace. We cannot announce
> such a move as it will lead to confusion to the volunteers,
> because the press will misinterpret it as surrender. We cannot
> meet the Secretary of State's public renunciation of violence,
> but it would be given privately as long as we were sure that we
> were not being tricked.

This extraordinary message secured the undivided attention of the British. Major set up a special committee consisting of himself, Mayhew, Kenneth Clarke, the Home Secretary, Douglas Hurd, the former Secretary of State, and Nick Lyell, the Attorney General to deal with the communications. Clarke was the most sceptical of the group. The committee authorised a reply saying that they 'understood and appreciated the seriousness of what has been said', that they would be 'influenced by events on the ground', and they would give a substantive reply when they had considered it.

When he was delivering the reply McLarnon said that this meant talks could occur if violence ceased for two to three weeks. A further message specified that there must be an end to violence before talks and that the British government would not adopt 'any prior objective of ending partition', but once again McLarnon and the Link put an optimistic gloss on it. Sensing weakness, McGuinness used BBC interviews to predict more violence if the government refused to drop its demand for a ceasefire before talks. He said, 'Unless there is a recognition that there must be change, I believe the IRA is very committed and very determined to prosecute the armed struggle to a final conclusion.'

That was on 15 March. On 17 March McGuinness let the mask slip, saying, 'We in the IRA and the Irish republican movement and Sinn Féin have put Britain to the test', and added, 'We must arm ourselves politically and any other way we see fit to remove Britain from this country.' On 20 March it became clear what he meant when the IRA exploded two waste-paper basket bombs in the centre of Warrington, killing two boys, Jonathan Ball, who died instantly, and Tim Parry, who died five days later in hospital. In an oral message the IRA expressed 'total sadness', adding, 'The last thing we needed at this sensitive time was what has happened.' The bomb was the second attack in Warrington within a month and Deverell, the more senior official, did not turn up to meet Sinn Féin in the house in the Bogside two days later. Kelly took it as a snub but perked up when McLarnon told him that Mayhew had given up all thought of marginalising or defeating the IRA. Indeed the British now accepted that 'the final solution is union. It is going to happen anyway. The historical train – Europe – determines that. We are committed to Europe. Unionists will have to change. This island will be as one.' The words, possibly intended as no more than a nod towards European convergence, would come back to haunt the British. McLarnon went on to suggest that there could be a meeting with senior civil servants after a two-week ceasefire. If the statement was ever an accurate reflection of British thinking it ceased to be after Warrington. Major wrote, 'I wondered whether to go public on the process and denounce the IRA for their perfidy. Only the possibility that this was their usual tactic of trying to seem, as they saw it "strong" to enable them to negotiate, stopped me.'

On 23 April, the IRA detonated a one-ton fertiliser bomb at Bishopsgate in London, killing one man and causing over one billion pounds worth of damage. On 1 April, Adams had been spotted entering Hume's home in Derry and their continued links had become public. To scotch criticism they agreed a joint statement which was issued the day after Bishopsgate and which pledged to try to 'change the climate away from conflict', and to search for agreement among the people of Ireland on how self-determination might be exercised. They added, 'We both recognise that such a new agreement is only achievable and viable if it can earn and enjoy the allegiance of the different traditions on this island.' McGuinness, who was also meeting Mansergh and other Irish government representatives in the Redemptorist Monastery in Dundalk, now took the two-week ceasefire proposal to the Army Council. He and Adams argued that since there was often a period without IRA operations, it was worth meeting the British request in order to explore McLarnon's stated commitment to Ireland being 'as one'.

The next big political event was the Northern Ireland local government elections where Sinn Féin reversed the long decline in its vote, emerging with 12 per cent, up a full point on 1989. The message which McGuinness and the leadership took from it was that the disclosure of the talks with Hume and the joint statement had widened Sinn Féin's appeal by associating the party with an effort to bring peace and, when no reply came from the British, there was a growing temptation to make the Link proposal and the offer of a ceasefire equally public in the hope of rallying nationalist support to the Sinn Féin position. The British sent McGuinness a message on 25 May that, in the light of the recent bomb attacks, a three-month ceasefire would now be required. The British message was sent the day after a massive IRA bomb destroyed Belfast's Grand Opera House and damaged the nearby UUP headquarters, injuring 13 people and costing sixty-two million pounds in damages. It was a dramatic vindication of advice that Mansergh had given McGuinness at their last meeting: he had told him that bombings would not move the British in the direction he wanted. In May, another ominous message, this time from the Irish government, pointed out that 'arms and equipment' would be one of the issues to be dealt with once peace was established. It was the first tentative hint of a decommissioning requirement.

In June, Beano Casey came out of hiding and was interviewed by the *Daily Mirror*. He gave details of his role as an informer and admitted involvement in several attacks. When he was subsequently arrested, McGuinness described it as 'a damage limitation exercise by the RUC, embarrassed by Casey's claims that his RUC handlers could have prevented attacks in which RUC members and others died'. Privately he was relieved that the potential for another supergrass had been reduced by Casey's damaging admissions of his own crimes. What was building up was not a supergrass trial but a television exposé. *The Cook Report*, a Central Television investigative series, had spent the best part of a year investigating McGuinness. Roger Cook, the show's presenter, specialised in exposing villains but the programme's insurers would not cover him to come to Northern Ireland to confront McGuinness. A reporter was dispatched to the Ridge Pool in Ballina, in the Republic, where he waited for weeks in the hope of catching McGuinness unawares.

In two programmes in August, Cook described McGuinness as 'Britain's Number One Terrorist', and produced an array of victims of terrorism and former IRA members. Raymond Gilmour, the former supergrass, appeared in silhouette to confirm McGuinness' IRA membership. Paul McGavigan testified that McGuinness had been present at his interrogation. The most powerful statement came from Rose Hegarty, who gave a first hand account of how McGuinness' assurances had lulled her son Frank into a false sense of security which led to his death. Although the RUC would not appear, Sir John Hermon, the retired Chief Constable, described Sinn Féin and the IRA as 'inseparable', and added that McGuinness had long been 'very central to what is going on'. McGuinness condemned the programme as 'the unsubstantiated claims of self-confessed liars, involving political opponents and the manipulation of grieving relatives', but added that he would not sue because his legal position was that he could not win in a British court. He added, 'I have never been a member of the IRA. I don't have any sway over the IRA. I am a political representative of the republican movement.' He claimed that he had behaved honourably towards the Hegarty family and that he had warned them that Frank's life would be in danger if he returned to Derry. Few believed him, and Ken Maginnis of the Ulster Unionists led calls for stronger laws, up to and including internment, to allow 'godfathers of terror' to be jailed. Mike Townson, the programme's editor, accused the government of adopting a 'hands-off policy' in their apprehension of McGuinness and added, 'McGuinness is treated with kid-gloves.' Stung by the accusation, the RUC launched Operation Taurus, a full-scale investigation into McGuinness' IRA links.

McGuinness' home circumstances were steadily improving. On 21 September he moved out of public authority housing to 11 Westland Terrace. The house was bought by his brother, Thomas, a builder, from Ita Bernadette McGurn, the previous occupier. It was an arrangement that allowed Martin, who would not have qualified for a mortgage, to claim Housing Benefit for any rent that he paid to Thomas. Martin's wife Bernie had a job working in a local café, which was promptly dubbed 'greasy Bernie's'. This along with his weekly subsidy of about twenty pounds from the IRA, helped boost the family income above the breadline level. The organisation also give him the use of a Ford Escort. McGuinness told two outright lies in an interview with *The Independent* in September claiming, 'the reality is that I am not a member of the IRA' and going on to deny that he had received any 'feelers' from the British. The main focus of the peace process was now moving onto the Hume/Adams proposals for a joint declaration. McGuinness, who was a member of an internal committee monitoring this process, told the BBC the proposal was intended 'to bring about a situation where the British government were acting as persuaders of the unionists'. Hume's original document had come close to this but had since been redrafted by the British and Irish governments to foreground the concept of consent. Hume, who disliked this tinkering, hit the roof in September when, as he prepared to travel to America, the Link told him that the British had declined the IRA's offer of a two-week ceasefire. He and Adams then decided to encourage progress on the declaration idea by issuing a statement to the public saying that the governments had in fact not yet responded to the offer. This proved something of a catalyst but recurrent violence continued to make progress difficult. The most serious IRA attack around this time was the bombing of a fish shop on the Belfast loyalist Shankill Road. It was intended to destroy UFF offices on the next storey and kill the leadership but instead wiped out 10 civilians and injured 57. Thomas Begley, one of the bombers, was killed in the attack, and when Adams acted as a pall-bearer at his funeral it became impossible for Major to adopt any declaration with, as one diplomat put it, 'his fingerprints on it'.

The Link may have intervened again to try and push things when on 2 November the British received a plaintive message: 'In plain language, please tell us as a matter of urgency when you will open dialogue in the event of a total end to hostilities?' McGuinness later denied sending it and the evidence is that he had now decided to expose the link publicly in the hope of achieving open dialogue. On 18 November he turned up uninvited at an Irish Congress of Trade Unions' peace rally in Derry to claim that he had been in 'direct and protracted contact and dialogue' with the British government at official level and without any preconditions, adding, 'Sinn Féin is quite ready to engage in talks at any time to create the conditions in which a peace process can be constructed and a political settlement reached.'

The British denied such contact had ever taken place but were rudely exposed when a definitive leak emerged from a Northern Ireland Office 'speaking note'. *The Observer* published the message from the DUP's Rev. William McCrea on 28 November. Mayhew was forced to confirm its contents and the government was seen to have breached the taboo on contact with Sinn Féin, as McGuinness had hoped. The joint Declaration, issued on 15 December, was a recognisable descendent of the Hume/Adams proposal but its teeth were blunted. Instead of being a persuader for unity, Britain would encourage and facilitate agreement among the people of Ireland, who had a right to self-determination but only 'in agreement between the two parts', and if there was to be a united Ireland it would be 'on the basis of consent, freely and concurrently given, North and South'. In the event of agreement being reached it would have to be ratified by the northern parties, by the two parliaments and finally in referenda held simultaneously in the North and South. The southern referendum would amend Articles two and three of the Irish constitution, which claim jurisdiction over Northern Ireland, to embody the principle of consent. In return for accepting the consent principle – considered a unionist veto by republicans – nationalists were given the assurances of institutional links between North and South and Ireland and Britain. All parties who had established a commitment to exclusively peaceful means would be allowed to join in dialogue with the two governments as the agreement progressed. As soon as Sinn Féin had established a ceasefire for three weeks, they would be admitted to preparatory discussions with British officials.

It all begged the question of how the republicans' commitment to exclusively peaceful means could be established so that they could be admitted to talks. Explaining the deal in the Dail that day, Dick Spring provided the answer. He said, 'Questions are being raised on how to determine a permanent end to violence. We are talking about the handing up of arms and explosives and are insisting that it would not be simply a temporary cessation.' Although Sinn Féin were to claim that decommissioning was sprung on them at a much later date it was in fact a feature of discussions from this time and was being mentioned as a test or precondition for entry to talks. It was a lot to put to the IRA at a time when opposition within the organisation led by the IRA's hard line Quartermaster, a Dundalk man, could normally muster between three and four votes on the Army Council. Adams and McGuinness played for time, demanding clarification of the declaration, which was already a remarkably lucid document. McGuinness also entered into a prolonged wrangle with Mayhew, which he largely won, over the precise nature of the exchanges. At one point Mayhew offered his resignation to Major over 'typographical errors' in the version of the messages that the government released and subsequently had to correct after McGuinness countered by issuing facsimiles of the original documents.

Within his own party McGuinness took things slowly, and did not commit himself one way or the other at a conference in Loughmacrory, Co. Tyrone, held shortly after Christmas, in which the Good Friday Agreement was discussed. The issue remained prominent within the party and was frequently discussed at further meetings but no vote was ever taken until McGuinness could be sure of a majority. It was a familiar Adams/McGuinness tactic that allowed them to talk out and flush out opposition. They used a similar strategy over abstentionism, which was discussed at three Ard Fheiseanna before the party finally committed themselves to it.

The American card came into play in September 1993 when Niall O'Dowd, publisher of the *Irish Voice* for which Adams was a columnist, led a delegation of influential Irish–American supporters of Bill Clinton, the new US President, to meet Sinn Féin. McGuinness told the BBC: 'They clearly indicated before they came that it would be most helpful if a period of quiet could be arranged to facilitate their visit and we went off to see what we could do.' He declared an unannounced ten-day break in IRA military operations to facilitate the visit and at the meeting with the Americans he told them that if they could produce a visa for Gerry Adams and if the Clinton White House gave permission to open an office in Washington that might persuade the IRA that politics offered a better way forward than violence. Reynolds also threw his weight behind a visa for Adams, lobbying Senator Ted Kennedy during a visit to his sister Jean Kennedy Smith, who was US ambassador to Dublin. There was a diplomatic tussle with Major, who asked that the visa be withheld until a ceasefire was declared and was backed by the State Department, but on 29 January 1994, Adams was granted permission to visit New York for forty-eight hours, during which he expressed support for a peaceful way forward. The visa was a major favour and the Americans made it clear that further concessions would be dependent on a ceasefire. Where McGuinness had once seen a ceasefire as the end point of negotiations he now began to see it as part of the process of trying to achieve British withdrawal. In February he told the Ard Fheis: 'If the British Government are prepared to say that the unionists will not have a veto over British Government policy and that guns, vetoes and injustices will all be left outside the door, then there is no good reason why talks cannot take place in an appropriate atmosphere.' Within the IRA he argued that the armed struggle had reached a stalemate and the question was now how to get the best possible conditions to move out of it.

On 20 February, McGuinness shouldered the coffin of his old comrade, Dominic 'Mad Dog' McGlinchey. Bernadette Devlin McAliskey, who had been the youngest MP when she attacked Home Secretary Reginald Maudling in the House of Commons after Bloody Sunday in 1972, joined him. McGlinchey, who frequently boasted that he had killed more than 30 people, was gunned down near his home in Drogheda, Co. Louth, in the Irish

Republic, as he left a telephone kiosk with one of his sons. It was ironic that McGlinchey, who had so little time for the democratic process in life, should in death have been carried to his final resting place by one former, and one future MP. His one-time IRA comrade, Francis Hughes, had been carried to the very same graveyard after his death on the 1981 hunger strike, when McGuinness gave his funeral oration. Today the two men lie nearby each other. McGuinness listened with the crowd to McAliskey's vitriolic speech, which eulogised McGlinchey – 'the finest republican of them all.' She had less kind words for the journalists who attended McGlinchey's funeral. They were curs and dogs, McAliskey lashed, 'May every one of them rot in hell.'

Adams and McGuinness soon discovered that their new allies in Dublin did not have infinite patience and in June, Reynolds, who had stuck out his neck on the visa issue, sent word through Mansergh that if a ceasefire was not called soon he was abandoning his support for Sinn Féin. McGuinness used the opportunity to ask for a few more concessions. He later said:

> I told Martin Mansergh that it was absolutely vital that the Irish government press for demilitarisation to show people effectively on the ground at grass-roots level that there was going to be fundamental change going to take place in their life. We discussed the issue of prisoners and different things which the Irish government could do in relation to improving the atmosphere and creating the very clear impression that nationalist Ireland had got its act together.

On 24 July, Sinn Féin held a special delegate conference in Letterkenny, Co. Donegal, by which time McGuinness and Adams had notched up enough concessions from Reynolds to proceed. They included the lifting of the Section 31 ban on radio and TV interviews, parole of prisoners in the south and a review of sentences in the Republic with a promise to press Britain to follow suit. McGuinness pitched his appeal for party unity telling delegates, 'We have been through much together, we have achieved much together and we should be proud of those achievements. We can and we will bring this struggle to a successful conclusion. Our message today is clear. Republicans want peace. Republicans demand peace. Republicans are united, determined and strong and looking to the future.' The Provos' last request to Reynolds was to secure a visa for Joe Cahill to visit the US to sell the ceasefire idea to supporters there. It was a tall order. Cahill was a convicted murderer and arms smuggler who had been monitored by the FBI during his meetings with George Harrison, the arms supplier, on previous trips to the US. Nevertheless, Reynolds swung it after a personal call to Clinton and Cahill arrived in America on 29 August. His pitch, according to Irish-Americans who attended some of the meetings, was that there would be a ceasefire, but that it could also be ended at any time and that the leadership should be trusted.

According to Phil Kent, a former IRA arms supplier now based in Canada, the IRA also passed to the White House details of their arms support network in the US and of individuals who, like himself, now supported the dissidents as part of the bargaining for permission to open an office and raise funds in the US. On 29 August, Adams and McGuinness attended an Army Council meeting where a ceasefire was approved in order to allow Sinn Féin to enter negotiations with the British and the other parties. The statement issued on 31 August avoided the word 'permanent' but gave no end point either. Instead it was described as a 'complete cessation of military operations' to create the right framework for inclusive negotiations. It was the first ceasefire in 19 years but, as McGuinness made clear during a visit to London in October, it was conditional on a successful outcome to the negotiations. In that sense, instability was built into it from the outset, an instability which was increased by the fact that McGuinness had overstated his case to get agreement from the Army Council. He said, 'If he thinks the SDLP and the Dublin government and ourselves will support assembly elections at the beginning of next year, I think James Molyneaux is living in cloud-cuckoo-land', and went on to predict that the British were about to disengage from Northern Ireland. Major quickly lifted the British restrictions on Sinn Féin's access to the airwaves. Even the loyalist community overlooked the IRA murder of three leading UDA members in the run up to the cessation and declared their own ceasefire on 13 October in which they expressed 'abject and true remorse' to their innocent victims. There were also direct and personal benefits to McGuinness. On 24 November, Jonathan McIvor, the Detective Chief Superintendent in charge of the RUC's C2 Criminal Investigation Department, drafted an internal memo covering the Operation Taurus investigation into the allegations made against McGuinness in *The Cook Report*, which was leaked to the authors. There were three potential witnesses in what McIvor described as 'this very important and sensitive inquiry'. He went on, 'A factor in this matter is that the UK government may soon be meeting senior members of Sinn Féin, including Mr McGuinness, to plan the future of Northern Ireland. Mid-December has been mentioned. Forwarded for direction please. ACC Crime is aware of this minute.' The document was classified 'Secret'. Detectives involved in Taurus were not given clearance to arrest and question McGuinness as they had wished. Some of them began to suspect that the peace process was his 'get out of jail free card'.

CHAPTER SIXTEEN

The Learning Curve

If we don't resolve the conflict, the potential for further conflict will always
be there. I am not making threats. I am stating a political fact of Irish history.
Martin McGuinness, *An Phoblacht/Republican News*,
10 November 1995

McIvor's prediction proved correct. On 9 December 1994, just three months
into the ceasefire, McGuinness bowled up to the doors of Stormont in an
armour-plated black taxi to meet British officials for exploratory talks. It
was a remarkable achievement. The Official IRA had waited five years after
their ceasefire to be accepted into formal political dialogue, but McGuinness
regarded the delay as irksome, 'a purgatory', as he later put it. Sinn Féin
leaders, now invited to official receptions but not permitted to meet
ministers, tried to buck the protocol by sidling up on the blind side of
dignitaries and shaking hands. Civil servants were deployed strategically
around ministers to grab the palm of any Sinn Féiner who approached. As
one put it: 'We headed them off at the pass while the ministers looked
disdainfully into the distance.' The Irish government had already set up a
Forum for Peace and Reconciliation in Dublin, open to all parties as a sort of
training ground for Sinn Féin's entry to full political dialogue. Adams took
the lead but McGuinness, who was focusing on the British, sometimes
attended as a substitute delegate. Sinn Féin delegates had to refer all
important decisions back to the leadership so that, even with the unionists
boycotting proceedings, it was often impossible to find common ground. In

the end they refused to put their names to the Forum Report because it contained a reference to unionist consent. It was a depressing precedent and a first straw in the wind that the republicans were not prepared for the give and take of democratic politics.

Just a few days before McGuinness' first exploratory meeting with British officials, the Forum devoted a session to the political obituary of Albert Reynolds who was deposed as Taoiseach after he lost the confidence of Dick Spring, the leader of the Labour Party, his junior partners in the coalition. With an arrogance born of the military mindset, Sinn Féin called for Reynolds to be kept on and McGuinness issued stern warnings, which had a somewhat ironic ring coming from the lips of an IRA leader, of the need for stable government. Spring ignored him and formed a new coalition with John Bruton of Fine Gael, something of a hate figure within Sinn Féin. It was a blow to Sinn Féin's confidence as they prepared to meet the British. One of their moorings had just slipped and they had seen that there was nothing they could do about it. The cosy picture that McGuinness had painted for the Army Council before the ceasefire was fading. Details of the basis on which the ceasefire had been agreed would be leaked to the unionists early in the spring, in the so-called TUAS (Tactical Use of Armed Struggle) document. It justified limiting the use of violence by reference to favourable circumstances which included John Hume (described as 'the only SDLP person on the horizon strong enough to face the challenge'), Bill Clinton (seen as the first US President to be decisively influenced by the Irish-American lobby) and the fact that the Reynolds administration was 'the strongest government in 25 years or more'. These combined to convince the leadership that ending violence would 'create the dynamic that would considerably advance the struggle', but, the unspoken subtext ran, it was only a tactical decision. The British were well aware that the Provo commitment was of this tactical nature, and, should they forget, they were regularly reminded by signs of IRA preparations, including surveillance of targets and the establishment of mortar positions, for a possible resumption of the campaign. Major decided to proceed slowly and to seek a definite commitment to peace from the Provos, either in the form of a statement that the war was over or in the form of decommissioned weapons.

In order to stabilise the situation within the IRA and sort out differences, McGuinness brought in Bobby Storey, the man who had organised the escape of 38 IRA prisoners from the Maze prison in 1983. He made the appointment after the dissidents attempted to bomb Enniskillen in January. The attack, in which Semtex leaked from the IRA by friends of the QM was used, followed an effort by McGuinness to reassure dissidents that the republican struggle was not being abandoned. 'McGuinness' approach was judged to be too abrasive," said a dissident source, 'He tried to lay down the law and he did it with the wrong people. That is one of the reasons for the bomb.' British officials were nervous before meeting Sinn Féin for the first time. One said, 'there had been a lot of agonising about the venue, would the Shinners come into Stormont with all its associations?' They need not have worried; McGuinness found it a heady and seductive moment. He said, 'When I stood on the steps of Stormont looking down the grand avenue that leads to the Newtownards Road, I felt that we had taken ownership for the first time of the place, that we had arrived and we had arrived politically and that we could build a new Ireland.' At the first meeting about six officials, led by the suave and unflappable Quentin Thomas, were present. McGuinness' team generally consisted of Lucilita Breatnach, the Sinn Féin General Secretary, Gerry Kelly, Sean McManus and Siobhan O'Hanlon, who took notes and reported directly to the Army Council. One of the British participants recalls, 'Quentin told them they were welcome here, rules of confidentiality were laid out and it was made clear that each side could take a break or go out into their suite of offices whenever they felt like it. It was a formal and formalised dialogue, though not tense in any sense. It wasn't unpleasant, people would laugh at double entendres, that sort of thing. We might take coffee together but we ate separately.' He went on:

> at the meeting Sinn Féin would outline their position on the national question, we would say that as a democratic government with no axe to grind we wanted to facilitate an agreed settlement. They were measured, even ponderous, statements. There was no negotiation and the Sinn Féin position did not change in the several months of talks. Each of us was out to test the other's commitment. They would frequently ask for ministers to be brought in but acquiesce in the situation when they weren't.

McGuinness impressed the mandarins. As one put it, 'Martin struck us as a formidable person: articulate, sharp and impressive all round. In some ways he reminded me of a bit of an old-fashioned peeler, he impressed people by his presence without having to say much or to issue any threats, and of course he could be quite tough.' After each meeting the agenda for the next one would be agreed. One civil servant recalled the culture shock as 'they lounged about in the car park amongst the civil servants' cars while the meeting went on.' He added, 'Things eased remarkably quickly. At a subsequent meeting I remember going down to the toilet and, if you remember, there are quite wide corridors in the castle. Martin was standing at the bottom of the stairwell surrounded by women, chatting and making small talk. He looked like a pop-star blinking at them. The guy undoubtedly has charisma and presence, it was remarkable how quickly he went from being bogey-man to getting accepted by people and being found fascinating on that human level.'

The British and Irish governments pushed things along by producing their *Frameworks for the Future* documents spelling out a joint vision. They elaborated on the commitments made in the Downing Street Declaration to the principle of consent and the possibility of a united Ireland. They also suggested a devolved power-sharing assembly and agreed north/south institutions to promote island wide cooperation. The unionists rejected the formula out of hand and this in itself recommended it to McGuinness. The British tried to freeze him out of talks with ministers but were crucially undermined when Clinton decided in March to lift the ban on Sinn Féin fundraising in the US and to grant a visa waiver to Adams who attended a St Patrick's Day reception at the White House and shook hands with the President. Major was furious and McGuinness capitalised on the situation to demand immediate talks with ministers while he side-stepped pressure to decommission by talking of the need to 'remove all the guns from our society'.

On 10 March Alasdair Frazer, the Northern Ireland Director of Public Prosecutions, stated that he considered the evidence available against McGuinness was insufficient to afford a reasonable prospect of obtaining a conviction. It was a bitter disappointment to the officers involved in Operation Taurus. They had been denied permission to question McGuinness and the Gardai had refused them access to one potential witness who was in protective custody in the Republic but, even so, they had amassed a considerable case. They had at least three possible witnesses, including O'Callaghan and two other men, who would have testified to McGuinness' membership of the IRA, his use of weapons and his presence during the torture of an informant. One detective said, 'We felt that if it had been an ordinary republican he would have been charged.' This worry lifted, McGuinness began issuing broad hints that the peace process might end if talks did not proceed without decommissioning. On Sunday, 19 March, for instance, he told Jonathan Dimbleby on the BBC programme *On the Record* that, 'the British government needs to get its act together, and it needs to tell people whether the peace process is over'. The IRA had carried out 69 punishment beatings since the ceasefire began. When the ban on ministerial meeting with Sinn Féin was ended in April they followed up the announcement by carrying out the murder of Mickey 'Moneybags' Mooney, a leading drugs dealer, using the name Direct Action Against Drugs (DAAD) as a cloak. When, on 3 May, John Major visited Derry and was greeted with widespread rioting, Mitchell McLaughlin took the opportunity to criticise the police for not using more crash barriers to prevent clashes.

McGuinness met Michael Ancram, the Northern Ireland Minister for Political Development, on 10 May for three-and-a-half hours of across the table talks at which Ancram lifted the ban on NIO (Northern Ireland Office) ministers meeting Sinn Féin councillors. In response McGuinness demanded a meeting between Adams and Mayhew. This was granted on 24 May at an investment conference in Washington where Clinton gave a speech calling for decommissioning. Adams told him, 'our lives are at stake', a reference, the minister thought, to the strains within the IRA. Mayhew spelt out three preconditions for talks – that the republicans must commit themselves to decommissioning, that they must agree modalities (i.e. the means) and that they must actually decommission some weaponry.

This was a step back from the previous British position, and indeed Spring's previous position, that all arms should be decommissioned before talks, but it was still too much for the Provos.

The next British proposal was for an international Commission to handle the decommissioning issue, a suggestion originating with Ken Maginnis, the Ulster Unionist Security spokesman. It was supported by Clinton, who was increasingly frustrated at the Provisionals' failure to deliver.

Father Alex Reid told Dublin of his fears that there would be 'bodies in the streets', suggesting that the lives of the Adams/McGuinness leadership would be a risk if they accepted the British proposals. The ceasefire, he was indicating, was shaky and the IRA were deeply divided. Rattled, the Irish government pulled out of a planned summit to launch the idea on 6 September.

That day McGuinness started a five-day tour of the US aimed at both fund-raising and promoting Sinn Féin's perspective. In a tub-thumping performance, he told a Noraid and Clann na Gael crowd in Philadelphia's Irish Center that, 'the IRA would be a laughing stock if they did it [decommissioned]'. He added, 'The British government only intends to use the establishment of an international Commission to force the surrender of the Irish Republican Army. Sinn Féin believes that's a mistaken way to move forward.' His visit was not confined to such traditional Irish-American venues. There was a fund-raising cocktail party at the Plaza Hotel in Manhattan and meetings with the editorial board of *The New York Times* and with Cardinal John O'Connor of New York. Debbie McGoldrick of the *Irish Voice* found that, 'McGuinness becomes visibly agitated' at the mention of a token act of decommissioning. He told her, 'The cities we come from – West Belfast, South Armagh, Derry – would undoubtedly interpret that as a surrender.' In a revealing comment he said, 'There might be a military agenda at work here – in other words, cause a split within the Republican family.' McGuinness went on to deny any divisions in republican ranks but it was clear enough that unity would only be preserved by a hard line against the British proposals.

A visit by President Bill Clinton to Northern Ireland on 30 November, the first by any US President, proved the catalyst for agreement between the British and Irish governments. After fraught negotiations, the Commission idea was formally endorsed by Bruton and Major hours before Airforce One touched down. The Commission was tasked to provide an advisory paper on the decommissioning issue by the New Year. It was to be chaired by Senator George Mitchell, Clinton's economic envoy to Northern Ireland, and was to include Harry Holkeri, former Prime Minister of Finland, and General John de Chastelain, the former Canadian armed forces Chief of Staff. At the same time the British government invited all parties to exploratory talks and expressed their intention of getting full talks underway by the end of February. Clinton's visit probably delayed the breakdown of the ceasefire. McGuinness, who by November was speaking in increasingly apocalyptic terms, described it at a news conference in Westminster as the last chance for progress, accusing Major of 'presiding over the death of the Irish peace process'. The visit also struck another blow against any effort to marginalise Sinn Féin. In Derry, McGuinness sat in the VIP section to hear the President. He and Adams were invited to a reception in Clinton's honour that was hosted by Mayhew at Queen's University. However, what Clinton had to say was less welcome. At Derry's Guildhall, he laid his cards on the table stating that 'this twin-track approach is I believe, a way to start that process where everyone can be heard,' and expressed strong support for the role of Mitchell, a personal friend. In Belfast he told those who would resort to violence, 'your day is over.' It was a play on the IRA slogan 'Tiocfaidh ar La' (Our Day Will Come) which was said to be the last words of Bobby Sands. Using their slogan in this way was seen as a challenge to some republicans, especially the QM and his partner who had been close to Sands.

By this stage the IRA was looking for an excuse to end the ceasefire, and active preparations were underway for attacks on military bases and on Britain. McGuinness knew they could not afford an open breach with Clinton – access to American influence was important and so was the money. Accounts lodged in the US by the Friends of Sinn Féin fundraising organisation showed that the party was raising an average of ninety thousand dollars a month and was on target to raise close to one million dollars in the first year of its American fundraising. Donors included celebrities such as Bianca Jagger, Oliver Stone, Anjelica Huston and Fionnuala Flanagan and, mainstream politicians, including Tom Hayden, Jane Fonda's former husband. The bulk of the money came from events arranged around visits by Adams and McGuinness where tickets costing up to one thousand dollars were bought by businessmen from more than 60 companies, as well as lawyers and even a judge. The accounts filed with the Justice Department showed that the money had transformed Sinn Féin into the wealthiest party in Ireland, buying a new building in Belfast for *An Phoblacht/Republican News*; clearing rates arrears on its Dublin and Belfast offices; buying a car for party officials and re-equipping the organisation with computers.

An IRA statement issued on 7 December put the blame on the failing peace process in the traditional quarter saying that, 'British bad faith and unionist intransigence has placed a huge question mark over the twin-track approach.' It accused Major of 'actively encouraging the Unionist proposition of a return to Stormont'. Now that the Americans had backed it the twin-track approach itself was no longer condemned, but its 'abuse' by the British was. Before meeting Mitchell and his commissioners, McGuinness resigned from the Army Council to avoid any suggestion that he was preparing to give up weapons and to avoid responsibility for the coming breach in the ceasefire. He was replaced by Sean 'Spike' Murray, an Adams supporter whose cousin, Danny McCann, was one of the three IRA members killed by the SAS at Gibraltar. George Mitchell had asked Sir Hugh Annesley, the RUC Chief Constable, whether, if they wanted to, Adams and McGuinness could deliver a decommissioning gesture before talks and had also been told that the issue could split the IRA. As a result, he suggested that the parties consider some decommissioning during negotiations rather than before them. His report also set out a series of principles of non-violence to which all the parties were asked to adhere. These included a commitment to exclusively peaceful means and to the total disarmament of all paramilitary groups in a way that was verifiable and to the satisfaction of the international Commission. Other principles included opposing the use of force by others and, most problematic of all for Sinn Féin and the IRA was that they had to 'abide by the terms of any agreement reached in all party negotiations and to resort to democratic and exclusively peaceful methods in trying to alter any aspect of that outcome with which they disagree'. Mitchell also suggested that holding an election as a doorway to talks might be an appropriate confidence-building measure. Mitchell, who had the backing of Clinton, had effectively ruled out the Tactical Use of Armed Force, which had been the basis of the IRA ceasefire. The strains on the cessation were now very great and they would become greater still if all-party talks were to start on this basis. The *causus belli* came when Major said that if there was no prior decommissioning then this election must go ahead as a condition for entry to talks. Adams immediately accused him of 'binning the Mitchell report', and expressed, 'implacable opposition' to the elections. Already the IRA had murdered six alleged drugs dealers under the DAAD flag of convenience, and intelligence reports were coming in of mortar distances being measured and timings being taken at the electronic gates of police and army bases. Still nobody seemed to see the breakdown coming. The British were working towards elections in May and talks in June and the unionists were gradually engaging with Sinn Féin. On 24 January Ken Maginnis of the Ulster Unionists was planning a televised debate with Mitchell McLaughlin of Sinn Féin. The event was recorded but never broadcast. That evening Gerry Adams phoned the White House and got Tony Lake, a senior Clinton aide. Adams said he had just received disturbing news about the peace process and when he was pressed for an explanation he hung up. Hours later the IRA announced its ceasefire was at an end and a bomb was detonated at Canary Wharf in London's prestige Dockland's financial and media area. It killed two people and caused eighty-six million pounds worth of damage. Both Adams and McGuinness had known that something of this nature was likely to happened since the previous winter, long before Clinton's visit.

In a sense the ceasefire had been doomed from the outset. The expectations of the IRA had been too high and they had misjudged the nature and depth of the British commitment to Northern Ireland. For centuries, Britain's involvement in Ireland had been predicated on strategic considerations, a realisation which had sunk deep into the republican psyche where it crystallised in the slogan, 'England's difficulty is Ireland's opportunity.'

The British knew that a deal was there to be done and despite the bombs no doors were permanently closed. By 26 February, just three weeks after Canary Wharf and amid peace marches throughout Ireland, McGuinness was again back in Castle Buildings, Stormont, at 3.00 p.m. to meet three British officials – Quentin Thomas, Chris Maccabe and Tony Beeton. He brought with him Gerry Kelly and Siobhan O'Hanlon. The meeting started testily, with McGuinness claiming that the 'Irish peace process has been sacrificed on the alter of expediency'. In words reminiscent of those Adams had used to Mayhew, McGuinness spoke of how the peace process had been undertaken 'at great personal risk to ourselves'. He accused John Major of lying about the 'war is over' message passed through the Link and said 'this was an attempt to assassinate me politically and actually'. It was a revealing comment, which exposed the tensions within the IRA, but it also proved wide of the mark. The Link, and not Major, had manufactured the message and the aim had been to push forward the peace process by making McGuinness' private position public. The British valued McGuinness, and, if anything, they had protected him. After the preliminaries McGuinness conceded, 'We don't have any objection to elections', though he regarded it as a 'time-wasting process', which had 'created the impression that he [Major] had moved to a Unionist agenda'. Asked by Thomas if they were close to agreement McGuinness replied, 'tantalisingly close' and assured the

British of Sinn Féin's continued commitment to its peace strategy. Thomas agreed to meet again, 'subject to events on the ground', and assured McGuinness of the government's 'commitment to finding a way forward', and to co-opting Sinn Féin into the political process. It seemed abundantly clear that everyone was still in the market for a ceasefire and talks. As a sign of good faith, each side briefed the other on what they would be saying to the press.

McGuinness was not, however, afraid to be identified with the men of violence. In early February, Ed O'Brien, a 20-year-old volunteer from Co. Wexford, was blown up on a London bus by his own bomb. Willie McGuinness attended the funeral while Martin led a black flag march through the Bogside in the bomber's honour. The Provos were maintaining the threat until such time as the Major government, which the IRA believed was hamstrung by unionist votes in the Commons, was beaten before they would make their next move. Men on the run were briefed that fresh negotiations were likely after an election had produced a more stable administration, whether the victors were Labour or Conservative. The position crystallised during the summer when David Goodall was sent to Clonard Monastery to warn Gerry Kelly that the government was prepared to start the talks without Sinn Féin. Kelly regarded the comments as a threat, but in reality it was a fairly empty one, for there was little prospect of Hume abandoning Adams to reach an agreement before the election. Sinn Féin contested the elections to all-party negotiations. A few days before polling, Adams said he was prepared to sign up to the Mitchell Principles of non-violence, a move which allowed the party to emerge on 30 May with 15.5 per cent of the vote, its best result ever. On 15 June, McGuinness led his delegation up to the gates of Castle Buildings where he was refused entry to all-party talks. Five days later a 3,500 lb bomb devastated the centre of Manchester causing up to three hundred million pounds worth of damage and injuring 200 people.

At times the campaign had a 'phoney war' feel to it. There were no restrictions on McGuinness entering Britain and he travelled there at the end of July to meet Kevin McNamara, the Labour MP, and Peter Temple Morris, a hibernophile Tory. He lost his way and ended up in the headquarters of MI5. No police were called and the building was not cleared. Instead staff allowed him to wait until he got his arrangements sorted out. The IRA's capacity and ingenuity were undiminished, but its *esprit de corps* was flagging. Volunteers were more reluctant to risk life and liberty when what was at stake was not the freedom of Ireland but an improved negotiating position in future talks. Increasingly, operations were abandoned at the first sign of danger. The technical coup achieved when two car bombs were detonated in British Army headquarters, Lisburn, killing one soldier in October, was down to the use of an identity card supplied by a former soldier. Notwithstanding, it was clear that the campaign was on borrowed time, and after each attack people tended to blame Sinn Féin. The Lisburn bombs had been timed to coincide with the Tory Party conference and John Major hit a raw nerve when he told delegates: 'This morning the IRA spat their hatred at the British nation. A British soldier died. I sent him there, Mr Adams, so spare me any crocodile tears. Don't tell me this has nothing to do with you. I don't believe you, Mr Adams, I don't believe you.'

Later that month an Army Convention was held and shortly afterwards Adams and McGuinness were reappointed to the Council where Thomas 'Slab' Murphy was elected Chief of Staff. On paper their hands had been tied – the council insisted that there would be no more ceasefires without a British declaration of intent to withdraw – but in practice they were gaining more control than before. The other members included McKenna, Keenan, Martin Ferris and the recalcitrant QM, now in a minority of one. In December, Adams and Hume put fresh peace proposals to the British government and in January 1997, Bombardier Stephen Restorick, shot down by a sniper as he checked a motorist's driving licence, entered history as the last British soldier to die in the Northern Ireland Troubles. Sinn Féin was now in the mood to win elections and do deals.

CHAPTER SEVENTEEN

Guns to Government

The people of Mid-Ulster can play a major role in rebuilding the peace process by casting their vote for Sinn Féin.

Martin McGuinness, *An Phoblacht/Republican News*, 1997

Omagh Leisure Centre, the squat modern building where the 1997 Mid-Ulster count was conducted, is not an historic or inspiring setting. Nonetheless, there was a feeling of destiny unfolding when Allister Patterson, the very same returning officer who had announced Bobby Sands' election victory 16 years earlier, called out the result from a makeshift podium in front of the counter of the 'Ramblers' canteen concession.

'McGuinness, James Martin, 20,294' – the room seemed to erupt around Rev. William McCrea, who realised that McGuinness had just taken his parliamentary seat. McCrea had refused to stand at the front to hear the results because it would have put him in too close proximity to his successor.

McGuinness thrust his right arm in the air in an impromptu ANC-style clenched fist salute. 'The roaring and shouting of them was desperate, it was certainly intended to be intimidating but I didn't expect anything else of them. I was called everything under the sun, they didn't think I was a child of my father,' said McCrea, a Christian fundamentalist. He felt McGuinness was smirking and staring at him from the platform. 'He has that steely eyed look, he reminds me of a mortician,' the DUP man added with a shiver.

For most of the 1997 election campaign McGuinness hadn't expected victory. The feeling had been that unionists would rally behind McCrea and that, with an IRA campaign on, voting for someone of McGuinness' ferocious reputation would prove a bridge too far for the middle-of-the-road nationalist voters he needed to win over to construct a majority.

During campaigning, McGuinness had turned the tide by stressing his commitment to the peace process and arguing that strengthening Sinn Féin's mandate would make a ceasefire more likely. It was a message which, his SDLP rivals pointed out, amounted to, 'Vote for us or we'll shoot.' McGuinness also pitched the election in terms of defeating the Tories and continued with his policy of demonising Major as the wrecker of the peace process. He told *An Phoblacht/Republican News:* 'My chief opponent in this election is the person who sabotaged the peace process. That person is the British Prime Minister John Major, the arch unionist. The people of Mid-Ulster can play a major role in rebuilding the peace process by casting their vote for Sinn Féin.'

In his acceptance speech McGuinness pushed home the message. 'What we require of the new British government is a real and determined attempt to rebuild a new peace process in this country. This is the most urgent task facing the new British Prime Minister, Tony Blair.' Outside in the street he was greeted by a sea of tricolours and carried shoulder high past the defeated Unionist. The outraged McCrea described McGuinness' election as an insult to the victims of violence, Catholic as well as Protestant. In the coming weeks McGuinness would lose no opportunity to use his IRA credentials to boost the idea of a renewed cessation.

The election produced a new Labour government, under the leadership of Tony Blair, which commanded a big enough majority to deliver on any undertaking it gave. The careless informality of Dr Marjorie 'Mo' Mowlam, the new Secretary of State, was a far cry from the patrician style of Sir Patrick Mayhew. Initially popular with both sides of the political divide, Mowlam affected a chatty, casual style, snaffling chips or cigarettes from politicians and often cursing to break the ice in discussions. Months later, McGuinness would ask her to stop constantly referring to him as a bastard.

The favourable political circumstances of a Sinn Féin victory at the polls and the new administration provided the context McGuinness needed in order to move the Army Council once more towards ceasefire. He began the groundwork with a series of engagements aimed at neutralising dissidents and promoting the idea of a renewed cessation, called from a position of political strength. The first was in Galbally Community Centre in County

Tyrone. It was a symbolic occasion, the tenth anniversary of the ambush and shooting of eight IRA members and one civilian by the SAS at Loughgall. The SAS's information had come from a listening device in one of the dead terrorists' homes but some IRA hardliners suspected that the unit had been set up by the leadership because of its opposition to any plans for a ceasefire.

In his address McGuinness put his own stamp on the memory of the 'Loughgall Martyrs'. He stressed, 'There is a need for a cessation, but a cessation must also come from the British and there must be credible negotiations that deal with issues like Loughgall and Bloody Sunday.' 'Loughgall,' he added, 'epitomises British "peacekeeping" in Ireland: kill the dissenters and the rebels and terrorise us into submission. British terrorism hasn't worked in 800 years and it won't work, not ever . . . The British ARE going to go, you know, because republicans definitely aren't going anywhere.'

A few days later, in London, McGuinness visited Roisin McAliskey, the pregnant detainee who had been dissuaded with such difficulty from standing against him in Mid-Ulster, publicly backing her case as he had promised. The main reason for his visit, however, was to press his claim to office space at Westminster. Peter Jennings, the Serjeant at Arms, had suggested that, despite refusing to take its seats or the MP's oath of allegiance to the Queen, Sinn Féin might still be entitled to privileges, including offices in the Palace of Westminster. Parliamentary passes would have entitled them to twenty-four hour access to the Commons with no searches, allowing them to use a range of facilities, including the House of Commons firing range. McGuinness and Adams hoped to appoint Siobhan O'Hanlon, a former bomber who escaped an SAS ambush while carrying out reconnaissance work for the planned bomb in Gibraltar in 1988, as the office manager. The proposal caused outrage and anger among MPs worried about the security implications. Andrew Hunter, one of several Tory and Unionist MPs under constant police guard due to IRA death threats, spoke for many when he said, 'I would be horrified to bump into IRA members in the bars and restaurants of the House.'

McGuinness' hopes on this point were finally dashed by Betty Boothroyd, the Speaker, who made a statement to the House on 14 May in which she introduced new regulations denying facilities to members who did not take their seats. The Speaker left a few days' grace until the Queen's

Speech on the 21st. Thirty-six hours before the new rules took effect, McGuinness and Adams turned up at the Commons. Mo Mowlam described the visit as 'propaganda' and McGuinness was determined to make the most of it, coming, as it did, on the eve of the Northern Ireland local government elections. He and Adams spent a day show-boating around the house, putting in an appearance in the Members' Lobby and getting shown round the actual chamber by Tony Benn, the veteran left-wing Labour MP. Benn, whom McGuinness later described as his favourite political figure, had earlier urged McGuinness to exploit another loophole by speaking in the Commons chamber during the election of the Speaker. He and Adams rejected the idea because of fears of a backlash from traditionalists if they spoke in Westminster. Benn had missed the point that Sinn Féin's objection was not just to the oath of allegiance but to the whole notion of dignifying British jurisdiction over Northern Ireland by representing Irish constituencies in the London parliament. Instead, they promenaded on the Commons terrace, admiring the view over the Thames and taking the opportunity to be filmed by TV crews from Westminster Bridge.

After McGuinness met the British government officials in Stormont Castle, he radiated optimism that the remaining problems could be overcome. In reality the meeting had been a ritual restatement of existing positions. McGuinness told Quentin Thomas and his team that he was seeking an end to 'British domination and British injustice'. They spoke of their eagerness to reopen full dialogue after an unequivocal IRA cessation, and the two sides agreed to meet again.

As the Stormont meeting took place, voters were going to the polls in local elections across the Six Counties, once more confirming the surge to Sinn Féin which had been evident in the Westminster poll. The party's position as one of the 'big four' Northern Ireland parties was confirmed when it won 74 seats or 16.9 per cent of the vote, a full percentage point ahead of the DUP.

This was a favourable political backdrop in which Sinn Féin could move but in the background the RUC were reporting to Blair and Mowlam that, despite McGuinness' talk of peace, the IRA were preparing renewed attacks once the elections were over as a means of 'managing their constituency'.

McGuinness attended a conflict resolution conference in South Africa sponsored by Nelson Mandela's Government and the US National Democratic Institute. The other main parties, including the Ulster

Unionists and DUP also attended but, ironically considering the venue, a strict apartheid was maintained between the unionist and Sinn Féin delegations. Something close to an incident occurred when Martin McGuinness advanced on David Trimble with palm outstretched at a dinner on Saturday. Trimble didn't see the funny side and complained to his South African hosts about his behaviour. Later that evening in the pub, however, the two politicians did manage to join harmoniously in the communal singing of 'Danny Boy', albeit from widely separated tables. The DUP, who attended the conference, boycotted the social side for fear of 'contamination' by Sinn Féin.

McGuinness regarded the gathering as one of the most memorable experiences of his life and Nelson Mandela's speech to delegates deeply moved him. The Sinn Féin leader said he was struck by Mandela's argument that 'You don't negotiate with your friends. You negotiate with your enemies.' The South African President made a point of showing the unionist table Lieutenant General Andrew Masondo, a former ANC commissar in Angola who had admitted ordering the execution of a suspected informer and now served in the Defence forces. 'I don't know what this country is coming to,' Mandela quipped, 'up at the other end of the table is an ex-convict. He calls himself a general. If I had known I was going to have to share a room with an ex-convict I would not have come here at all. I have my reputation to think of.' The analogy with Sinn Féin was obvious.

On 13 June McGuinness received a document from the Northern Ireland Office promising that a cessation would be rewarded by entry to talks at the end of July. In the background, however, the tempo of violence was once more picking up, to remind the British of what the IRA was capable, and to still dissent. In some areas local IRA leaders, let off the leash after the election pause, saw the recent political successes as evidence that a 'ballot and Armalite' approach was still viable. Just three days after the document was received, on 16 June, two community police officers were cut down by the leader of the IRA's hardline North Armagh Brigade as they patrolled in Lurgan, Co. Armagh. In a statement the brigade said the attack had been preceded by several weeks of surveillance. It was a deliberately provocative act in the lead up to the July marching season, at a time when Mowlam was personally involved in negotiations aimed at defusing the annual row over the Orange Order's plans to march down Portadown's Garvaghy Road, just a few miles from the murder scene and in the Brigade area.

Incensed, Blair announced that he was breaking off all contact with Sinn Féin but it was clear that the offer of talks was repeated within days in the House of Commons. Despite worldwide condemnation of the murders, and despite an RPG-7 rocket attack on an RUC vehicle in North Belfast, the sanction lasted no more than a couple of weeks. McGuinness used the annual Wolfe Tone commemoration in Bodenstown to warn that, 'Rather than eyeballing us, governments and political leaders should be applying themselves to making change and to creating justice.' He went on, 'Decommissioning has not yet been removed as an obstacle in the negotiations.'

In the background Mowlam had decided – on strong security force and civil service advice that it was 'the least worst option' and would prevent widespread attacks by the dissident loyalists – to force a limited Orange March through Garvaghy Road on 6 July. She was determined to keep her channels open to McGuinness who was privately using his limited influence with former republican prisoners in the leadership of the Garvaghy Road Residents Association to damp down the dispute. In return the Orange Order had assured Mowlam that they would help her defuse the situation by rerouting a number of contentious parades in Belfast. Publicly, however, McGuinness strongly opposed the decision. In Bellaghy, the day after the Drumcree march was pushed through, he took part in a demonstration against another Orange march and claimed to need stitches after being hit on the head with an RUC baton. In fact, according to eyewitnesses, his injury was caused by a piece of wood thrown at the police by demonstrators.

By early July, British officials had taken three telephone calls from McGuinness. Letters from McGuinness had been received on 20 June and 2 July and a reply – approved by Mo Mowlam – was sent to him on 9 July. The essential elements being sorted out in these contacts were that the negotiations to which Sinn Féin were admitted should be without preconditions and that they should not be stalled if the IRA failed to decommission in parallel with talks, as Mitchell had recommended. Mitchell's proposal, a step away from prior decommissioning, had been accepted only with difficulty by Trimble's Ulster Unionists. Before he would risk recommending a renewal of the ceasefire at the Army Council, McGuinness was determined to reduce the proposal to an aspiration. He also needed to be able to tell the other IRA leaders that the talks would not preclude any outcome, including a united Ireland and the release of prisoners. He also demanded 'confidence building measures' from the British, particularly on the prisoners issue as a means of winning over the Council.

The required cave-in on the decommissioning issue was contained in the reply sent on Mowlam's behalf to McGuinness on 9 July. It spelt out that decommissioning would not stall talks provided any ceasefire was unequivocal, that Sinn Féin signed up to the Mitchell Principles and that the parties made their best efforts to achieve decommissioning. There would be a review mechanism on progress which was, essentially, in the hands of George Mitchell. The letter did not go as far as McGuinness would have liked on prisoners, but it did promise that tariffs would be set for four more IRA lifers in Britain, that a process of repatriation of IRA prisoners in British jails would get underway and that security classifications would be reviewed.

It concluded, 'What now needs to be cleared up without further delay is whether the IRA will declare a genuine and unequivocal ceasefire, which alone can permit Sinn Féin to join the political negotiations when they get under way in September.'

McGuinness realised that he was now approaching the British bottom line. All that remained was for the concessions to be made public and the charade of no contact with Sinn Féin publicly abandoned. If this happened Adams and McGuinness would recommend a renewal of the cessation when they attended the IRA Army Council on 18 July. On 16 July a document encompassing the watered-down proposals on decommissioning was pushed through the Commons without debate and on 17 July, the Northern Ireland Office released the letter to McGuinness together with a claim that they were not negotiating a ceasefire.

At the Army Council, held shortly before a Sinn Féin Ard Comhairle meeting in Dublin, McGuinness and Adams outlined the situation as they saw it. The essential argument was that the circumstances leading to the abandonment of the last cessation had now changed and that, in the new political atmosphere, further delay would threaten the nationalist consensus to the point where the SDLP and Irish government might enter talks without Sinn Féin. If that happened the IRA would be left with a choice of losing the initiative and acquiescing, or seeking to destabilise any resulting settlement by military means over a period of years. The probability was that if the IRA looked like succeeding in this it would face an unprecedented security crackdown by both the British and Irish governments and hostility from the rest of the nationalist family. They would, McGuinness argued, then be denied the option of pursuing the present opportunities for political movement, the release of prisoners and a rundown in the security presence.

A permanent commitment to non-violent means had been avoided and the IRA could continue to keep its options open should the British break their word and inclusive negotiations did not proceed. Indeed, following an IRA convention at the end of 1996, the IRA's 12-strong Army Executive, dominated by old-timers, was charged with reviewing any future ceasefire every four months. A final decision on any renewed ceasefire would be taken by another IRA convention in the spring of 1998. In the meantime preparations for a possible return to violence would continue and targets would continue to be recced and lined up so that, if the need arose, the IRA could strike at short notice.

Behind all this lurked the realisation that the security forces were already taking their toll and that the circumstances for continuing the campaign were not good. As Professor Paul Bew wrote in the *Sunday Times*, 'the return to violence had cost the IRA more than is sometimes realised: key operatives – the type who could produce effective "spectaculars" – were lost.' Even for the hawks a renewed cessation offered an opportunity to regroup. As one IRA member put it, 'the military as well as political arguments for it were quite simply unanswerable, it was an offer you couldn't refuse.'

The ceasefire statement, when it was issued to Charlie Bird of RTE next morning, spoke of 'an unequivocal restoration of the ceasefire of August 1994' in order to 'enhance the search for a democratic peace settlement through real and inclusive negotiations'. The sub-text was clear: no negotiations, no settlement, the option of violence was still open and the IRA continued to arm, train and import arms. They built links in both Southern Africa and the US for the supply of new and untraceable weapons which could be used in 'deniable' operations, whether robberies or attacks on criminals and dissidents who got in their way. Even if there was no return to the campaign, the IRA would be able to credibly threaten one and to control the streets and to protect its members in its areas of strength.

The process of consolidating the ceasefire started straight away. Within twenty-four hours McGuinness and the other members of the Sinn Féin delegation were admitted to their new offices in a brutalist medium rise block in Stormont's Castle Buildings, provoking a permanent withdrawal from the talks process by the DUP and UKUP. Later in the week the British and Irish governments ignored a rejection of their decommissioning proposals by all the unionist parties and announced that all inclusive talks would begin on 15 September.

McGuinness began preparing for a trip to the US by meeting a delegation of Irish American businessmen and opinion formers in Belfast. They included Niall O'Dowd, the publisher of the *Irish Voice*, and the financier and philanthropist, Chuck Feeney. Feeney was later to finance restorative justice projects, favoured by Sinn Féin as an alternative to the RUC and to punishment beatings in republican areas. Bill Flynn, Chair of the Mutual of America Insurance Corporation, predicted that the Sinn Féin leadership would be invited to the White House soon and promised to help with the cost of their trip. A few days later McGuinness and the other Sinn Féin leaders met Mowlam and Paul Murphy, her Welsh-born Political Development Minister, for the first time at Stormont. There were two hours of talk, at the outset of which they presented her with a paper saying that discussions must include political and constitutional change, an equality agenda and demilitarisation. McGuinness, the chief negotiator, urged the British side to persuade the unionists to embark on a process of Irish reunification, ignoring the fact that the main problem facing Mowlam was getting the unionists into the talks at all.

A first sign of unionist intentions came a week later when Ken Maginnis, the Ulster Unionist security spokesman, agreed to a televised debate with McGuinness on BBC. It was a largely set piece affair in which Maginnis described the republican leader as 'the godfather of godfathers' and accused him of involvement in the killing of hundreds of innocent people. McGuinness played up the positive, saying he was pleased that unionists were now reacting positively to a desire among ordinary Protestants for the talks process to continue.

On 6 September McGuinness joined Adams and O Caolain on a five-day trip to America. From the start, the red carpet was rolled out for the three MPs by Irish America. During their stay, McGuinness met President Clinton's National Security Adviser, Sandy Berger, in the White House, Secretary of Commerce William Daly, and Senators Ted Kennedy, Chris Dodd, Robert Torricelli and Alfonse D'Amato.

After a dinner in Sinn Féin's honour, which had to be moved from its original venue to the larger Waldorf Astoria hotel, McGuinness broke off from the rest of the schedule to travel to California and visit three fugitive Maze escapees, against whose extradition he had argued at the White House. The visit over, he was fêted in San Francisco, showing his skills in working a room when he mingled with guests and posed for photographs at the city's 'Ireland 32' bar and restaurant. At a formal rally in the city's Russian centre he was presented with the freedom of the county and city of San Francisco by Mayor Willie Brown, an honour he said he was accepting on behalf of 'the risen people, particularly those who need the keys to unlock the hundreds of jail doors not only here in the US but in Ireland and Britain'.

It was all a morale-boosting backdrop for the move which would risk splitting the IRA when, on 9 September, Sinn Féin would sign the Mitchell Principles of non-violence and enter talks. As soon as they did so the US Department of Justice said that they were halting the extradition of six IRA fugitives on the advice of Madeleine Albright, the Secretary of State, who had advised them it would advance the peace process. For the families of Robert McErlean, Matthew Morrison, Gabriel 'Skinny Legs' Megahey, Brian Pearson, Noel Gaynor, and Gerald McDade, McGuinness had delivered the US government.

Despite the sweeteners, it was evident that the IRA would take damage from Sinn Féin's new found commitment to non-violence. Within three days of Adams signing the principles, McGuinness organised an IRA interview with *An Phoblacht/Republican News* in which the organisation stated that it disagreed with the principles and was not bound by them. A few weeks later he chose a 'release the prisoners' rally in the republican heartland of Coalisland to state that Sinn Féin's bottom line in talks would be British withdrawal and smashing the union.

Trouble was brewing in Dundalk, home to the IRA's influential Quartermaster (QM) and his equally influential girlfriend. A short, impetuous, thickset man in his forties, with a bad temper and a piercing stare, the QM took a militant line from the safe harbour of the Republic and was regarded as a 'long rifle' by McGuinness. Eamon Collins, a former IRA intelligence officer, described him as 'a tough little guy and a bit of a brute. He used to beat people up after an operation if they didn't carry it out the way he desired'.

As soon as Adams signed the Mitchell Principles on behalf of Sinn Féin, the QM moved. Rather than wait for the scheduled Army Executive review of the ceasefire on 20 November, he lobbied for the Army Executive, of which he was a member, to call an extraordinary army convention.

His main target was the fifth of the Mitchell Principles, which committed Sinn Féin 'to agree to abide by the terms of any agreement reached in all party negotiations and to resort to democratic and exclusively peaceful methods in trying to alter any aspect of the outcome with which they may disagree'. This, he claimed, meant renouncing the armed struggle and accepting the unionist veto at talks. He wanted Adams, who had signed, and McGuinness, the chief negotiator, expelled from the IRA for treachery.

McGuinness' trips to places like Galbally, Bellaghy and Coalisland had not been in vain and he calculated that he was now strong enough to meet the challenge head-on. His supporters on the Executive went along with a motion which declared the Mitchell Principles to be against the IRA's constitution and referred Adams' actions in signing them to the Army Council. The Council then said Adams had a special dispensation in his capacity as Sinn Féin president.

The executive responded by calling a convention, held in October in Gweedore, Co. Donegal. It came shortly after Tony Blair met and shook hands with McGuinness and Adams for the first time at the talks in Castle Buildings. Immediately afterwards Blair was mobbed by loyalist protesters when he attempted a meet-the-people session in Connswater Shopping Centre, East Belfast. On 9 October the Ulster Unionists, but not the DUP, for the first time sat down in direct talks with the Sinn Féin and the British and Irish governments.

The mood music, with the British and the unionists at each others' throats and McGuinness pursuing the objective of Irish unity in direct talks, was near perfect when the Convention met. The meeting authorised Sinn Féin to continue the dialogue and to give whatever undertakings it liked on the understanding that the IRA would not be bound by them. In 1998 a new convention would review the position. 'Adams and McGuinness were told: come back and show us what you have got – then we will decide,' an RUC source said.

The sting for the QM came when, in the Executive elections, key delegations from South Armagh and Belfast voted against him and he was thrown off. In a fit of pique he resigned from the IRA and a close female friend also left in sympathy.

Without the Quartermaster's vote, and the vote of his female ally, a close friend was removed from the Army Council and replaced by Brian Gillen, the OC of Northern Command and an Adams supporter. Thomas 'Slab' Murphy was reappointed Chief of Staff and Martin Ferris from Kerry, and Brian Keenan, who organised the British bombings in the 1980s, also joined the Council. McGuinness and Adams had turned a coup into a purge – successfully isolating the opposition and increasing their room for manoeuvre.

As soon as McGuinness returned to the Mitchell talks he used his discretion to make a crucial breakthrough, agreeing for the first time to discuss a Northern Ireland assembly at Stormont. He was, as the QM had foreseen, now firmly on the road to becoming a British Minister at Stormont.

CHAPTER EIGHTEEN

The Long March Away From The Gun

Tony Blair needs to crack the whip on the unionists . . . He has to tell them that the game is up and that he is British Prime Minister and he is a British Prime Minister with a very powerful mandate.

Martin McGuinness, *Charlie Rose Show*, *PBS*, 13 March 1998

As 1997 closed, McGuinness' long march away from the gun was irreversible, yet his place in government had still to be secured through the stalled talks process. This made him vulnerable and, over and above issues arising from in the talks process, his priorities had to be keeping the republican movement together and avoiding a formal return to armed conflict.

When the talks broke at the end of 1997 McGuinness had vetoed a draft agenda agreed between the unionists and the SDLP. Mitchell wrote in his book on the negotiations that 'rarely in my life have I felt so frustrated and angry as I did on that day.' The visible impasse heralded a spiral of loyalist and republican dissident killings. Shortly after Christmas the INLA murdered Billy Wright, the UVF leader in the Maze, in what they said was an attempt to stop attacks on Catholics. It had the opposite effect and drew sections of the UFF into the fray. Mo Mowlam took the unprecedented step of visiting the UFF, and other prisoners in the Maze, to ask for their support with the negotiations and to stop the killings. She was widely praised for her courage but the murders continued until Sir Ronnie Flanagan of the RUC stated publicly that the UFF were involved and the UDP, their political wing, were expelled from the talks. In response to the loyalists' action, the IRA flexed its muscles by murdering two alleged drugs dealers and Sinn Féin was, in turn, temporarily expelled from the talks. McGuinness, a member of the Army Council that approved all potentially fatal attacks during the ceasefire, played it down. 'I see all this as another challenge, another obstacle, and out of this has to come a real peace process,' he said, adding that Sinn Féin were 'down but not out'. What really mattered was that Blair kept delivering on the republican agenda. In early February the Prime Minister announced a full public inquiry into the events surrounding Bloody Sunday, under the direction of Lord Saville. It was something McGuinness had raised at every opportunity since he first met Blair the previous October.

The talks in Belfast approached their climax on 7 April when Mitchell tabled a paper summing up a possible framework for agreement. Tony Blair and Bertie Ahern, the latter straight from his mother's funeral, personally joined discussions and, after three days of near round-the-clock talks an agreement emerged in the early hours of 10 April. The final hurdle had been the release of paramilitary prisoners, a point on which McGuinness had stalled, insisting that they should all be out within one year rather than the three that the British were proposing. When the loyalist parties refused to back Sinn Féin and Bill Clinton personally phoned Adams to remonstrate, McGuinness finally accepted a compromise of two years, a good result in the circumstances and one which delighted the prisoners. Elsewhere he had not done so well.

The centre-piece of the agreement was a 108-member power-sharing assembly at Stormont that McGuinness had fruitlessly opposed to the last.

Policing was fudged: the agreement specified a 'new beginning' and a service representative of the community as a whole but left the details to an independent commission with international membership that would report by the summer of 1999. Full decommissioning was envisaged by May 2000 and all parties were committed to using their best efforts to achieve it. On the constitutional front the Irish Government agreed to replace articles two and three of its constitution, which asserted sovereignty over the north, with an aspiration that unity be brought about with 'the consent of a majority of the people, democratically expressed, in both jurisdictions of the island.' This last provision was a decisive defeat for McGuinness on what he repeatedly described as a 'touchstone issue'. He opposed this consent principle to the last and fought to minimise constitutional change in the republic.

The annual Sinn Féin Ard Fheis on 18 April had to be adjourned until 10 May before a vote could be taken but in a detailed report to the conference McGuinness conceded that the agreement 'clearly does not go as far as most nationalists and republicans would wish. But it is the basis for advancement'. For republicans his phrasing was uncomfortably reminiscent of the words that Michael Collins used to recommend the Anglo-Irish Treaty of 1921. Collins described the treaty as, 'not the ultimate freedom that all nations desire and develop to, but the freedom to achieve it'. As Sinn Féin's chief negotiator in 1921 Collins, like McGuinness, was regarded as an incorruptible IRA stalwart, but he had left himself dangerously exposed by signing the treaty in London without referring back to the movement. On his return the majority backed him and he helped form a government but the IRA was split, sparking the Irish civil war in which Collins himself was killed by the anti-treaty minority. This 'Collins factor' goes some way to explaining McGuinness' inflexibility in negotiations and his reticence in publicly endorsing what he believed was the best deal achievable. In any case, he was prohibited by IRA standing orders from advocating the taking of seats in a partitionist assembly, such as the one being proposed for Stormont. It would take an Extraordinary Army Convention on 2 May to change the rules before he could speak in favour of the deal at the resumed Ard Fheis. The Provos were wooed with a range of sweeteners from London and Dublin. Nine prisoners were released early from their sentences in the republic and the five members of the Balcombe Street Gang – 1970s London bombers – were transferred to Ireland. They were even allowed parole to attend the Ard Fheis, where McGuinness embraced them and they, in turn, welcomed the agreement as a basis for progress.

The Convention had an offer it couldn't refuse. If the republican movement rejected the agreement then, under the rules of sufficient consensus, devolution could proceed without Sinn Féin. The agreement was also likely to pass in the referenda, leaving republicans with a choice between acquiescing and trying to destroy a settlement approved by the Irish people. McGuinness even risked suggesting a further change in the IRA's rules to allow the Army Council the right to dispose of weapons as they wished. This had been the situation prior to 1996 when the QM and his followers had succeeded in having power over arms reserved for the more broadly based Convention. McGuinness argued that now the dissidents had left the movement their motion should fall but when the idea proved divisive he deferred it to a further convention in six months. An IRA statement described the Good Friday Agreement as falling 'short of presenting a solid basis for a lasting settlement', and stated bluntly, 'Let us make it clear that there will be no decommissioning by the IRA. This issue, as with any other matter affecting the IRA, its function and objectives, is a matter only for the IRA to be decided upon and pronounced upon by us.'

Anthony McIntyre, a former IRA commander who is now an academic, saw this as the moment when 'the IRA virtually voted itself out of existence as an offensive fighting force', adding that the organisation now had 'little purpose other than to further the aims of the Sinn Féin leadership, most notably in the area of suppressing internal dissent'. An interview McIntyre conducted with a sceptical IRA member gives a flavour of the internal debate. The IRA was, he [the IRA member] believed, reduced 'to functioning as a defence against any possible loyalist backlash, or additionally acting as a guarantor against any attempt by the Brits or unionists to renege on the Stormont agreement thus denying it any offensive role against the Brits'. The republican movement was, in his view, deprived 'of any of its traditional revolutionary vestige'.

The reconvened Ard Fheis, which the British gave 27 prisoners special parole to attend, voted by 331 votes to 19 to alter the party constitution to allow Sinn Féin to take seats in the new assembly, but not in Westminster, and recommended a 'yes' vote in the referenda. To sweeten the pill McGuinness pointed to unionist pain, saying 'unionism's problems are 100-fold ours because its time as a dominating force is finished'. The agreement passed the dual referenda with 71.1 per cent support in the north and 94 per cent in the south. However the built-in instability of the result was revealed in a *Sunday Times*/Coopers & Lybrand exit poll which showed that only 55 per cent of Protestants had voted 'yes' while the figure for Catholics was 96 per cent. The fragility of the new unionism was soon confirmed in the actual assembly elections. The anti-agreement DUP and UKUP were neck and neck with the UUP, and for the first time the SDLP (22 per cent) scored marginally more than the UUP (21.3 per cent). Sinn Féin achieved its highest ever share of the vote, 17.6 per cent, confirming its position as one of the province's 'big four' parties. In Derry, however, the results were disappointing to some and as soon as the election was over the IRA were forced to act on its new role as suppressor of dissent. The main target was Michael Donnelly, a veteran locally revered as one of the 'hooded men' who received compensation at the European Court after being subjected to inhuman and degrading treatment during the early days of internment. Donnelly had called for a boycott of the election and had criticised Sinn Féin's stance as a sell out. Three days after polling, on 28 June, armed men burst into his house late at night as he sat watching a *Star Wars* video with his ten-year-old daughter on his knee and his family around him. The attackers sprayed the room with mace and identified themselves as IRA members, according to Donnelly's wife, Martina. The intention was clearly to abduct and shoot him. One weapon went off when Donnelly and his son, Deaglan, attacked the gunmen with a heavy stainless steel teapot and an iron bar they managed to wrench from another member of the gang. Two of the unit left a trail of blood to the car when they fled. Both Donnelly's legs had been broken and a bone protruded from one of them. His arms were also severely bruised. After visiting him in hospital the next day, his distraught wife Martina, herself a veteran republican, went to confront McGuinness in his home on Westland Terrace. The IRA leader was friendly when he answered the door. She said, 'I think he thought maybe I was up looking for clemency, to beg, to apologise. When he saw how I was taking it, he became very aggressive.' As he usually did when confronted by victims of IRA violence, McGuinness denied all knowledge, saying he had been in England. When Martina refused to believe him, 'he jabbed his finger at me and said "your husband has been calling me a traitor all around this town for the past year."' She replied, 'You are a traitor, you'll be running the government now for the British,' at which he slammed the door in her face telling her to keep her voice down so as not to distress his children.

Donnelly is representative of a number of people beaten and intimidated by the Provos in Derry and elsewhere following the election, most of whom were afraid to give interviews to the authors. A disturbing factor in this case is that the police, who were quickly on the scene, did not succeed in apprehending anyone despite the fact that there was DNA evidence, including blood, and that two of the attackers were fairly badly hurt. A mace canister, a bullet and other material were also recovered and the attackers' names became widely known in Derry within days. Since it involved guns and could well have proved fatal, the attack was undoubtedly authorised at Army Council level. 'It shows that McGuinness and some of his henchmen are a protected species, they are safe from arrest as long as they do not attack the British forces or the loyalists. It is the price our community pays for their peace process,' Donnelly believes.

A summer of violence, in which the IRA killed at least one man in a punishment attack, culminated in the Real IRA's car bombing of Omagh on 15 August in which 28 people were massacred, most of them Catholics. The Real IRA were a hard-line dissident group who broke away from PIRA in 1998. Desperate to distance himself from the violence but yet unwilling to endorse security moves against the bombers, McGuinness described the attack as 'indefensible', and said he believed that nationalist and republican supporters of the peace process would put pressure on the bombers to stop. In the immediate aftermath of the bombing, McGuinness sent a representative to ask whether he would be welcome at the homes of some of the bereaved. Victor Barker, a Surrey solicitor whose family had moved to Donegal and whose 12-year-old son James died in the bombing while on a day trip to Omagh, was among those who told McGuinness to stay away. McGuinness attended the funeral anyway. 'I wasn't aware of it at all until I got in the church and I was on the point of actually walking out and taking James' remains with me but the priest calmed me down,' Barker said. Later, however, he rang McGuinness and arranged a meeting for the Gateway Hotel in Buncrana early one Sunday morning. McGuinness came alone but insisted on sitting in an open area on the hotel's landing. Barker asked him, 'I want you to tell me, Mr McGuinness, who is responsible for the Omagh bomb.' McGuinness replied, 'everyone knows'. Barker then asked McGuinness if he had any part in the bomb and McGuinness agreed to put his hand on the Bible to underline his seriousness of his denial. McGuinness, who had by this time been appointed to liaise between Sinn Féin and de Chastelain's Commission, wrote a brief, hopeful personal message in a book of remembrance that Victor Barker maintained for his dead son. It read, 'A Chara [my friend] James, The work of justice and peace will continue until we succeed. When we do, that will be a most fitting memorial, Siochan [Peace] Martin McGuinness.' McGuinness offered to do anything he could to help and later Barker realised that an appeal for information would be very useful. 'When I tried to phone him he wouldn't take my calls,' said Barker, who then wrote to the Sinn Féin office. The reply he eventually received was from Gerry Adams who said such an appeal was impossible because of, 'continuing concern at the criminal justice system'. Other families took Sinn

Féin's sympathy at face value and appreciated it. McGuinness later told how he had walked resignedly away after a woman he had met at the funeral of Libby Rushe, one of the victims, refused to shake hands with him. He said, 'I heard a voice behind me calling and it was the young woman. I went back to her and she said, "I am sorry for turning away. I am a unionist and I am hurting," and she started to cry. I said that we were all hurting but that we were doing our best, and she said, "I know you are doing your best."'

The Omagh bombing was swiftly followed by strengthened anti-terrorist legislation and a ceasefire by the RIRA. Leading dissidents had been visited and warned off further violence by leading republicans including Willie McGuinness and Tony Millar, a former member of McGuinness' 1970s bombing teams. A glimpse of the changing relationship with the British government came when Mo Mowlam, the Secretary of State, expressed her appreciation to the republican movement for trying to restrain the dissidents.

The Omagh massacre on 15 August 1998 changed the mood in Northern Ireland. The first-face to-face discussions between Trimble and Adams took place soon after. Two days later the new Northern Ireland Assembly held its first session but optimistic hopes were dashed when the UUP insisted on the decommissioning of IRA weapons before a power sharing Executive, which included Sinn Féin, could be formed. Trimble wanted Sinn Féin penalised by being excluded from government but McGuinness argued that the party had fulfilled all its obligations by using its best efforts to achieve decommissioning. He spelt out the situation as he saw it after a meeting with Blair:

> David Trimble cannot move on without Sinn Féin, or any other party, to the Agreement. Nor can the two governments allow him to stall the full implementation of the Agreement in order to placate the rejectionists in his party any longer. He should resolve to face down the rump within his party which is intent on maintaining the politics of pre-Good Friday Unionism. He must tell them that they have had their day.

It was a call on Trimble to split his own party in order to facilitate republican unity as McGuinness approached that year's second Army Convention, held in early December. The Irish government believed that the convention would now give the power to dispose of weapons back to the Army Council, on which Adams and McGuinness sat along with Martin Ferris and one other Senior Sinn Féiner. This gave them a majority and the assumption was that they would be prepared to move once the convention was over. Blair's statement was a public repetition of private assurances that there would be no gloating by the British if the IRA moved. In the drive for decommissioning, violence deployed by the IRA within the nationalist community was now accepted as 'housekeeping' which did not constitute a breach of the ceasefire or result in sanctions against Sinn Féin. Up to 22 November the IRA had been involved in 79 beatings and shootings and the loyalists in 109. In January 1999 the IRA would murder Eamon Collins, a former IRA intelligence officer from Newry who had turned against violence and had become a best-selling author and commentator. Collins' main offence was to give evidence for the *Sunday Times* in a libel action brought by Thomas 'Slab' Murphy, the IRA Chief of Staff. The paper had given Collins money with which to move house following the trial but he had decided to remain living only a few miles from Murphy. As was so often the case following embarrassing killings, McGuinness expressed sympathy to the bereaved and threw a smoke-screen around the murder. 'Eamon Collins made an awful lot of enemies in the course of the years and any one of these could have been responsible for his death,' he said. At the Convention, Murphy, who had been humiliated in court and who had seen many secret IRA operations, including the names of his Libyan contacts, exposed, resigned as Chief of Staff. A few days later, when the Army Executive came to appoint the new Council, he was prevailed on to stay, with Brian Keenan as his deputy. The Convention also ratified the continuation of the ceasefire and confirmed the IRA's support for Sinn Féin's current strategy. Although control over weapons was restored to the Army Council, it was clear to McGuinness that there was no consensus for making an early concession. With his agreement the council took a cautious approach, ruling out any movement for the immediate future.

In the early months of 1999 the Irish government was increasingly frustrated with the IRA's failure to decommission and it was clear that, as official liaison man with de Chastelain, McGuinness was stalling. The General had given him a list of 12 questions, asking him about the 'modalities' (methods) of decommissioning and whether explosives might be destroyed as a first move but he had answered none of them. Publicly

McGuinness ruled out decommissioning for the foreseeable future, saying, 'in the context of such an ungenerous response from unionism, Sinn Féin has stretched the Irish republican constituency to the limit in the process. And not without taking damage or suffering defections. The republican constituency can go no further.' There were private warnings, two in the week following 7 February 1999, that Irish government patience was running out. Nonetheless McGuinness and the rest of the Sinn Féin leadership were taken by surprise when the rebukes became public on Sunday, 14 February in an interview that Ahern gave to the *Sunday Times*.

The first question he was asked was whether he would regard Sinn Féin as a suitable coalition partner in government in the republic. Ahern replied: 'our view is that decommissioning in one form or another has to happen. I am on record in recent months as saying that it is not compatible with being part of a government – I mean part of an executive – that there is not at least a commencement of decommissioning, and that would apply in the North, it would apply in the South.' He drove home the point repeatedly, there was no mistaking what he was saying.

That morning the BBC's David Frost interviewed Mitchell McLaughlin who, at first, declined to comment on 'this sensationalist report'. When Frost told him Dublin had confirmed the story McLaughlin described the situation as a crisis. In Dublin, Ahern had gone to mass after authorising the confirmation and when McGuinness, who spoke to him regularly on Sundays, phoned the Taoiseach's home to complain he got an answering machine. For the rest of the morning Paddy Teahon, the Secretary General of the department got it in the neck from McGuinness who hinted at breakdown if the government didn't retract. Teahon authorised a holding statement saying the Taoiseach didn't want Sinn Féin barred but an executive couldn't be formed without 'an understanding of how the implementation of decommissioning – which is part of the implementation of the Good Friday Agreement – would be taken forward.' McGuinness grasped at this straw of comfort, 'Mr Ahern made it clear that he has not said, as was reported, that Sinn Féin should be barred from the Executive and he also told me that he had made it clear in the interview that there are no preconditions in the Agreement.' However, in the Dail on Tuesday Ahern cut away the ambiguity. 'I don't detract from what I said in the *Sunday Times*,' Ahern told the chamber, adding, 'I attended a number of meetings in the past few weeks with Martin McGuinness, his colleagues and officials. I also met him directly . . . I am sure Mr Martin McGuinness would not agree with many of the things I said in the interview, but he would be aware of them as being my views.' McGuinness handled the situation expertly, turning the pressure to decommission back on those who deployed it against him in order to win further concessions from them. The basic strategy was to hint that decommissioning could occur, indeed would already have happened, if various measures were taken. He said in interviews that it would be 'further advanced' if an executive had been founded in 1997 and hinted that if Blair would only force Trimble into talks with him – 'liberate Mr Trimble from the position that he has adopted' – then anything was possible.

Eventually Blair set a deadline of 30 June for agreement on a deal to include decommissioning and the establishment of the executive and other institutions. Before that date Sinn Féin received a further boost in the European parliament elections in which they contested all the seats on the island of Ireland. Mitchell McLaughlin, Sinn Féin's Northern Candidate, ran the Ulster Unionists close for the third seat, being eliminated at 17.3 per cent of the poll, just a third of a percentage point below the Unionists. McGuinness pointed out that the combined nationalist role, at 300,000, was the highest ever. In the south Sinn Féin trebled its vote.

Despite his strong position McGuinness said in an *Irish Times* article that he hadn't even asked the IRA to begin decommissioning. 30 June came and went without agreement and, in early July, when Mo Mowlam attempted to trigger devolution the unionists did not attend. Blair had set the June deadline on Mowlam's insistence after she had assured him the unionists would have no choice but to come to heel. When, instead, the process crashed it raised inevitable questions about her judgement and her grasp of detail. After the summer she was replaced by Peter Mandelson, and George Mitchell was called back to chair a new review of the operation of the Good Friday Agreement. Mandelson was a formidable political operator who had been sent by Blair with a mission to get the unionists into government with Sinn Féin and to secure sufficient movement from the Provisionals to keep them there. The Mitchell/Mandelson combination proved effective – Mandelson commanded the confidence among unionists that Mowlam lacked, while Mitchell's patient, unflappable diplomacy was, as one participant put it, 'like adding Prozac to the tea'.

Relations began to thaw at a dinner in Whitfield House, the US ambassador's residence, where, for the first time, McGuinness, Adams and

Gerry Kelly sat round a table with Trimble and the rest of the unionist leadership. Before the meal started Mitchell made an unusual announcement – no politics were to be talked that evening. It proved an effective strategy. With an expression between dismay and disgust, Gerry Kelly, pigeon-holed by most unionists as the man who bombed the Old Bailey, leaned across the table to Trimble and his two lieutenants, Reg Empey and Dermot Nesbitt, to advise them, 'at least keep off fishing, if you mention that to Martin he'll have us here all night.' However Ken, now Lord, Maginnis, recalls, 'it didn't work, there was a lot of talk about fishing. Jim Wilson on our delegation was another enthusiast. There was all sorts of chit chat . . .'

Over the meal and the succeeding days the two delegations began to interact on a more human level and as the stereotypes broke down each delegation began to suspect that their opposite numbers did indeed want devolution to work and the violence to end for good. It was the beginning of a certain degree of trust and McGuinness was bullish to the press. 'We've achieved a cordial atmosphere and we've achieved greater understanding of each other's positions. However, we have to achieve agreement,' he declared.

Throughout the talks McGuinness sometimes relieved the tension by fly-tying or playing soccer. In one of over 40 games played during the Creggan festival in late October, when he appeared in a team called 'The Exiles' alongside Mitchell McLaughlin, he broke his thigh and appeared for a time in plaster. He used the mishap to divert attention from a more humiliating setback, which he never mentioned publicly. It came a couple of days earlier when the European Court unanimously rejected his claim that he was illegally excluded from using House of Commons facilities and claiming expenses. The Court described the allegation as, 'manifestly ill-founded'.

Mandelson worked in the background on the unionists and the deal that eventually emerged required them to move first, with less than cast-iron assurances that the Provos would reciprocate. If the Ulster Unionist Council approved entry into government with Sinn Féin by the end of November then decommissioning might start seven weeks later at the end of January and be completed within four months. These moves were in turn part of a delicate choreography, sequencing, which would build up to the full implementation of the Good Friday Agreement including the North-South bodies and the new beginning in policing. Trimble sold it to his Ulster Unionist Council. He also gave Sir Josias Cunningham, his Party Chairman, a post-dated letter of resignation, to be activated if there was no decommissioning by the end of January 2000. On 29 November, Mandelson succeeded in triggering devolution. McGuinness had been expected to pick the Agriculture Ministry because he represented a rural constituency but instead he picked Education, one of the highest spenders, while his colleague, Bairbre de Brun, picked Health.

When the new executive – the first in Northern Ireland's history to include Unionists and Republicans – sat round a table for the first time for a 'class picture', McGuinness was clearly nervous and took the seat reserved for Michael McGimpsey, the Ulster Unionist Minister for Culture. 'Hello Mr McGimpsey, Hello Mr McGimpsey', Trimble called over to him laughing. 'Trust me to be the first one to make a mistake,' said the Derry man with a broad smile, which even the unionists found infectious.

CHAPTER NINETEEN

Conclusion: An End to the IRA?

In many ways Martin McGuinness is an exemplary man. He is a good father, a good husband, a strong churchgoer, I believe him to be honest and upright in his personal conduct. No, my only quarrel with Martin was with the legitimacy and morality of using violence for political purposes.

Bishop Edward Daly, *Financial Times* , 4 December 1999

Bugger me, I thought, this is a murderer and terrorist talking about spending more on integrated education.

Dr Marjorie 'Mo' Mowlam MP, April 2001

On 8 May 2001, Peter Robinson, the Democratic Unionist Party MP and Member of the Local Assembly for East Belfast moved a debate in Stormont: 'That this Assembly has no confidence in the Minister of Education, Mr Martin McGuinness MP.'

McGuinness did not speak in the debate, but his hooded pale blue eyes flickered at Robinson's opening words:

A document was sent to my home recently, and I read it out in the House of Commons. The document outlines the present Army Council membership of the IRA. It indicates that the Chief of Staff is Thomas Murphy, and the Assistant Chief is Brian Keenan. The other members are Martin McGuinness, Gerard Adams, Martin Ferris, Patrick Doherty and Brian Gillen. The Headquarters Staff are as follows: the Quartermaster is Kevin Agnew; the Adjutant General is Martin Lynch; Bernard Fox is in charge of the Engineering Department; the Director of Education is James Monaghan; the Director of Finances is Patrick Thompson; the Operations Officer is Sean Hughes; the Director of Intelligence is Robert Storey; and Patrick Murphy and Kevin McBride are in charge of Internal Security – although I suspect that they will have to get new jobs after this. These are the people in charge of the Provisional IRA today. That information is on the record at the House of Commons, and it is now on record in this House.

Robinson's staccato words were accurate. McGuinness has maintained control of the IRA like a vice since his early days as the first leader of Northern Command in 1976. There have been few changes in the Army Council since then. Brian Keenan, one of the most influential men in the secret world of international arms dealing, rejoined the Army Council shortly after his release from prison in 1993 after serving 14 years of a 21-year sentence for masterminding 18 terrorist outrages. In early 2001, Keenan travelled to Colombia to set up a joint IRA/Farc (Revolutionary Armed Forces of Colombia) training camp. Jim 'Mortar' Monaghan, named by Robinson as a member of Staff, is the man who designed and developed the IRA's homemade mortar from its 1974 prototype, the Mark One, to the sophisticated Mark 18 Mortar, 'the barrack buster'. At the time of writing, Monaghan was one of three IRA men being held in the infamous La Modelo jail in Bogotá, where they were charged on 23 August 2001 with travelling on false documents and aiding terrorism.

Thomas 'Slab' Murphy was a founder member of Northern Command Staff and Pat Doherty, McGuinness' close friend from Donegal, replaced Daithi O Conaill as OC Southern Command shortly afterwards. The relationship between Gerry Adams and Martin McGuinness has its foundations in their joint membership of the 1972 IRA delegation that met William Whitelaw in Chelsea. The two men remain close. In 1984, Adams convalesced in McGuinness' grandmother's house in the Illies as he recovered from gunshot wounds he received in the loyalist attempt on his life in March that year.

This parliamentary tactic had been employed before by the DUP. On 4 February 1998, during a debate on the Public Processions (Northern Ireland) Bill, Robinson's party leader, Ian Paisley MP, MEP, MLA read an extract from an article he said was written by 'a Roman Catholic journalist from the Bogside.' He continued:

> This journalist says about Mr McGuinness: 'How dare you, big chief republican, current killers' mouthpiece, former killers' colleague, clamour for prosecutions. If we inquired into the entirety of the violence of the early 1970s with half the vigour you want for the Bloody Sunday investigators, who would stand accused beside the paratroopers?' 'I think General Sir Robert Ford (Commander of Land Forces in Northern Ireland in 1972) in particular is going to come under the microscope,' you said. It's a pity you could not go under with him. Perhaps the search for truth and justice will someday uncover the role of command you had in another land force of the time. Mrs Rose Hegarty must long to know. 'Who is Rose Hegarty?' The article continues, saying to Martin McGuinness, 'you promised, on bended knee, that her son was safe to return from exile. He was in hiding from the IRA who had threatened to kill him. You promised and cajoled and charmed her into telling him to come home. A few boys would question him and he'd be free to go, you told her. His sister drove him to the appointed place. His sister, unwittingly, drove him to his death. He was shot and his body unceremoniously dumped.'
>
> Those women long for the truth behind that atrocity. They won't hold their breath waiting for you to speak it. As Sinn Féin spokesman, your truths, like your morality, are selective. Your double standards are sickening . . . Sinn Féin should shut up . . . they have covered a dirty, murky, bloody past of their own in a way that makes Widgery look positively Godly.

McGuinness is a grandfather now, but back in 1972, he was just 21 and eager to flex his muscles in his first chance at command. After almost 30 years, his early enthusiasm remains undimmed.

While Martin McGuinness, Chief Negotiator for Sinn Féin, took part in the negotiations which led to the Good Friday Agreement, the secret army he belonged to trained, targeted, imported weapons and even, on occasion, killed. On 17 June 1999, police believe Scott Gary Monaghan, a Scotsman who has served time for bombing offences in Belfast, tried to murder Martin McGartland, a former RUC agent within the IRA who resettled in Tyneside under a new identity after his cover was blown. McGartland was seriously injured in the attack and has been campaigning for his attackers to be charged ever since. In 2001, Sergeant Ian Mills, a victims' liaison officer with the police at Tynemouth Area Command wrote to tell McGartland who his attackers were. One suspect, Monaghan, had been released from prison early under the terms of the Good Friday Agreement, and the other, Harry Fitzsimmons, had been a member of McGartland's unit. McGartland is one of the most vocal and courageous of the many 'exiles' that cannot return to Northern Ireland for fear of IRA reprisals.

While the RUC and the Garda Siochana tended to agree that the IRA had no firm plans to go back to war, they realised that they maintained the capability to do so. Like a nuclear deterrent in inter-state relations, the IRA's arsenal was a powerful bargaining tool in the talks, especially when the arms were not used. Republican targeting exercises, often carried out under the very nose of surveillance teams, might be accompanied by repeated IRA assurances that they 'posed no threat to the peace process', but police were in no doubt that they still constituted a form of gunboat diplomacy, which could at times have its uses. There was little doubt in the mind of the British that if republicans wished, they could return to violence.

These were the cards that history had dealt McGuinness, and he was not in a hurry to surrender any of them. British suspicion of republican intentions emerged graphically just eight days after he took office when a bug was discovered in a car that he had used to meet the IRA during the Mitchell review. Mowlam had personally sanctioned the listening and tracking device found in the vehicle, as she later confirmed in a television interview. MI5 later briefed the *Sunday Times* that the twenty-thousand-pound device had also been intended to help locate IRA weaponry. The target of the surveillance was an IRA intelligence officer, Martin Lynch, whose unsuspecting wife owned the car. Adams tacitly confirmed the vehicle's status as IRA transport when he stated that it was used by both Martin McGuinness, Sinn Féin's chief negotiator, and himself when they travelled to meetings with the IRA. He accused the British of endangering the peace process, describing the affair as 'an outrageous breach of faith which must be addressed at the highest levels'. His complaints were largely ignored.

Peter Mandelson, who took over as Secretary of State after Mowlam, was an astute observer of human nature. Of McGuinness, he said, 'If you were in his bad books, he would treat you in a very tough, usually unpleasant, way. If you were in his good books, he was completely charming.' The two men were not close. Mandelson did not like the habit McGuinness had of jabbing him in the chest at moments of tension, and McGuinness regarded his detailed expositions of the political constraints on British action as little more than excuses for delay. When Mandelson shared his impressions of McGuinness with Gerry Adams, the Sinn Féin President told him, 'Well, the nice thing about Martin is that he *is* so human – so emotional, quick to anger, quick to charm, quick to show his humour, always reacting very sharply in a situation. Martin takes everything very seriously, expresses himself very passionately.' Mandelson continued, 'In a sense, I know what he was saying. On the other hand, there was an aggression, almost a violence sometimes, in the way he expressed his point of view, and attacked you for your own, which was off-putting and not very constructive.' Mandelson found that, 'Martin would come with an agenda – actually both he and Gerry would come with exactly what they wanted to say and what they wanted to hear from you. Martin would oftentimes talk to you as though you were being deliberately perverse, quite stupid. How could you not see this, why can you not see our point of view, why can you not realise that the British Government has got to do this?'

One particular occasion when Mandelson and McGuinness crossed swords was after Mandelson temporarily suspended the Assembly and other institutions in February 2000 to avoid triggering Trimble's resignation: 'You will look back on this day and realise that you have destroyed what we achieved. This is the worst decision anyone has ever taken – what you have done is of such historical magnitude.' The Secretary of State felt: 'It was all calculated to make you feel that you had indeed done something of earth-shattering destructiveness, that you had really wrecked things. It was meant to make you feel utterly awful and unnerved. When you are first on the receiving end of something like that, it does take you aback, it does make you think, and you do of course reflect on it. But it was a speech I got many times subsequently, on many different occasions.'

246

Mandelson found McGuinness to be an intransigent bully in negotiations; even so, he had to admit that Sinn Féin's tactics were among the most effective he faced as Secretary of State. While the Provos were constantly chiselling at his position, negotiating and moving from one issue to another, the Ulster Unionists expended all their political capital more or less fruitlessly on the issues of policing and decommissioning.

As McGuinness played hardball with the British in his demand for the full implementation of the Patten report into the future of the RUC, he took every opportunity to drive a wedge between them and the Unionists, squeezing every situation until the pips squeaked. McGuinness would even exploit divisions within the IRA and dissident attacks to extract further concessions with which to bolster the Sinn Féin leadership. As part of his game plan, McGuinness stretched the consensus with the SDLP to its limits, using the spectre of breakdown and violence to frighten the larger party away from a deal with unionism. It was a predatory relationship, aimed at hollowing out their support in order to supplant them.

In the short term, McGuinness would often use Hume's party to decisively influence the Irish government's Northern policy and, through Dublin, could often induce Clinton to pressurise the British. If McGuinness could play the sophisticated spin-doctor, he could also do the common touch. An initial flurry of protests at state schools, orchestrated by the DUP, died away when the reality sunk in that there was nothing to be gained from antagonising the Education Minister. The civil servants liked McGuinness. Unlike Minister of Health, Bairbre de Brun, he did not press his staff to learn Irish or waste departmental budgets on bilingual statements. One civil servant said, 'There was some initial trepidation but he is basically very easy to deal with and not at all temperamental. He has a few clear objectives and he follows a brief intelligently.' His one controversial proposal was the egalitarian one to abolish selection at the age of 11, which he had failed himself. With the well-honed skill of a politician, he floated the proposal off to an independent commission, covering his back against any fallout.

His high-budget Education portfolio allowed him an opportunity to spend government money, particularly in constituencies that Sinn Féin held or was targeting, and provided an opportunity for him to soften his public image by having photographs taken with young children and clergy. McGuinness was eager to put his hard man reputation behind him. In conversation he cultivated the diffident, almost academic, image of a shambling grandfather, prone to clumsy, if innocent, faux pas. After his daughter, Grainne, gave birth, he charmed the press outside Hillsborough Castle by announcing, 'It's a boy, six foot, three inches – I mean six pounds, three ounces.' His backwoods style may well have been contrived, like the story he repeated with self-deprecating glee at every leg of his American tour in 2001. As McGuinness took the podium, he would tell the apparently spontaneous yarn of the Chinese woman who had grasped his hand, exclaiming, 'Are you David Letterman?' to which McGuinness replied, 'Well, at home they think I'm Art Garfunkel.' According to Nic Robertson, the CNN journalist who followed him, 'It brought the house down every time.'

McGuinness made attempts at outreach, inviting leading churchmen, Protestant as well as Catholic, to lunch with him at Stormont. He told CNN of one Protestant Church leader who suggested, 'Martin, this situation would move along an awful lot easier if you would say you were sorry for the events of the last 30 years.' McGuinness, an IRA leader throughout the Troubles, replied, 'The responsibility lies with successive British governments, right through those decades, who turned their heads away from what was happening in the North of Ireland. It is very easy to blame a little black boy in Soweto, or to blame a little Catholic in the Bogside. It's very easy to salve your conscience and wash your hands of all of that and place the responsibility on a small person as if they were to blame.'

Criticisms of past IRA actions are characteristically met by McGuinness in one of two ways. The first is 'what-about-ery', a blatant attempt to change the focus to the sins of others. The second, accompanied by a sorrowful shaking of the head, was an exhortation to leave the wrongs of the past behind, for after all, are we not all victims? As McGuinness explained to Nic Robertson, 'I think that the legacy of the Troubles is something that we are going to have to deal with, because there's pain in this for everybody and on all sides. But I do think that it's a serious mistake to attempt to apportion blame and responsibility for that around the shoulders of people in this city who decided, because of the oppression that was being used against them, to confront the British Army.' This, however, was not his attitude to the Bloody Sunday Inquiry, where he demanded full disclosure. McGuinness resisted requests to give evidence to the Saville Inquiry for as long as possible and was among the last to give a statement. As Lord Saville of Newdigate pointed out to McGuinness' solicitor, Barra McGrory, when he applied for full interested party status for McGuinness on 13 December 2000, the Inquiry 'had no reply to that letter in April, a reminder was sent in May and another reminder was sent in July; another in July and to none of those letters was a reply sent.' McGrory was left to apologise for his client, who, he suggested, had not been aware of the 'full gravity of his personal situation in respect of these proceedings'.

At the time of writing, the suspicion of a smoke-screen still lingers over the accounts given by both the Ministry of Defence and the IRA to the Inquiry. Several IRA members who had been active at the time of Bloody Sunday were 'visited' after news broke that McGuinness had decided to give evidence. After being politely asked if they intended to follow McGuinness' example, any who said they did were bluntly warned not to proceed.

His image as the IRA's trustee in the peace process, the hard man whose unquestioned integrity could be wheeled out to convince hardline republican doubters, has begun to move out of focus, to dissolve into the new persona of the genial, fly-tying grandfather with a common touch – an image he is clearly keen to promote. Martin McGuinness would now like us to picture him more at home with a fishing rod than an Armalite. The hoary mantle of the IRA has slipped from McGuinness' shoulders and looks as though it might be assumed by Brian Keenan, the international Marxist and arms trader, whose suspicions of McGuinness' role in his own arrest in Operation Hawk in 1979 have never entirely faded.

The puritanical image of Martin McGuinness has also relaxed with the years. He once said, 'I don't drink and I don't like dancing, but I do like to go out to socials where there would be ceilidh dancing and a bit of crack and traditional music.' As a teenager, he had experimented with alcohol, but renounced it to maintain his guard when he joined the IRA. Previously, he would only have drunk occasionally and in private, in the house with Bernie, whereas now he takes the odd glass of wine, usually a West Coast cooler, in company. The softening of his image since the ceasefire has allowed the man once called 'Britain's No 1. Terrorist' to admit to more homely pursuits. McGuinness admits himself that he is a little heavy-handed with the garlic when he follows his favourite Delia Smith recipe for meatballs – something his daughters told him when they were dating as teenagers. The man who in 1985 denied being Chief of Staff of the IRA with a smile, saying that if it were true he would regard it as a compliment, now cheerily admits that he enjoys hoovering, if he has the time.

His regular reading includes each week's *An Phoblacht/Republican News*. He used to read the *Sunday Times* until around 1993, but by 10 June 1996, as he told the *Media Guardian*, he had 'grown dispirited by its biased coverage of Northern Ireland.' He relaxes by reading *Trout & Salmon* Magazine, 'which transports me to the lakes, rivers and mountains where I feel most at peace.' Among films he has enjoyed are *Braveheart*, starring Mel Gibson, and *Into the West*, starring Gabriel Byrne. McGuinness enjoys RTE's *Questions & Answers*, as well as its BBC equivalent, *Question Time*, and considers John Humphrys of BBC Radio Four 'tough but fair'. Less serious viewing includes wildlife programmes and *Last of the Summer Wine*.

McGuinness' political hero, 'apart from Bobby Sands and the other hunger strikers', is Tashunka Witko (Crazy Horse) of the Oglala Sioux, who was run through with a bayonet by a US soldier while imprisoned. 'His dying words were: "All we wanted was peace and to be left alone."' His long-time favourite leisure pursuit is fishing, however, and perhaps by now he has fulfilled his ambition for a holiday salmon fishing in the Scottish Highlands, from where he was excluded for so many years under the Prevention of Terrorism Act in 1982.

McGuinness summed up his future vision for the IRA in an interview with Emily O'Reilly in *The Observer*, when she asked him where they went from here: once decommissioning had been resolved; the assembly was up and running and the Good Friday Agreement had been fully implemented. Poker faced, he replied, 'The old IRA existed in the south for years. They attended commemorations, they buried old comrades, and they did so peacefully. It's an odd question in my opinion. Why should we worry about it?' The image is of some cherished antique, the pike rusting in the thatch, even while partition flourishes and British rule continues.

With the benefit of hindsight, and in terms of whether or not it has achieved its stated objectives, the IRA campaign has been a waste, both of time and of life; and this is something which many veterans find deeply troubling. The political differences between Sunningdale and the Good Friday Agreement are too minor for either the campaign or the massive loss of life that intervened to be logically or morally justified. However, life is not lived with hindsight; to argue against the decision to end the campaign on the best terms available – and McGuinness did get the best terms – is to argue for the continuation of a struggle which experience has shown to be futile. In any case, one major factor distinguishes between the Good Friday

Agreement and Sunningdale: under Sunningdale, Sinn Féin would not have attained power, nor McGuinness, ministerial office.

McGuinness' great achievement is to have steered his movement through almost 30 years of largely fruitless violence; to emerge, not defeated as they might otherwise have been, but, with his hand on the tiller, as one of the most powerful forces in Irish politics. It is an achievement not so much for his community, as for his comrades.

A police officer who has spent the best of his career career studying him observed:

> McGuinness has been an extremely cold and ruthless man and he has had a very keen sense of self-preservation. Where others have died, he has lived; and his tactics have only been restrained by what his followers would tolerate, not by humanitarian concerns. Yet I would have to admit he is a religious man and apparently a loving father, he has his own integrity and he is not corrupt. From all that we can see, there is no sign of him going back to terrorism.

Many who spent their careers despising him for his role in the IRA now, almost against their will, find him a likeable and engaging individual. His old gift of devoting all his attention to one individual, so evident when he flattered and groomed young Derry men for the IRA is also a valuable commodity for a politician. One man who watched McGuinness and Clinton together says, 'It's no contest – no one can work a room like McGuinness, not even the President. He could charm the birds out of the trees.'

Lord Maginnis, the recently retired Ulster Unionist Party MP, a former UDR Major, found McGuinness the most likeable of all the Sinn Féin members he has met during the talks process. 'If I hadn't a fairly serious grievance,' Lord Maginnis admitted, 'if I wasn't thinking about the way in which terror was conducted, I probably would find McGuinness quite a palatable companion – there is an earthiness and directness about him which can be quite attractive, whereas I still wouldn't like Adams. I find him laughable because he is so pompous. Things are never going to be right between people like McGuinness and myself, there are too many bad memories, but for our children and our children's children, things will inevitably be different.'

Martin's younger brother Willie, an activist like him, has avoided the hardship suffered by most IRA volunteers. In fact, he is now Chairman of Iona Enterprises, a community development programme. He is also carving out a niche in the security field for himself. On 6 March 2001, Paul Greengrass, a film director for the January Films production *Bloody Sunday*, thanked 'Mr William McGuinness and his colleagues who provided security and stewarding.'

In July 2000 former MI5 officer David Shayler revealed that MI5 and the Metropolitan police anti-terrorist squad had kept regular surveillance on a cousin of Martin McGuiness, Cyril 'Jimmy' McGuinness. Writing in *Punch* magazine, Shayler claimed that bungling by MI5 in 1992 allowed McGuinness to escape arrest. Two months after the Bishopsgate bomb in London on 24 April 1993, the Met issued a photofit picture of Cyril McGuinness, but by that time he had gone on the run to the Irish Republic. In November 1995, he was fined one thousand five hundred pounds for refusing to complete an embarkation card at Cairnryan ferry port. Shortly after the Docklands lorry bomb which had marked the end of the first ceasefire on 9 February 1996 and had killed two people, he was arrested in Britain again – bolt cutters found in his car after a police search were allegedly linked to the theft of agricultural fertiliser in the south of England. The six-foot man, who lived in a mobile home at Rosslea, Co. Fermanagh at the time, was released on police bail and returned to Northern Ireland.

In 1990, his former brother-in-law, Joseph McColgan, was sentenced to four years in prison by a Florida court after being found guilty of attempting to export a Stinger missile to Ireland without a licence. The FBI caught McColgan as he tried to hide the missile in a suitcase. When arrested, McColgan told the FBI, 'I am just a poor Irishman on holiday.' His comments provided some light relief to jurors. On 4 April 2001, Joe McColgan assured the Bloody Sunday Inquiry that 'I would not know an IRA gunman if I seen one.' He also claimed never to have discussed the events of Bloody Sunday with his former brother-in-law, who he had never even asked if he had been on the march.

His mother, Peggy, has certainly become more politicised, telling *An Phoblacht/Republican News* on 25 January 1996, as she reflected on her own experiences: 'Hundreds of tragedies have affected me: Bloody Sunday, deaths of volunteers, children murdered by plastic bullets, the lists is endless. I agonise to this day over the horrific deaths of the hunger strikers. These people were starving themselves to death for justice and all I could do was join in the daily protests or lead a crowd of women in saying the Rosary at the street corner every night. The frustration I felt to try and relieve their pain was terrible.'

One remarkable feature of his career, remarked on by colleagues, policemen and unionists alike is the fact that he has managed to avoid serving any major term of imprisonment. For a man who has been involved in violence and intrigue for many years he has emerged from it in remarkably good shape. He bears no injuries and his family, unlike the families of many republican and loyalist activists, is functional and unscathed. None of them have been imprisoned or deprived of either parent because of the Troubles, which their father did so much to orchestrate.

His mother Peggy worries, as she told the BBC's *Real Lives* programme in 1985, about him: 'Any mother would worry who had a son involved in a political struggle. I worry all the time about his safety and about all the family.'

At least twice loyalists have threatened his life; initially when his first marital home was targeted for a bomb attack; and once when Michael Stone was plotting to kill him. On each occasion, he received timely warnings from sources he never acknowledged and changed his movements. In 1992, he admitted the possibility of an attempt by loyalists to assassinate him, saying, 'I'm conscious of that and it doesn't worry me at all. I have no fear of them whatsoever, absolutely none. I think that taking sensible precautions like being careful, not having a regular routine, assists you in protecting yourself.'

When Mo Mowlam was Secretary of State, McGuinness' name was on a list of 30 republicans to receive home security grants at taxpayers' expense, which was submitted to her by Sinn Féin after she accepted their demand that the RUC should not be involved in the assessment procedure.

Ian Phoenix, the head of the RUC's surveillance unit who was killed in the Chinook crash, recorded in his diaries that surveillance of McGuinness and other Sinn Féin leaders was officially curtailed on 27 September 1993. Phoenix challenged the decision, considering it to be a result of political pressure. Some have hinted that McGuinness may have been protected by the British state at some level. It seems beyond rational belief, however, that he was an informant or agent. For much of his life, he lived in relative poverty; too many of the IRA operations of which he had knowledge were carried to a successful conclusion, and over too long a period, for McGuinness to have been a security force agent. The republican struggle would not have continued as it did if

McGuinness had been seeking consistently to subvert it from within. Much of his apparent luck is explained by what the police officer referred to as 'his very keen sense of self preservation.'

Some former IRA men say that McGuinness rarely took the same chances with his life and liberty as others, and held back from the worst of the action. However, there can be little doubt that a prosecution could have been mounted against him if it had been a priority. Sean O'Callaghan and Robert Quigley were just two of the potential witnesses who would have been willing to give evidence against him. Operation Taurus, the RUC's concerted and major effort to prosecute him in the 1990s was ended in circumstances where charges might have been expected and where senior police officers warned of political sensitivities.

One possible explanation for his apparently charmed existence is that McGuinness was selected at an early stage by the British authorities as someone who could prove useful, and was preserved in a leadership position with future negotiations in mind. It is standard international intelligence practice to leave the leadership of paramilitary or subversive groups intact. If security measures remove the top tier of leadership, a new generation of Young Turks will have to spend years going through the learning curve their predecessors have already experienced. In the intervening years, they will secure their position through militancy. Preserving the leadership does not prevent the security service from attacking the organisation itself, narrowing the leadership's options and even, when necessary, taking out more militant factions who show serious signs of escalating the campaign and threatening the leadership's grip on the levers of power. It is a classic technique, and some attempt at it must have been in place even as Lord Widgery prepared his report in the months that followed Bloody Sunday in 1972.

By the mid-1970s, British policy had abandoned earlier models of stamping out the first signs of an uprising with saturation level troops for the more sophisticated option of the long haul of Ulsterisation, containment and ultimately, political negotiation. It was at this point that McGuinness met British ministers and officials when he was plucked from the obscurity of the Bogside to join the delegation to meet William Whitelaw in Cheyne Walk. Dennis Bradley, the former priest who was the central link between McGuinness and British Intelligence, bears witness to the constant contacts between republicans and the British authorities. Bradley, now an Oscar-winning filmmaker, stresses that McGuinness was never a blind militarist:

McGuinness' great contribution is that he knew, even quite early on, that the war could not, nor should it, go on forever; and that violence in its own right had no role to play. At an early stage I knew that if there was political movement it would allow McGuinness' head to move into that and that he would have some authority, and I use the word some authority, within that situation to bring other people with him.

Oatley, an able and decent man, emerges from the Troubles as something of an Irish Lawrence of Arabia, a British agent who grew to appreciate the republican perspective, and who had a sense of mission. He surfaced during the 1981 hunger strike as 'Mountain Climber', where republicans became convinced, probably through misunderstanding him and certainly mistakenly, that there were better terms available to them than those they were being offered through the official channels of the Irish Commission for Justice and Peace. Oatley's contribution may not, in the end, be remembered as the most positive, either for the hunger strikers or, at a later stage, for the peace process. The Irish government certainly regarded his activity as an impediment to real negotiations with the Provos. Genuine progress towards a ceasefire was made only after the secret diplomacy of men like Oatley had been replaced by more or less open political dialogue.

However, the contribution of the secret diplomats may have been more positive for McGuinness personally. Oatley's final act before retiring from MI6 in 1991 was to visit McGuinness in Derry to give him an analysis of the way forward. Afterwards, Oatley spoke warmly, even admiringly, of the republican leadership. He wrote of Adams' and McGuinness' courage in the *Sunday Times* in October 1999, saying: 'They decided to take a risk. I was a witness to their decision. For many years, circumstances have allowed me an occasionally intimate view of political developments within the republican movement. I became aware of the leadership's broadening attitudes, re-examination of the effectiveness and justification of the armed campaign and willingness to enter into dialogue with people who could offer fresh perspectives.'

Was it a leadership that Oatley and his colleagues saw the value of preserving?

Glossary

ANGLO-IRISH AGREEMENT: November 1985. Resented by unionists because it gave the Irish Republic a formal consultative role in Northern Ireland affairs

APPRENTICE BOYS (OF DERRY): A Protestant male marching order which commemorates the siege of Derry of 1689

APRN: An Phoblacht/Republican News, the Sinn Féin weekly paper. *Republican News* first appeared in Belfast in 1970. It was originally a monthly publication. The Dublin-based *An Phoblacht* started at the end of 1969 when the republican movement split. The two merged as *An Phoblacht/Republican News* in 1979 and came under the direction of the new Northern leadership. *APRN* is owned and under the direct control of the IRA

ARD COMHAIRLE: Sinn Féin's central committee

ARD FHEIS: A Sinn Féin delegate conference

ASU: Active Service Unit, a paramilitary cell composed of 4–6 people

AUXILIARIES: Auxiliary IRA

B SPECIALS, B MEN: a part time section of the RUC abolished in 1970

BLANKETMEN/WOMEN: Republican prisoners who protested about privileges lost when special category status was ended by refusing to wear prison uniforms, choosing to wear only their prison-issue blanket, 1976–81

CONTINUITY IRA: The military wing of RSF

CUMANN: A party branch

CUMANN NA MBAN: Women's IRA

DAIL, DAIL EIREANN: Lower House of the Irish Parliament

DET: Fourteenth Intelligence Company – a section of the British Army which deals with undercover surveillance

DISSIDENTS: Real IRA (RIRA, sometimes referred to as 'Cokes') who emerged as a result of dissent following the IRA ceasefires of 1994 and 1997. They were responsible for the 15 August 1998 bomb at Omagh which killed 31 people including unborn twins. The Continuity IRA (CIRA) is linked to Republican Sinn Féin (RSF)

DUP: Democratic Unionist Party, extreme Protestant party, led by Rev Ian Paisley

FIANNA (EIREANN): Youth wing of the IRA

FIANNA FAIL: The largest party in the Irish Republic

FREE DERRY: An area around the Bogside and Creggan estates of Derry from which British troops were excluded until July 1972

FIANNA GAEL: The other main political party in the Irish Republic.

FREE DERRY CORNER: Marks the entrance to the area

FRU: Force Research Unit, section of British military intelligence which handled informants and agents in Ireland

FULL INTERESTED PARTY STATUS: Witnesses who give evidence to the Bloody Sunday Inquiry are entitled to the advice of an independent lawyer during that process, the costs of which are normally met out of public funds. Those who are granted full interested party status then have the right to legal representation during the hearing of any evidence relevant to them

GARDA SIOCHANA: Irish Republic's Police force. A single officer is called a Garda, plural is Gardai. Female officers are known as Ban Gardai (singular Ban Garda).

GHQ: General Headquarters Staff: the people appointed by the Chief of Staff to head the departments responsible for the day to day running of the IRA

GOOD FRIDAY AGREEMENT: Also called Belfast Agreement, 1998; backed by the British and Irish governments and all the major Northern Ireland parties except the DUP

IICD: The Independent International Commission on Decommissioning, chaired by General John de Chastelain

INLA: Irish National Liberation Army, the military wing of the IRSP

INTERNMENT: Imprisonment without trial

IRSP: Irish Republican Socialist Party, a militant group that broke away from Official Sinn Féin in 1974

JARK: military intelligence slang for tampering with weapons to insert a tracking device or render the weapons unreliable

LINK: The name given to the group made up by Father Dennis Bradley and two Derry businessmen who liaised between the IRA and the British authorities

LONG KESH: Prison where paramilitary prisoners were held in Nissan huts. Phased out after the Maze was built on the same site. Provos continued to call it Long Kesh in protest at the ending of special category status

MAZE: Northern Ireland's largest prison for terrorist inmates. Opened in 1976

MOUNTAIN CLIMBER: code-name for Michael Oatley, an MI6 officer who liased with the Provos

NAAFI: Organisation that provides canteen facilities for servicemen and women

NIO: Northern Ireland Office

NORAID: Irish Northern Aid. US based Republican fund raising group

OGLAIGH NA HEIREANN: Irish for IRA

OIRA: Official IRA. Originally the majority faction when the IRA split in 1970. More left wing than the Provos, they declared a ceasefire in 1972

OIREACHTAS: Irish Senate and Dail

ORANGE ORDER: a Protestant male marching order, closely aligned to the Ulster Unionist Party. Its meetings are held in Orange Halls

PDF: Prisoners Dependants Fund, a republican fund raising group in Ireland

PEELER: A policeman

PIRA: Provisional IRA. Split from the Officials in 1970. Unless otherwise specified, mentions of the IRA after 1972 refer to PIRA

PREVENTION OF TERRORISM ACT: Similar to the Special Powers Act

PROVOS: refers to the Provisional Republican movement, including both Sinn Féin and the IRA

RIRA: Real IRA, hard line dissident group who broke away from PIRA in 1998 because they disagreed with Sinn Féin's entry into politics and the

IRA ceasefire. Sometimes referred to as 'Cokes'.

RSF: Republican Sinn Féin. A breakaway group that emerged in 1986 after Sinn Féin voted at the Ard Fheis to end abstention from the Dail. Its two leading spokespersons included Daithi O Conaill and Ruari O Bradiagh who is still its President

RTE: Radio Telefis Eireann, the Irish state TV and Broadcasting body

RUC: Royal Ulster Constabulary, Northern Ireland's police force

SDLP: Social Democratic and Labour Party. The main moderate nationalist party in Northern Ireland led by John Hume

STICKIES: a nickname for the Official Republican movement

SUNNINGDALE: Agreement to set up the power-sharing Executive made up of Brian Faulkner's Unionists, the SDLP and the Alliance Party on 21 November 1973

SUPERGRASS: Member of paramilitary or criminal group who gives evidence in court against other members

TANAISTE: Deputy to Taoiseach.

TAOISEACH: The Irish Prime Minister

TONE, THEOBALD WOLFE: Leader of the United Irishmen's uprising of 1798, regarded as the founding father of Irish republicanism. He cut his throat in his prison cell, rather than be hanged by a British rope

UDA: Ulster Defence Association, largest loyalist paramilitary group, also known as the UFF (Ulster Freedom Fighters)

UDR: Ulster Defence Regiment. A regiment of the British Army recruited in Northern Ireland for home service and containing a part time element. It was founded in 1970 to replace the B Specials and amalgamated into the Royal Irish Regiment in 1992

UUP: Ulster Unionist Party, the major unionist party in Northern Ireland

UVF: Ulster Volunteer Force, the oldest loyalist paramilitary group

VISA WAIVER: Document which allows a person normally banned from entering the US to visit it

Notes

A Note on IRA Structures

The supreme policy making authority of the IRA is the Army Convention, a delegate conference. Conventions are held every four years in time of peace but only when necessary if a campaign is in progress. The convention elects an Army Executive, mainly composed of veterans, which arbitrates on policy matters and appoints the Army Council – responsible for the overall conduct of the campaign. It appoints a Chief of Staff and General Headquarters Staff to handle the practicalities of running the campaign.

Locally, the IRA is organised into Brigades, each of which has a Brigade Staff, some of which are divided into Battalions. The most basic unit of organisation is the ASU (Active Service Unit).

Chapter One

Invaluable information about Derry at the start of the Troubles can be found in Niall O Dochartaigh, *From Civil Rights to Armalites* (Cork University Press, 1977)

Chapter Two

The *Irish Times* article quoted from was written by Nell McCafferty, published on 19 April 1972.

Kevin Toolis interviewed Martin McGuinness for a chapter in his book, *Rebel Hearts* (Picador, 1995).

Chapter Three

References to the police and army are taken from documents placed before the current Inquiry into Bloody Sunday, chaired by Lord Saville of Newdigate.

The Italian photographer Fulvio Grimaldi mentioned that Barney McFadden's house was a good place to find out information about the IRA and other matters during his evidence to the Bloody Sunday Inquiry on 26 June 2001.

Quotations from James Doherty are taken from author interviews and an unpublished interview carried out by Dean Nelson, editor of the Scottish edition of the *Sunday Times*.

Eamon Mallie & Patrick Bishop, *The Provisional IRA* (Corgi, 1987).

Peter Taylor, *Provos: The Ira and Sinn Fein* (Bloomsbury, 1997).

Sean MacStiofain, *Memoirs of a Revolutionary* (Gordon Cremonsci, 1975).

Chapter Four

Martin McGuinness announced in May 2001 that he would give evidence to the Bloody Sunday Inquiry. In his statement, he confirmed that he had been second-in-command of the Provisional IRA in Derry at the time of Bloody Sunday.

There are persistent rumours that other former senior IRA figures, including the OC, were 'visited' by current senior IRA men after McGuinness' announcement, in an attempt to prevent them giving their own version of events. Those quoted here who saw McGuinness on the day are adamant that he tried to attack the army on several occasions, none of them successful. They would like it recorded that, in their view, nothing could have justified the Army's murder of 14 unarmed civilians on Bloody Sunday, a point with which the authors are in complete agreement.

Father O'Gara is mentioned in *Peggy Deery*, Nell McCafferty, (Attic Press, 1988).

The quotes from Father (later Bishop) Edward Daly are from an interview with Kathryn Johnston in December 1981.

A good account of Bloody Sunday can be found in Peter Pringle and Philip Jacobson, *Those Are Real Bullets, Aren't They?* (Fourth Estate, 2000).

Chapter Five

Eamon McCann, *War and an Irish Town* (Penguin, 1974).

Martin McGuinness told the *Irish News* of his fondness for 'spuds, cabbage and pork ribs, a la Peggy' on 10 May 1997.

Colin Wallace wrote about the incident with Major Hugh Smith in the *Mail on Sunday* on 3 October 1999.

The account of Martin McGuinness' speech in 1972 is taken from an article by Mary Holland in the *Irish Times*, 9 November 1999.

Frank Thornton's article appeared in the *Daily Express*, 11 April 1972.

A good account of the meeting with Whitelaw appears in Peter Taylor, *Provos: The IRA and Sinn Féin* (Bloomsbury, 1997).

Jill and Leon Uris, *Ireland: A Terrible Beauty* (Corgi, 1976).

Leon Uris, *Trinity* (Corgi, 1976).

Chapter Six

Shane Paul O'Doherty, *The Volunteer*, (Fount, 1993).

Central Television's *The Cook Report* on Martin McGuinness was broadcast on 21 and 31 August 1993.

Peter Taylor's book, *The Provos*, has a good account of the 1974 negotiations, (Bloomsbury, 1997).

Chapter Seven

Merlyn Rees, *Northern Ireland: A Personal Perspective* (Methuen, 1985)

1978 Secret Army Intelligence Report first published in Sean Cronin, *Nationalism* (Academy Press, 1980).

The quotations from Peter McMullan are taken from the *Kansas City Times*, September 1979.

Chapter Eight

Good accounts of the IRA's American links can be found in Jack Holland, *The American Connection* (Viking, 1987) and Jack Holland, *Hope Against History* (Hodder & Stoughton, 1999).

In May 1998 Sean O'Callaghan gave evidence to a Dublin court where he gave details of the IRA's contacts with Syria, GRU and other groups.

Chapter Nine

We have relied on interview material with Father Alec Reid conducted some years ago and on more recent interviews with Willie Carlin. Raymond Gilmour has signed a confidentiality agreement with MI5 and the quotations from him are taken from interviews conducted before this came into force.

Mairtin is the Irish for Martin, and Fiachra was one of the four children of Lir who were turned into swans by their stepmother in the Irish legend.

Chapter Ten
The quotations from Sean O'Callaghan are taken from evidence he gave in a Dublin court in May 1998.

The authors interviewed Raymond Gilmour on several occasions between 1993 and 1996 and have quoted from his police witness statements.

The description of the supergrass evidence given by Raymond Gilmour in 1984 is contained in an article by Nell McCafferty, 'Supergrasses', *Belfast Bulletin*, No. 11, Workers Research Unit.

Chapter Eleven
This chapter draws on material from interviews with a number of undercover agents and their handlers. These include Sean O'Callaghan who gave Liam Clarke a written account of his life during his time in prison.

Other material is drawn from Willie Carlin, 'Martin Ingram' and 'Rob Lewis'.

The authors interviewed Raymond Gilmour in 1992, before the secrecy agreement imposed on him by MI5.

We also obtained access to a number of RUC documents relating to the abduction of Paul McGavigan.

Barrie Penrose provided valuable insights into the *Real Lives* affair.

Chapter Twelve
The account of the Frank Hegarty episode draws on conversations with Hegarty's mother and sisters and an account given by 'Martin Ingram', one of Hegarty's handlers, and by an RUC source with knowledge of the investigation. We have also drawn on published and broadcast accounts, particularly Central Television's *The Cook Report* and BBC's *The Long War*. Ingram is the subject of various injunctions for alleged breach of the Official Secrets Act in allegedly giving interviews to Liam Clarke. The interview material used here was given before these came into force.

Material relating to Brendan Casey was supplied by Ted Oliver who interviewed him at length for the *Daily Mirror* in 1993.

Quotations from Adrian Hopkins are taken from his unpublished statements to the French authorities.

The account of Loughgall draws on conversations with former military intelligence officers and published accounts by Jack Holland and Brendan O'Brien.

Chapter Thirteen

Quotations from Michael Stone are taken from interviews with Liam Clarke and Trevor Birnie of UTV Live, from his statements to the police, from Martin Dillon, *Stone Cold* (Arrow, 1993), and from the BBC's *Endgame* documentary series.

The intercepted communication was first quoted by Jack Holland in *Hope Against History: The Ulster Conflict* (Hodder and Stoughton, 1999).

Liam Clarke interviewed Michael Williams and his family in 1990.

Chapter Fourteen

The authors spoke to Liz Flood in the early 1990s and have a statement that she wrote entitled *My Story*. Other quotations are taken from the inquest.

The IRA gave Kevin Toolis access to their evidence against Flood and his taped confession for Toolis' book, *Rebel Hearts*.

Some quotations from McGuinness are taken from a statement he issued in 1994 on his contacts with the British. Both Sinn Féin and the British government issued versions of the contacts at that time. We have also relied on interviews with Michael Oatley, Denis Bradley and others.

Eamon Mallie and David McKittrick, *The Fight for Peace: The Secret Story Behind the Irish Peace Process* (Heinemann, 1996) is a useful account of the 1990–96 period, and we have drawn on some interview material in it. It also contains the various drafts of the Hume/Adams document and the Downing Street Declaration.

Liam Clarke interviewed Kathleen Gillespie a few days after her husband's death.

Statistics are taken from McKittrick et al, *Lost Lives* (Mainstream, 1999) and Colonel Michael Dewar, *The British Army in Northern Ireland* (Arms and Armour Press, 1985, 1996).

Chapter Fifteen

The material on Gerry Holmes, whose story is told here for the first time, is from a private source.

Gerry Adams, *An Irish Voice: The Quest for Peace* (Mount Eagle, 1997), gives Adams' views and recollections of some events from June 1993 until July 1997.

Some McGuinness quotations on the negotiations have been taken from the BBC series *Endgame* which was broadcast in 2001 and contains useful interviews with the main players.

The quotations from Dick Spring are taken from the *Dail Record*, available on the internet. They record a similar comment on 1 June 1994.

John Major: The Autobiography (HarperCollins, 1999); Mallie and McKittrick, *The Fight for Peace* are valuable resources on this period as is the 1993 Sinn Féin pamphlet *Setting the Record Straight* which is available in the Linenhall Library, Belfast.

Chapter Sixteen

The BBC *Endgame* documentary series has provided useful background and some quotes from McGuinness.

John Major: The Autobiography (HarperCollins, 1999), is a very useful reference for this period.

We have drawn on notes gathered at some of the meetings between Sinn Féin and the British.

Comments about what men on the run were told are drawn from an interview with Dermot McNally, one of the 1983 Maze escapees who was still at large when he spoke to Clarke.

Chapter Seventeen

The source of much of the information in this chapter was the *An Phoblacht /Republican News* website, http://irlnet.com/aprn/

Chapter Eighteen

Adams' account of the meeting with Blair is contained in his book *An Irish Journal* (Brandon, 2001).

Anthony McIntyre's comments and his IRA interview are available on the internet at http://rwg.phoblacht.net/ira.html

Most of the quotations that are attributed to McGuinness about the pre-

Good Friday negotiations come from his report to the 1998 Sinn Féin Ard Fheis that was reprinted in full in *An Phoblacht/Republican News* on 23 April 1998.

McGuinness referred to the funeral of Libby Rushe in the Northern Ireland Assembly on 14 September 1998. Quotations are taken from the official record.

The passage involving Victor Barker is based on Victor Barker's account and records.

The account of McGuinness' dealings with Ahern after the *Sunday Times* interview is mainly contained in the official Dail report.

Chapter Nineteen

We would like to thank Nic Robertson of CNN for providing us with transcripts of interviews in his documentary, *Dying for Peace*, which was broadcast in June 2001.

References to Ian Phoenix's diaries are from Jack Holland and Susan Phoenix, *Policing the Shadows* (Hodder and Stoughton, 1996).

Index